The Experience of Meaning

The Experience of Meaning

JAN ZWICKY

McGill-Queen's University Press
Montreal & Kingston · London · Chicago

© McGill-Queen's University Press 2019

ISBN 978-0-7735-5742-0 (cloth)
ISBN 978-0-7735-5743-7 (paper)
ISBN 978-0-7735-5850-2 (ePDF)
ISBN 978-0-7735-5851-9 (ePUB)

Legal deposit second quarter 2019
Bibliothèque nationale du Québec

Printed in Canada on acid-free paper that is 100% ancient forest free (100% post-consumer recycled), processed chlorine free

This book has been published with the help of a grant from the Canadian Federation for the Humanities and Social Sciences, through the Awards to Scholarly Publications Program, using funds provided by the Social Sciences and Humanities Research Council of Canada.

We acknowledge the support of the Canada Council for the Arts, which last year invested $153 million to bring the arts to Canadians throughout the country.

Nous remercions le Conseil des arts du Canada de son soutien. L'an dernier, le Conseil a investi 153 millions de dollars pour mettre de l'art dans la vie des Canadiennes et des Canadiens de tout le pays.

Library and Archives Canada Cataloguing in Publication

Title: The experience of meaning / Jan Zwicky.
Names: Zwicky, Jan, 1955– author.
Description: Includes bibliographical references and index.
Identifiers: Canadiana (print) 20190054328 | Canadiana (ebook) 20190054387 | ISBN 9780773557437 (softcover) | ISBN 9780773557420 (hardcover) | ISBN 9780773558502 (ePDF) | ISBN 9780773558519 (ePUB)
Subjects: LCSH: Experience. | LCSH: Meaning (Philosophy) | LCSH: Meaning (Psychology)
Classification: LCC B105.E9 Z95 2019 | DDC 121/.68—dc23

Set in 11.5/14 Adobe Garamond Premier Pro
Book design & typesetting by Garet Markvoort, zijn digital

CONTENTS

Preface vii

Introduction: What Is Gestalt Thinking? 3

Poetry and Meaninglessness 22

Simplicity and the Experience of Meaning 59

Plato and Gestalt, or Why There Is No Theory of Forms 75

"Show, Don't Tell" 96

Music 109

The Inscape of Being 147

Appendix: A Few Outstanding Questions 175

Notes 185

References 211

Acknowledgments 225

Figures and Illustrations 229

Index 231

PREFACE

It is easy to demonstrate that gestalt comprehension — our grasp of wholes and how they hang together — informs many aspects of our lives, from our ability to recognize our favourite jazz standard in an unfamiliar arrangement to the construction of compelling proofs in mathematics. It is equally easy to demonstrate that for the last sixty years few have paid serious intellectual attention to these phenomena and that philosophers in the Anglo-American tradition have ignored them since the Enlightenment. Recent scholarly attention has been engaged instead with mechanistic epistemologies — models of thinking that proceed by aggregation of elements — or with the gleeful deconstruction of such models. The result is that as an intellectual culture we have lost sight of meaning. For the experience of meaning — 'getting it' — is the gestalt phenomenon *par excellence*.

The aim of this short book is a recovery of interest in the experience of meaning. The opening chapter introduces the concept of gestalt insight, and subsequent chapters show gestalt thinking in operation in several theatres: mathematics and physics, poetry, music, literary composition, and Plato's ancient theory of forms. I intend these investigations as provocations to further research and reflection, not as definitive accounts.

Stirrings of new interest in early twentieth-century gestalt research are evidenced by the recent publication of seminal texts in English translation. But so far, the presumed audience has been psychologists and neuroscientists. The discussion needs to be widened, for the issue is of vital cultural importance. The Ivory Tower, if it was ever a reality, is now clearly a fable. Research programs at universities are not culturally isolated; they do not reflect the goal of pure inquiry. Increasingly, they are driven by funding opportunities that reflect the agendas of corporate donors, and the results of those research programs in turn shape general cultural priorities.

For example, many of us live now caught up in the nexus of Big Data. We find this situation troubling but feel powerless to escape. How did Big Data come to dominate our lives? It did so in part through an alliance between capitalism and mechanistic technology. But whence the power of that alliance? Underlying it, at its root, lies a particular conception of thinking — thinking as calculation — which has itself eroded our ability to see its limitations. This conception is excessively narrow — it ignores gestalt comprehension — but it holds us captive. It has fostered correspondingly limited conceptions of truth and reality that have done an immense amount of damage, not only to our private lives but to the planet. From the intellectual standpoint that dominates technocratic culture, Gestalt theory appears to be a pointless, if not laughable, enterprise because it has been unable to specify machine-programmable formulæ that govern gestalt insight. It is my view that this is a problem with the standpoint rather than the theory.

A number of these essays grew out of talks intended for general audiences. They represent a widening of earlier investigations into what I have called lyric philosophy. Lyric is a fundamentally integrative, rather than analytic, mode of thought; it is one species of gestalt understanding. In the final essay, I explore relationships among lyric poetry, lyric philosophy, and other members of their genus.

Extensive notes and references are provided, but in an effort to keep the discussion readable, they are not marked in the text. Readers interested in the details will find them, cued to page number and phrase or name, at the back of the book. Where the reference is general in nature and both the author and title are mentioned in the text, I have not added a note; complete bibliographic information can be found in the list of references. Unless otherwise indicated, translations are mine.

JZ • Heriot Ridge, Quadra Island • February 2019

❧ The Experience of Meaning

ॐ Introduction
What Is Gestalt Thinking?

What is gestalt thinking? This is a question like 'What is logical thinking?' The difference is that we believe the second has a crisp, clear answer, while the first doesn't. Our confidence, however, is not entirely well founded.

Consider Gottlob Frege's well-known essay "The Thought: A Logical Inquiry." It opens with this sentence: "The word 'true' indicates the aim of logic as does 'beautiful' that of aesthetics or 'good' that of ethics." After an attempt to "outline roughly" what he means by 'true,' Frege concludes that "it is probable that the content of the word 'true' is unique and unidentifiable." He can't explain further. You either get what he's driving at, or you don't. Frege then turns to the main task of his essay, a logical inquiry into the nature of thought, and says, "Without wishing to give a definition, I call a thought something for which the question of truth arises."

Or consider Willard Van Orman Quine's attempt to define logic in the preface to *Philosophy of Logic*: "[L]ogic is the systematic study of the logical truths. Pressed further, I would say that a sentence is logically true if all sentences with its grammatical structure are true. Pressed further still, I would say to read this book."

Susan Haack, with characteristic directness, says at the beginning of *Philosophy of Logics*, "Because I have to begin somewhere, I shall take for granted an intuitive idea of what it is to be a formal system."

In other words, the idea of logical thinking is an impression of a thing, a something, a 'that,' which is gathered from a number of instances, which can be only imperfectly codified, and which is rooted in, bound up with, many other human activities, practices, and concerns in a way that makes explicit, non-circular definition impossible. The idea of logical thinking is, in short, a gestalt.

All understanding — not only of what logic is, but of what science is, what systematicity and analysis are, what we mean by 'beauty' and 'moral excellence' or 'language' or 'philosophy' — involves grasp of a gestalt. This fact has been aggressively neglected in Western European culture for at least four centuries. (By contrast, it has been fundamental to much Asian thought about thinking.) We have, in the West, convinced ourselves that the idea of gestalt thinking is too fuzzy and vague to be taken seriously. It is, however, no more fuzzy or vague than many notions that we do take seriously. My aim in this introduction is, then, to precipitate a gestalt of the notion of gestalt thinking.

ૐ

The word Gestalt means 'shape' or 'form.' It came to prominence in German philosophy and psychology with the work of Christian von Ehrenfels in 1890. Von Ehrenfels was interested in melody. Take "Row, Row, Row Your Boat," for instance. Most of us couldn't specify the sequence of relative pitches if our lives depended on it. But we can, almost without effort, hum the tune. We recognize it instantly, regardless of what key it's played in. This means, von Ehrenfels argued, that we don't perceive melody in an aggregative fashion — first one note, then the next, then the next — and then stick these elements together with some sort of epistemic glue. The thing we hum and recognize, the thing we remember, is the melody as a whole, its aural shape. Von Ehrenfels called this shape "Gestalt quality" — something that was, he claimed, more than the sum of its parts.

The next generation of Gestalt theorists — notably Max Wertheimer, Wolfgang Köhler, and Kurt Koffka — demonstrated that this immediate apprehension of 'shaped' wholes informs a great deal of our perception and thinking, not just music. Like many European psychologists of the day, they were well versed in philosophy. Wertheimer in particular was interested in the educational and socio-political implications of Gestalt research. By the mid-1930s, all three had emigrated to the US — Koffka by choice in 1927, Wertheimer in 1933 because he was a Jew, and Köhler in 1935 because his public denunciations of Nazi policies had

4   The Experience of Meaning

made him a political target. Despite considerable contemporary interest in their views, Gestalt theory was eclipsed in North America by behaviourism. It also declined in postwar Germany, but for reasons that are less clear. Mitchell Ash speculates that pressures included the early deaths of some key figures, a burgeoning interest in quantified 'personality diagnostics,' and Gestalt theory's insistence that language is not the source of meaning.

Gestalt comprehension is insight into how things hang together. It is perception *that* a thing or situation hangs together; and it is sensitivity to structural echoes between that thing or situation and others. Wertheimer, Köhler, and Koffka embraced von Ehrenfels's observations to this effect and began controlled experiments to extend them. But they took exception to von Ehrenfels's claim that a gestalt is more than the sum of its parts. A gestalt, they argued, is *different* from the sum of its parts. In his 1925 essay "Über Gestalttheorie," Wertheimer says:

> There are contexts in which what happens in the whole is not derived from how the individual pieces are put together, but where, on the contrary — this is the heart of the matter — what happens in a part is determined by inner structural laws of that whole.

Of almost equal importance, they maintained, was the fact that we perceive wholes first and parts later. What we call the 'elements' of a thing are, epistemologically speaking, not elementary: they are the product of analysis. So-called elements are abstracted from an initial perceptual experience; they are not its foundation. As Michael Wertheimer, Max's son, puts it, "parts do not become parts, do not function as parts, until there is a whole of which they are parts." Great poems, great theorems in mathematics, lyric insights of any kind do just this: they present a whole in a manner that invites us to see parts we'd never noticed before, and to see them in connection with parts we thought we knew, but now see differently. They change the way we view things. We become aware of something very like an ecosystem.

Two important caveats: Gestalt theory does not claim that all wholes have this character; some, like bags of marbles, are mere aggregates. Nor does Gestalt theory suggest that in wholes that are deeply integrated, the parts somehow pop into existence at the behest of the whole. The parts are distinctly, independently real. Once they have come to our attention, parts can be isolated in perception — that is, we can focus on them — and in some circumstances they can be plucked from their contexts for separate examination. (A caddis fly from a pond; a hair from a head.) It is what parts *do*, the way they behave, that is determined by the 'inner lawfulness' of the whole. (Though, of course, what they do affects what they are; the situation is indeed metaphysically complex.)

The illustration Wertheimer offers is the unfolding event of a symphony performance. In many contexts, the right answer to the question *Why did that viola just emit an F-natural?* isn't *Because its C-string was stopped at the ratio 4:3*; nor is it *Because the cellos just played a B-flat*. The right answer is very often, *Because that's how Beethoven's Third goes*. Or, as Aristotle might say, you don't have an explanation until you've grasped the formal cause; a thing's form is what it *is*.

Comparison with Aristotle's views on causation might seem to muddy the waters, as the details of those views are notoriously difficult to pin down. Their obscurity, I believe, is no accident; and I also believe that it is related to difficulties in the exposition of Gestalt theory. I suspect that Aristotle and Wertheimer were trying to draw attention to related features of the world and our knowledge of it. Wertheimer doesn't want to deny that the unfolding event of the symphony could exist without viola players sometimes playing Fs when cello players play B-flat any more than Aristotle wants to deny the existence of efficient causes — the physical actions of the musicians and the physical responses of their instruments. Both Wertheimer and Aristotle want to say that in general, or frequently, a list of efficient causes won't tell you *what's going on*. That list will not generate *understanding*.

But where Aristotle's tone is that of someone stating the obvious, Wertheimer's is often desperate. "Piecewise" methods in logic, science, and mathematics, he argues, have obscured what any intelligent *unschooled* child can see. Members of post-Enlightenment European and colonial cultures can't, anymore, see the facts for what they are because we have so profoundly committed ourselves to an erroneous view of what the facts must be.

The attack on piecewise methods constitutes the socio-political wing of Wertheimer's project, his critique of educational theory and practice. But what of his metaphysical commitments? Does he believe, as Aristotle does, that nature as a whole has, like the Beethoven symphony, a final cause? As far as I can tell, he doesn't. Nor does he appear to believe — unlike Wolfgang Metzger, another important Gestalt theorist — that the mind imposes coherence on events; there is not a whiff of Idealism in the way he presents his views. And yet Wertheimer does not, unlike his friend Köhler, explicitly argue against the Idealist position, either. What emerges most clearly in the 1925 essay is his impatience with ungrounded philosophical debate and his commitment to "concrete scientific work." What he wants are the *facts*: about the world and, even more urgently, about how humans (and some other animals) perceive and think. The philosophical status of the facts will be clarified once we have a better idea of what they are. Wertheimer suspects (as do I) that a full appreciation of the facts will necessitate a fundamental overhaul of a great deal of philosophical vocabulary.

ॐ

Wertheimer's example notwithstanding, there are two philosophical questions on which I wish to dwell briefly. The first is this: How can Wertheimer maintain that the unfolding event of the symphony is "not derived from how the individual pieces are put together"? Surely the occurrence of the symphony depends just as much on what the players do as what the players do depends on it. The part- and whole-processes appear to be interdetermining.

That is: It is possible to play "Row, Row, Row Your Boat" in a minor key, and have it still be recognizably "Row, Row, Row Your Boat." Change enough of its structure, however — its time signature, the rhythmic proportions of its melody, many of its intervals — and it won't be "Row, Row, Row" anymore. (How much is enough? There is no rule or recipe.) This seems to be a case where, as the music unfolds, the dynamic relationships among the parts appear to be determining the whole; they give rise to it. Good practising poets will tell you that the same thing appears to be true of poems: the quip attributed to Oscar Wilde about spending the morning taking out a comma and the afternoon putting it back in is no joke. The presence or absence of a comma can indeed affect the meaning of an entire poem, not merely in a grammatical sense (which would be unsurprising), but by affecting the tone of a phrase, which in turn affects the cadence of a stanza, which ultimately conditions our reading of the whole.

In the musical case, the determination of the whole by the behaviour of its parts seems to be especially clear if we remove the score from the picture and consider what happens when musicians get together to jam on a tune they're still working out. Yet here's where things start to get really interesting. I can attest from personal experience that when an ensemble is 'cooking' or 'in the groove,' it feels, to the musicians, as if *the music is playing them*. The experience is not as uncanny when charts are involved (as they are in a string quartet), but it is equally ecstatic. I don't know a good jazz, chamber, or folk musician who doesn't live for such experiences and I've never met anyone with a better explanation than the one I've just given. It is, I believe, such phenomena — what happens when the music plays you, or when the complete solution to a mathematical problem suddenly declares itself, or when you know where you should be on the ice in two seconds in order to receive (out of nowhere) the puck — that Wertheimer was attempting to place centre stage. There is indeed no 'piecemeal,' calculative explanation for these events, one that starts with individuals' conscious ideas about what to do next and builds the whole up out of these elements. You let go — you stop trying to 'do' anything — and the music, or the solution, or the game effortlessly happens through you. These experiences feel the way a flock of sandpipers skimming and twisting over surf looks.

And yet, and yet — even if philosophers were willing to accept this testimony at face value and take it as corroborating the existence of wholes that determine part-processes — there is also no question that musicians in a hot ensemble are reacting to one another. They listen with immense pleasure and delight to their fellows, and they respond — with absolute confidence — to what others do. They co-respond. The whole is determining what the parts do, but the parts are also interdetermining one another and determining the whole. In such situations, the slightest gesture — the flick of a wing — can irrevocably change the shape of what happens.

To summarize: Some wholes are indeed mere aggregates. (A deck of cards, a pallet loaded with bricks.) And some are like symphony performances: they have an explicit *antecedent* and overarching form. Yet others are like marshes or forests or lyric poems in the process of being composed: structures all of whose aspects are in dynamic interrelation with each other and with the whole. In such wholes, the interdetermining response and co-response of distinguishable parts is at least as apparent, at least as discernible, as the shifting, integrated whole that is, at any moment, being realized through their presence. However, the unfolding symphony performance no less than the marsh is an integrated ensemble in which each part has a place, or functions in a way, that enables the whole to be, stably, what it is.

The aspect of Aristotle's view most clearly present in Wertheimer's is that *structure is real*. What the Gestalt theorists add to this claim is that, at least in some cases, we perceive the structure clearly and sharply before we distinguish its interdetermining aspects from one another. The evidence is overwhelming that they are correct. Do such structures pre-exist, in a robust metaphysical sense, their apparently interdetermining aspects? That's one possible explanation, and sometimes it seems that they do. That they do in all interesting cases is Plato's view. In a general way, it is also Kant's — though Kant tried to solve the attendant metaphysical quandaries by insisting that all metaphysical structure is epistemological in origin. (And Hegel then tried to locate the origin of epistemological structure in language — thus post-structuralism.) None of these views is intuitively satisfying. They are, however, testaments to the depth of the challenge. If we admit that the apprehension of structure, whole and unmediated, is the foundation of our experience of meaning, we can construct no *merely* materialist-mechanical story of how the mind interacts with the world. I believe this means that materialist-mechanical accounts of the world are not wholly correct. It is, however, by no means clear what, if anything, to put in their place.

The second philosophical question that requires attention before we can turn to the facts is this: What are we talking about when we speak of a 'gestalt'? A perception, 'in the mind'? A thing, 'out there,' in the world? This question may seem simply to be an attempt to get Wertheimer to declare for or against Idealism, but it is not. Idealists, too, distinguish between phenomena that *appear* to have mind-independent existence and phenomena that do not.

Gestalt theory was, and still is, primarily intended to answer the question *How do we see?* With the development of optics and the investigation of retinal images in the seventeenth century, some aspects of seeing became straightforwardly explicable and others became mysterious. For the retinal image itself does not distinguish, for example, between a trapezoid erected in two dimensions parallel to the plane of the retina, and a square tilted in a third dimension. Nonetheless, we make such distinctions both accurately and instantaneously, without effort, hundreds of times a day. How do we do it? The Gestalt school rejected the theory that we (and other animals) register separate features of an isolated retinal image and, based on experience, proceed to draw conclusions about those features, reasoning our way to a correct interpretation of the image. No one had been able to propose a plausible account of the reasoning (which, if it exists, has to transpire with extraordinary speed); nor had anyone designed an experiment that successfully demonstrated that we register separate features first. Pointing to these lacunae, Gestalt theorists argued that we register — without calculation — internal relations among aspects of visual arrays.

What is a gestalt? A gestalt is *what we perceive*. What sort of thing is *what we perceive*? This question has no happy answer because of the way in which Western intellectual history delimits the 'sorts' that a thing might be. To say that a melody is a gestalt is in no way to deny that it is, as we say, 'veridical.' But it is not, thereby, to denominate it an 'object,' like a rock or a rock star. We can say, with some degree of truth, that Wertheimer was primarily concerned with perception and not ontology, and that this concern colours his use of the term 'gestalt.' But the nature of what we call perception has not been resolved, nor has the relation between perception and ontology. This much is clear: many of the primordial terms and assumptions of our standard philosophical gestalt of perception — that it involves some 'mental' 'registration' of a 'reality' that is either 'external' or 'projected' — are *interdefined*. The question of what a gestalt 'is' carries all the historical freight of ancient debates, even though Gestalt theory, as Wertheimer developed it, was an attempt to step outside that discussion. To say 'see' or 'perceive' or 'know,' in a scholarly context, is to invoke the whole apparatus, even if one is attempting to avoid engaging with it. I believe that this, in part, is why Wertheimer had such trouble writing.

ﻉﻭ

The Experience of Meaning

I propose at last to take Wertheimer's advice and now set philosophical discussion to one side. We need some concrete examples.

Think of what happens when you see a face. You don't, contrary to received computational wisdom, first perceive bits and pieces — a blue eye, a 45-millimetre-long nose, a squarish chin, another blue eye, a 50-millimetre-wide mouth with narrow lips — and synthesize these in a judgment or inference. ("Yes, it adds up to Joe, my old friend from high school.") You see, first, the face. ("Good heavens! Joe!" or sometimes — "Good heavens! It's, um, er ..." — you have to search for the name although you know the face; "... it's Joe!") Only subsequently, and usually only if prompted (perhaps you wonder how he is and search for signs) do you notice individual features. ("Those eyes: he's had a hard time." Or, perhaps, a facelift.)

In one of its simplest forms, this perceptual tendency is demonstrated by what Max Wertheimer called the *phi* phenomenon. Set up two individual lights and turn them on and off in sequence, one after another, repeatedly. When the interval between flashes falls in a certain range, a viewer positioned a certain distance away from both lights will not see first one light flash, then the second one, and then the first again. She will perceive a single light moving continuously back and forth between the two positions. This is an important case to foreground because it shows that our tendency to perceive gestalts — wholes rather than collections of parts — can get it wrong. Overwhelmingly, however, it tends to get it right. How do we know that it tends to get it right? Because we're still here, both as individuals and as a species; because you do immediately recognize your old friend; because you do correctly call that glimpsed diving silhouette for a grebe, and because you can hum along with a rockabilly arrangement of "Row, Row, Row Your Boat" that you've never heard before (and hope you'll never hear again). These and many other commonplace perceptual achievements are incomprehensible on a building-block model of perception, which assumes that we start with perceptual 'atoms' that we somehow 'reason' into coherence.

There are two ways in which we become aware of gestalts. In some cases, we move from a chaotic situation — a jumble of lines, concepts, sounds, or data — to a situation in which we discern pattern or structure: the face springs out at us; the identity of the culprit dawns. Ben

Shahn, the painter and printer, was referring to this kind of experience when he described the "so-called genius" as "only that one who discerns the pattern of things within the confusion of details a little sooner than the average man." Here are two illustrations:

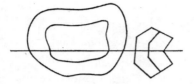

Fig. 1
What single-digit integer is contained in this figure?

At first, Figure 1 may appear to be nothing more than a doodle — two accidentally irregular closed figures bisected by an equally irregular line. Once the numeral is seen, however, it springs out every time.

Fig. 2
What is this?

This figure, too, appears to have no meaning; and then suddenly, when we see it as a word connected to its mirror image, it does. The effect is the mental equivalent of dropping a crystal of sodium acetate into a supersaturated solution.

In other cases — the second type of gestalt experience — we see one thing as another; our perceptual or conceptual experience undergoes a kind of restructuring.

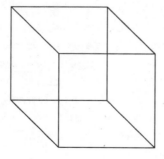

Fig. 3
Necker cube

12 The Experience of Meaning

A beautiful abstract version of this sort of shift occurs with the Necker cube, which can be seen with its front face pointing down and to the right, or with its front face pointing up and to the left. The first time we are exposed to the figure, it is usually stable in one orientation and we have to be invited to perceive it in the other. But, once we've experienced the shift, we can re-perform it at will.

Another example of a figure that illustrates our capacity for gestalt shifts is the so-called Rubin vase:

Fig. 4
Rubin vase

When we look at this figure, we see either a central chalice, in white, or two human profiles facing each other, in black. For most people, these two gestalts alternate; but it makes no sense to say one is more basic than the other, nor to say that the drawing is 'really' just splotches of paint that we can 'interpret' as we choose. Our experience is not of interpretation — it doesn't involve thinking through or puzzling about what we've seen. It is an experience of direct perception: we see one of the figures immediately, and the second shortly afterward (especially if we've been told it's there). The relevance of this figure for poetry is obvious — it's an example of metaphor in action, of seeing one thing (two faces in profile) as another (a chalice) on the basis of profound, inalienable, shared structure.

Here is yet another example, a standard visual proof of the Pythagorean theorem that depends on seeing that the area of the square with

What Is Gestalt Thinking?

side *c* has to be *the same as* the combined areas of the squares with sides *a* and *b*.

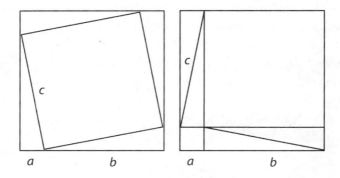

Fig. 5   *Proof of the Pythagorean Theorem*

Should we, in fact, call such experience perception? Or does it involve *con*ception, thinking of some kind? Or is it a combination of the two? This is a question that greatly interested Ludwig Wittgenstein. In the phenomenon of 'seeing-as,' he suggested, "[m]any of our concepts *cross*." Recent neuropsychological research confirms the existence of 'perceptual-cognitive phenomena' — that is, situations in which large patterns of neuronal activity in the brain interact with the local activity of particular perceptual neurons. The phrase 'perceptual-cognitive phenomena' is technically precise, but clumsy. Speakers of English have long used the vocabulary of sense experience to indicate that they *understand* — "I see!", "I hear you!", "I feel I'm on the right track." I propose to continue in this vein and to avoid the use of technical terms. It may be that one of the things respectful attention to gestalt capacities will teach us is that the traditional distinction between sense perception and thought is empty.

Early Gestalt research focused almost exclusively on overtly visual phenomena — the kinds of shifts and restructurings illustrated by the *phi* phenomenon, the 'buried numeral 4' problem, and the mirror word problem. (Although the examples given above involve synchronic images, it is important to remember that temporally extended gestalts —

the *phi* phenomenon and melody — were fundamental to early Gestalt theory.) In later years, Wertheimer's interest turned to gestalt recognitions that have no overt physical component. He was particularly intrigued by their occurrence in mathematics, citing the famous story of young Karl Friedrich Gauss as an example. We don't have Gauss's own testimony, which may be why the story has developed a life of its own. The version I'll tell comes from Wolfgang Sartorius, the source closest in time to Gauss. (It is slightly different from the version Wertheimer tells.) Sartorius says that one day Gauss's schoolmaster told his pupils to sum a sequence of successive integers and Gauss got the answer immediately, putting his slate, according to the custom in his class, on a table designated for the purpose, and saying "Ligget se" ("Here it is"). He then, according to Sartorius, quietly waited an hour for the others to finish, at which point his slate, at the bottom of the stack on the table, was found to have the correct answer.

Later accounts specify the sequence that was added — many give it as 1 to 100, some give it as 1 to 1,000, others as 1 to 10 (Wertheimer's version), and yet others as another sequence. Some accounts also describe the method Gauss used, although Sartorius doesn't. The key facts are these: the boy was given some arithmetic series or other and saw, almost instantly, what the sum was. How did he do it? The most plausible suggestion is that he did what many mathematicians have since done when contemplating similar problems: he declined to view the problem piecemeal, and saw it as a structural issue about the whole sequence. In any arithmetic series, the first number added to the last will give the same total as the second number added to the second-last; and the same total as the third number added to the third-last; and so on. If the sequence is 1 to 100, each pair sums to 101: $1 + 100 = 101$, $2 + 99 = 101$, $3 + 98 = 101$. And we can see why: in each pair, the same amount is added to the first number and subtracted from the second.

$$\longrightarrow$$
$$1 + \ 2 + \ 3 + \ldots + 48 + 49 + 50$$
$$100 + 99 + 98 + \ldots + 53 + 52 + 51$$
$$\longleftarrow$$

Fig. 6
Summing 1 to 100

What Is Gestalt Thinking?   15

All you need to know to figure out the sum of the whole sequence is how many pairs you have. In the 1-to-100 case, it will be 50. 50 times 101 is 5,050. Presto.

Some of the most illustrious discoveries in the history of science and mathematics are examples of such gestalt shifts: Poincaré's famous description of his recognition that the transformations he had used to define Fuchsian functions were identical with those of non-Euclidean geometry; or Newton's equally famous account of the origin of his conjecture about the nature of gravity. Wertheimer and his colleagues maintained that all productive thinking — thinking that involves insight, thinking that precipitates an experience of meaning — involves the apprehension of gestalts. As far as I can tell, they were right. Gestalt comprehension is the foundation of a great deal of problem-solving, of understanding or 'getting it,' and is also the wellspring of much creative work in both the exact sciences and the arts. It is a basic form of intelligence.

ॐ

We frequently use the vocabulary of recognition to describe our experiences of insight, and this is no accident. Whether the problem is understanding what your friend meant when she said "Uh-oh" in that peculiar tone of voice or calculating the sum of a long sequence of integers without tediously adding them up one by one, the experience is indeed one of *re*-cognizing a situation.

The word 'recognition,' however, implies, as does the word 'insight,' that we've grasped something true — and not all gestalts are veridical. Wertheimer's first laboratory experiment — the one involving the so-called *phi* phenomenon — was in fact designed to demonstrate the intransigence of a demonstrably *false* gestalt. Kepler's vision of the relations of the planetary orbits to the five perfect solids proved illusory — although it struck him with such tremendous force that it continued to inspire his thinking even after he himself had demonstrated that it was false. What this reveals is that the experience of meaning is not always an experience of truth. What it does *not* show is that gestalts are generally unreliable, much less that they are merely 'subjective' impressions. The

16   The Experience of Meaning

phi phenomenon is as 'objective' as perceptions get — everyone sees one moving light instead of two lights flashing on and off in sequence.

"But surely," someone will protest, "gestalts aren't as 'real' as elementary sensations. The downward-projecting box and the upward-projecting box are just interpretations of an array that is, in fact, neither." But this misses the point that our immediate experience of the Necker cube is of one box or the other; 'an array of lines that is neither' is an *abstraction* from immediate experience. I don't want to deny that 'elementary sensations' exist; I'm not expert enough in neuropsychology to know one way or the other. I want only to note that there is no perceptual evidence that they are the building blocks of our experience of the world. They don't exist *the way* what we call *things* do. "I stand at the window and see a house, trees, sky," writes Wertheimer. "Theoretically I might say there were 327 brightnesses and nuances of colour. Do I *have* '327'? No. I have sky, house, and trees." Are skies, houses, and trees, melodies and faces, real?

They are what we perceive.

•

Although gestalt comprehension is fundamental to accurate, reliable perception, to problem-solving, and to the experience of meaning, in many ways it appears to be different from what we, in contemporary North American culture, usually regard as intelligence. For example, gestalts tend to shift or coalesce suddenly, in a flash. They aren't the result of processes with discernible steps which elapse through time. And although you can work on the requisite intellectual muscles by developing skills that require gestalt comprehension — making music, for example, or following Ikea assembly instructions — there's usually no technique or method for precipitating a given gestalt. If you don't get it, the best you can do is ask someone to trace the outlines again — and hope. Once you do get a gestalt, though, it tends to make a strong impression. Unlike some of the results of calculative intelligence, gestalts, once comprehended, are hard to undermine.

However: our inability to guarantee that a given gesture or diagram will precipitate the right gestalt for everyone, or, even, for anyone, does not mean there is no right gestalt to precipitate. It does not mean there is no point in trying to tell the truth, or in trying to listen to it being told. It means only that there is no formula for success. Meaning isn't structured in a way that will allow it to be made by a machine; there is no series of steps that can assure insight into the nature of the world. The process cannot be digitized. It is not programmable. This is because the perception of gestalts does not, by definition, occur in piecemeal, stepwise fashion: gestalts are wholes and perception of them occurs all at once and also as a whole.

And although recipes are not available, the question *How do we become proficient in gestalt comprehension?* nonetheless has a clear answer: practice. In a reductive context, this answer may appear to be circular: how can we practise recognizing gestalts if we don't know how to recognize them? Yet it is just the answer Aristotle gave his fellow citizens about how to become virtuous, and he expected to be understood. Aristotle expanded a little: he suggested that we hang out with those known for excellence. Acquire some experience of how they go about their lives. Follow in their footsteps. Copy them. It's the same advice you'd give to someone in fifteenth-century Florence who wanted to become a painter, or to someone in an eighteenth-century Haida village who wanted to learn how to carve. That is: becoming proficient in gestalt comprehension, like learning to be virtuous, learning to paint, learning to carve, is an *art*. There's no civilization in the world, except perhaps our own, that does not understand a great deal of what learning *is* in these terms.

Connected to the absence of algorithms for precipitating gestalt insight is another characteristic that literate post-Enlightenment culture finds extremely problematic: gestalt comprehension appears, in at least some instances, to be at odds with language-use.

In 1916, Wertheimer had a series of conversations with Albert Einstein which formed the basis of an essay on Einstein's thought processes in developing the theory of relativity. "These thoughts," Einstein said, referring to his crucial insights regarding simultaneity, "did not come in any verbal formulation. I very rarely think in words at all. A thought comes, and I may try to express it in words afterward." When Wertheimer pressed him, saying, "many report that their thinking is always in words," Einstein merely laughed.

Some forty years later, Konrad Lorenz claimed that his ability to recognize distant birds in flight was disrupted when he consciously tried to distinguish the details on which — he thought — his identifications depended. He described this as gestalt perception's "sensitivity to self-observation" and elaborated: "Rationally controlled attention to perceived details apparently disrupts the equilibrium that must exist between those details if they are to come together in a unified Gestalt." Why? Lorenz quotes Goethe: *Das Wort bemüht sich nur umsonst, Gestalten schöpferisch aufzubaun* — "words strive in vain to bring to life the forms we see." This is so, Lorenz says, because it's not possible to put "the innumerable, multi-directional relationships" that comprise gestalts into the "linear, temporal sequence of spoken language." He speculated that a failure of memory was involved.

More recent research confirms Lorenz's (and Goethe's) observations, but disputes Lorenz's view that inadequate memory might be the culprit. Jonathan Schooler, an American psychologist, contends that the problem is structural: we can't talk about certain aspects of gestalt perception because the cognitive capacities involved in analysis and verbal description actually interfere with the cognitive capacities involved in shape-recognition and insight. There's no describable series of steps, as there is with problems that require only analysis. To attempt to articulate the thought processes involved is to undermine them. Or: we can try to talk, but we won't do a very good job, either of talking or gestalting. The experience of poets in this regard is especially striking: even when the gestalt is a word-complex — a poem — it appears that the *thinking* that produces the poem does not occur (or does not occur entirely) in words.

ॐ

Gestalt thinking fundamentally involves the spontaneous perception of structure: not analytic order — one brick stacked on another — but what might be called resonant internal relations.

Resonance is to gestalt comprehension what valid consequence is to deduction. It names the relation that must hold among parts if the whole of which they have become parts is to be a gestalt. In a culture that identifies thinking with the aggregation of atoms or elements, acknowledgment of such wholes can be hard to come by: the dominant epistemology makes them, literally, unthinkable. Critics of Gestalt theory, like logical positivists, especially dislike the concept of 'internal relations.' Virgil Aldrich provided a classic statement of the complaint:

> Wertheimer's [manner of speaking] tantalizes the painstaking reader with the impression that something important is being said, something that needs to get said as a corrective for the old associationist and rationalist psychologies; but precisely *what* is being said remains an enigma. This reviewer, for one, wishes that as great a psychologist as Wertheimer had written at least one whole chapter of *Gestalt* theory of learning without once using the semi-metaphorical term 'inner.' Doubtless there are 'inner meanings' to be apprehended, but a theory of these should contain some literal analysis of the term, to provide means to identify and manipulate them in an objective way.

No metaphors! Literal analysis! Objectivity! — This is not a critique of Gestalt theory but a statement that it must be wrong. One way of attempting to understand the Gestalt project is to say that Wertheimer put the concept of metaphor — more precisely, the concept of significant similarity and the notion of internal relations on which it depends — where standard theory puts the concept of epistemological atoms. The appeal to internal relations isn't an attempt to avoid the issue; it's an attempt to state what the real issue is.

Or: we should expect to feel some discomfort with Gestalt theory's observations and proposals, its failure to produce predictive algorithms, the pressure it seems to put on the standard distinctions between thinking and perceiving. Our way of talking in literate post-Enlightenment society is epistemologically loaded: reductionism, and the ideal of context-independent, algorithmically specifiable processes that reductionism subserves, are part of the texture of 'educated' speech. That texture won't allow us to express what is fundamental to gestalt comprehension in compelling terms. This is why it is crucial to keep reminding ourselves of our actual experience of meaning, those times when our breath has been taken away, when our vision has been altered. When we focus on this experience, we know, immediately, that it is important: it

The Experience of Meaning

is one of the grand reasons for getting out of bed in the morning. And so, if we keep its image before us, we will want to tell the truth about it; we will be willing to struggle to find a way to do so. We will wrestle with our standard ways of talking — where else are we going to start? — and be willing to see past them, or through them, to insights that we can't articulate in their terms. Ultimately, if we stick with the project, insist on being honest with ourselves about our experience, we will be led to a new grammar of thought. Because there is overwhelming evidence that we do, often, think and perceive things in ways that standard aggregative theories cannot account for, I think it is reductionist prejudice that has to go, not gestalts. This is not to say that aggregative synthesis is *not* a kind of thinking. It is to say that it is not the only kind there is, and that it is not always the most important kind.

&

What, then, is gestalt thinking? It is an attempt to perceive the shape of things, their inner and outer attunements, their melody. Gestalt thinking and gestalt insight are present wherever we look, though our ability to recognize and therefore to acknowledge them has been eroded by the ideal of mechanization. This ideal — in its eighteenth-century form of physical mechanism, its twentieth-century form of industrialized physical mechanism, and its twenty-first-century form of digital mechanism — grounds the West's pursuit of what it calls progress. There can be no question that the advent of machines has made life easier for countless numbers of human beings. There can also be no question that the rise of mechanization has not made meaning easier to apprehend. To grasp a gestalt, on the other hand, just is to apprehend meaning.

✌ Poetry and Meaninglessness

THE PLEASURES OF GESTALTS

ALL CARDS, REMOVE YOURSELF

Grandparents were.
Chapter life.
Some people do not know

To say that the organization
We are accidents.
Lost the next day from a convenient
*   location.*

Report an accident
No freedom to use it.
Ezekiel.

— Jim Murdoch

A friend of mine, a widely educated scholar involved in the arts, wrote to me recently confessing that, although as a child he had wanted nothing more than to write poetry and thought of himself as a lover of poetry, he could read very little of what is now published under that name. He finds it meaningless. My first response (and my response to my friend) was that it has always been thus: there has never been a time when there were not a great many bad or indifferent poems written for every good or great one. I had to concede that the internet has made a difference to our sense of what is publishable — it now includes everything. But was this the source of his dismay? On reflection, I found myself increasingly curious. I couldn't help admitting that I understood my friend's problem; he was at least partly right — one of the striking things about some contemporary poetic dross is its apparent meaninglessness. Would this complaint have been lodged against Edwardian poetic dross? Florentine? Athenian? I remembered having seen "scandalous," "clumsy," "hideous," "trivial," and "dull, dull, dull" in the historical critical record, but not, before the advent of Dada, "meaningless." (All good poems are alike, we might say; all bad ones are epochally defined.) Meaninglessness, then, appears to be a particularly twentieth- and twenty-first-century concern. Why should this be so?

It might seem that with the mention of Dada, I've answered my own question. Dada set out, in 1916, to *be* meaningless: it wanted to destroy the complacency, the pretentiousness and vapid aestheticism that its members felt had precipitated a continental war. It aimed to offend logic and reason; it wanted to shock cultivated taste. Its promulgation of collage technique and 'readymades' laid the foundation for both surrealism and postmodernism. For better or worse, its interest in both mechanical and random composition is still with us. Why is meaninglessness our age's poetic *bête noire*? Ask Tristan Tzara.

And while you're at it, ask Ezra Pound and T.S. Eliot: high modernism appears to be part of the problem, too. Its adherents also distrusted 'bourgeois' institutions, the easy, ennobling sentiments of run-of-the-mill Victorian verse. Unlike the Dadaists, however, they didn't think the answer was to dispense with meaning; they thought the answer was to resuscitate it. They were impressed by what Darwin, Nietzsche, and Freud had to say about human nature's darker side and weren't keen to see psychological truth straitjacketed by nice literary manners. They wanted to tell it like it was. Stream of consciousness emerged as an important technique, along with an interest in multiple points of view. Imagism, which refuses to impose discursive continuity on insight, is a direct outgrowth of both techniques. The results can be hard to follow. Couple this with a simultaneous erosion of literacy — owing to a laudable attempt to fully democratize the public school system and the absence of sufficient funding for the project — and you end up with a body of literature that is for many readers as unintelligible as Dada's successors strive to be.

But this, while it traces the history of the phenomenon, doesn't really answer the question. What made Dada's program so potent? How did it become any part of the artistic mainstream, influencing European and colonial sensibilities so strongly that young artists who may not even have heard of the movement now compose according to its precepts? Dadaists themselves might point to the ongoing need to protest the atrocities and inanities of life in the technocratic hegemony. And plenty of postmodern art would bear them out. But that need doesn't explain the way unthinking collage, the poem as unfocused grab-bag, has caught on among those who are completely uninterested in cultural reform. My suggestion is that the superficial resemblance between the artifacts of Dada and high modernism constitutes the background to this problem: it paves the way for the belief that art is supposed to be unintelligible. In the foreground, however, is a quite distinct phenomenon: the pleasure that many of us (though not my friend) take in meaningless compositions. That pleasure, which underwrites our tolerance for overt meaninglessness, is bound up with a basic way in which human beings think.

Consider 'cut-up technique,' popularized by William S. Burroughs in the middle of the last century and now frequently pursued as a workshop exercise. It goes like this: Find or write something that makes straightforward sense. Write it out on paper. Then take scissors and cut what you've written into scraps — individual words and phrases. Mix these up. Lay them out randomly, but with discernible line-breaks. Nudge here and there for local effects (punctuation, the odd article or preposition added or eliminated). Maybe omit a few chunks. There's your poem.

> *write Write written*
> $\qquad$ *scissor*
> *article odd line breaks randomly*
> *individual*
> *punctuation nudge*
> $\qquad$ *local effects*
> *there on paper*

The question is why this works. For assuredly it does. Not always, and not always with brilliant results. But certainly more frequently than the curmudgeons among us might expect. The exercise repeatedly gives its practitioners what I have heard referred to as 'the poetry buzz.' What is 'the poetry buzz'? My hypothesis is that it is a version of the energy release associated with the exercise of gestalt intelligence. It doesn't matter whether we're confronted with the lyric equivalent of the Theory of Relativity or a linguistic version of the lights in Wertheimer's *phi* phenomenon experiment: the mind naturally reaches for gestalts, and it comes up with them, warranted or not. When you are confronted with something that you've been told is a poem, getting a gestalt, any gestalt, gives you the poetry buzz.

That is: The mind likes to do what it does. It feels good to 'get it,' to 'see' the solution to the problem in arithmetic, to identify the flash of a Cooper's hawk on the wing in dense forest. This is what the experience of meaning *is*: the perception, in challenging circumstances, of a gestalt. And experiencing meaning is an evolutionary pleasure; it's what the mind is for. In the good old days, before smelting and electricity, our lives depended on accurate shape recognition. Like many other evolved capacities, we exercise it by default. Running well, throwing well, recognizing what's out there well — we enjoy what we're fitted for.

So, confronted with an apparently random assortment of words and phrases, or what seems to be a grab-bag of private images and jottings, we nonetheless try to form a gestalt — especially if we've been cued that what we're looking at is 'a poem' and not a grocery list. Often we're successful: Aha! We experience what Sharon Mesmer, a leading flarfist, is reported to have described as "a little pop in [the] mind." The more problematic the initial array, the more powerful the release, the louder the pop. The bigger the poetry buzz.

What's flarf? The epigraph by Jim Murdoch at the beginning of this essay is an example. Flarf got started as a protest movement. In 2000 a New York poet named Gary Sullivan set out to expose the International Library of Poetry as a sham. The ILP routinely solicited entries in what it called 'poetry contests' — and declared every entry it received a winner. Each 'winner' was then invited to pay $50 for a copy of an anthology featuring their poem. Sullivan's grandfather got suckered by this little Ponzi scheme and Sullivan decided to take revenge. He submitted the absolutely worst poem he could come up with; it was just terrible. When he 'won,' he showed the poem and the congratulatory letter to a group of friends, who in turn submitted their own terrible poems to the ILP. And then — here's the interesting thing — they got hooked. The practice took off. Sullivan subsequently wrote a piece titled "Flarf

Poetry and Meaninglessness   25

Balonacy Swingle," which gave the movement its name. Drew Gardner developed its signature technique, which involves typing unusual terms into a search engine and then collating the results. (This is the technique that was used to generate "All cards remove yourself.") It's now a growth industry, both in terms of the primary production of artifacts and in terms of the secondary critical literature that's being written about the artifacts. And hardly anyone is laughing.

Not that flarf is, by itself, the problem; it's simply one apotheosis of our willingness to accept meaninglessness. Its value as an exemplar lies in Mesmer's articulation of why it appeals. Her answer is the key to the phenomenon as a whole.

'Aleatory' is the fancy Latin-based word for compositions that involve randomizing techniques like compiling search results from the internet or cutting up a straightforward composition and tossing the bits in the air. Meaningless poetry can be generated in other ways, too, though. It can be produced by the non-random algorithms advocated by groups like Oulipo — substituting for every noun the next noun in the dictionary, for example; or deleting every word that contains a 't.' (Applying both rules in sequence, and depending on the dictionary, we might get: "Can be produced by non-random / algoses, by grouses like ounce — / for every noup, noup. In dicyanide / for exangulous; or every wore.") Or meaningless compositions can be generated by simply distorting the lexicon and syntax at will, as some adherents of the L=A=N=G=U=A=G=E school advise. The 'theory' of such writing often explicitly invites the reader to project a gestalt. Indeed, the L=A=N=G=U=A=G=E school contends that forcing readers to project gestalts teaches them that they, and they alone, are responsible for the creation of meaning in all contexts, thereby undermining capitalist myths about the ownership of intellectual property. Machine constraints — for example, "write an intelligible narrative in which only the vowels a, e, i, and o appear" — can also be used to produce work that is not overtly incomprehensible, but which is nonetheless frivolous: meaningless in the way that a word game is meaningless. The results can be readily understood as far as they go, but they are, primarily, amusements, distractions from the difficulty of real engagement with the world, ways to show off one's cleverness. The aim of such compositions isn't to get the poetry buzz; it's to win.

26   The Experience of Meaning

In contexts where the aim is to force readers to project a gestalt, the buzz, if it occurs, is like a sugar high — empty ontological calories that tell us nothing about the world. This doesn't matter unless we become addicted, refusing real lyric food in preference to stuff that doesn't nourish us. The parallel is exact. Too many pops scored with our scissors and gluestick, and we become uninterested in getting out there to forage for real gestalt calories. Why bother, when we can visit the worldwide literary convenience store and grab the equivalent of a Coke and donut? The result for our literary diets is the same as it is for our physical ones: we want sugar in everything and we see no need to learn to hunt, garden, or cook.

Nonetheless, aleatory fooling around in small doses can — like sugar in small doses — sometimes give us just the kick we need to get going on a project. Many poets who write perfectly intelligible poems play with random fragments or machine poetry as a way to warm up, to stretch their lyric muscles and get the gestalt juices flowing. And, just to make things really difficult, it sometimes happens that, by accident, the randomly generated juxtapositions or the rule-governed distortions actually pick up on a way the world really is. (If I toss fifty pennies in the air, it's possible they might land in a pattern that resembles a maple leaf.) Is it a problem, when this happens, that we can't tell — unless we know the compositional history — that the poem is making those connections by accident or through insight? I don't think so. The problem is that we can get so entranced by the game that we forget to go back to work.

And poetry *is* work. It is the work of telling the truth, that is, of perceiving and responding to the real. In all ages and in all cultures, it springs from the discernment of complex, non-linear, integrated, and therefore resonant structures in the world. That is why poetry is also real food. (In the next section, I'll address the concern that the world doesn't really exist, that humans are the sole source of meaning, which they always already invent.) Of course, the world does, and the poem may, include machines, games, and our own delight in both. The task of the poet is to use language — a naturally linear medium that lends itself to the specification of discrete particulars — to gesture towards the resonant structure she has discerned so that we, as readers, can see through the poem to a way the world is. (If readers consistently end up focusing on the finger pointing at the moon instead of the moon, then we, as poets, have not done our jobs. The post-structuralist will ask if the gesture of pointing is not itself a part of the world — if the poem can point to machines and games, why can't it point to itself pointing? It can. And some great poems do. Again, the thing to watch out for is becoming addicted to the trick.) The difference between real and meaningless lyric poetry is this: the real poem, a resonant linguistic structure, stands in a real resonant relation to a resonant structure in the world. The real poem is a gestalt that enacts, or responds to, a way the world, or some part of it, is. The genuinely meaningless poem may have moments of local coherence, but it does not, as a whole, hang together with the world. There is no resonant structure in the world to which it stands in resonant relation.

As technocracy has burgeoned, gestalt comprehension has become less and less visible as a way of understanding the world. Under the press of colonialism, capitalism, resourcism, consumerism, and exponential human population growth, the natural world, human cultures, and relations among nonhuman and human cultures have disintegrated. As a consequence, the resonant gestalts of lyric vision are harder to come by. Insight of any scope is difficult to achieve, difficult for artists to render, and difficult for audiences to appreciate.

In countries with large gross domestic products relative to their populations, the world in which human gestalt capacities evolved is no longer with us. Those capacities are not required for navigating; for knowing where food and water might be found; for hunting or for tending plants; for cooking and preparing food; for reading the weather; for reading the behaviour of nonhuman animals; for reading the behaviour of other humans. Instead of skill in such matters, we have global-positioning systems; Siri; self-regulating houses; the processed ready-to-eat products of food marketers; work environments sealed from the weather; texting. Intelligence is everywhere represented as computation — in the popular press, in business, at the university. Our gestalt capacities are active, but they are harnessed by marketing agencies and political interests to manipulate us. We are vulnerable to such manipulation because our gestalt intelligence is underdeveloped. We no longer exercise and refine gestalt capacities in situations that matter — we don't use them to discern vital

28   The Experience of Meaning

truths about the world. As a result, we are not motivated to become more proficient gestalt thinkers and we become ever more vulnerable. The deep pleasure of the experience of meaning eludes us.

Thus, in the literary sphere, the bewilderments of high modernism are re-enacted and deepened, with predictable results. Don't 'get' a lot of the recent canon? Does it all just seem like a bunch of words? Does 'interpretation' appear to be nothing more than seeing shapes in clouds? Light bulb: What if it *is* all just a bunch of words! At least we can let everyone in on the secret. We can turn poetry into a randomized compilation that isn't supposed to make profound sense — using techniques anyone, or even a machine, can master — and the folks who want to play cloud shapes can have at it. At least there's no more pretense around 'inspiration,' no more suggestion that we need to be serious about the results, no more anxiety that there might actually be something the poem is about which we should strive to understand.

It is on this point, though not on others, that aleatory, machine, and distortion techniques make contact with the ethos of cool. If you're going to be cool, it's extremely important not to be seen to care about meaning. This we might call avoidance of meaning, however, rather than embrace of meaninglessness. For it's easy enough to grasp — we are meant to grasp — the despair and the nostalgia for more earnest times that underlie cool's sophisticated and ironic surface. Cool is in fact deeply angry at the cultural betrayal of earnestness through ubiquitous advertising and political spin. It feels powerless to resist them — it is a plugged-in urban genre. But if we mistake its superficial frivolousness, its rhetorical costume dramas and its fascination with camp for vacuity, we have misunderstood it. Cool does not thrum with the resonance of reality; it's afraid that if it tries, it will be duped by yet another social construct. But it genuinely mourns that it's lost touch. It enacts an engagement with the emptied outline of reality, with reality conceived as negative space.

To summarize: there are four intersecting factors governing the rise of meaningless poetry:

(1)   the emptiness of late-nineteenth-century European culture, which gave rise both to Dada and to high modernism; and

the ongoing breakdown of nonhuman and human cultures, which extends and deepens the difficulty of achieving or appreciating genuine lyric vision of any scope;
(2) the failure of educational practices to develop the literary muscles in readers that would enable them, at least some of the time, to distinguish difficult compositions from meaningless ones;
(3) the effect that the proliferation of both very difficult poems and fun aleatory compositions has had on the general perception of 'how to write poetry'; and, crucially,
(4) the addictive gestalt sugar-pop that humans get from aleatory and other determinedly meaningless compositions.

The first three factors, or at least aspects of them, are old hat; the fourth, however, is one to which we've paid little attention. It is what sustains us in our tolerance for meaninglessness. That, and our mammalian compulsion to comply, our atavistic desire to hang out with the herd. Although many of us sense the moral vacuum at the centre of 'anything goes,' we feel powerless to do anything but salute. We're afraid that if we don't pretend that anything that calls itself a poem is a poem, we'll be accused of elitism and bigotry. I believe, passionately, that it's time to stop erecting tribal barricades and excluding perspectives. But I do not believe that the only alternative to exclusion is a consumerist shrug.

We often employ the vocabulary of recognition to talk about what happens when we perceive gestalts — bird-shapes, old friends. But didn't Uncle Ezra teach us that real poetry must 'make it new'? He did; and I agree. How, then, if poetry is supposed to 'make it new,' can it have anything to do with recognizing a way the world is? If we already know what the poem is telling us, how can it surprise us? Isn't 'making it new' a vote for precisely the kind of linguistic experimentation I've rejected?

According to Roo Borson, *Fresh is always fresh*. This is Pound's imperative in the descriptive mood. It tells us how to recognize that someone has made something significant: what they've made *stays* new. It continues to surprise with every reading. Mathematicians have noticed this about good proofs: they 're-surprise' those who think them through anew. This recurring surprise is what makes a proof satisfying. And it's the same with the arts. The connoisseurs, the experts, are those who continually re-savour masterpieces, who re-experience, each time, what they experienced the first time: the shock of meaning.

A great poem offers us this shock. It is always fresh because each time we read it, our mind experiences a gestalt shift with a pay-off: truth. 'Recognize,' then, does not mean 'see the same old same old'; it means re-cognize — that is, experience the *shift* in gestalts. To be a lyric artist is to have a capacity for this sort of structural insight plus the ability not simply to state the insight but to show it: to create something that allows other minds to experience the same shift.

The work of lyric art focuses our attention on real structures in the real world: it allows us to experience real connections among these structures. It achieves this through an enactment that is also a pointing. P.K. Page insisted on drawing a distinction between verse and poetry. Verse, for her, was not defined by its formal prosody and rhyme: it was defined by the fact that it was consciously made up by the writer. She reserved the word 'poetry,' whether formal or free, for poems that seemed to spring from a source outside her and spoke themselves through her:

> I am far from sure that I am the perpetrator of my own work. By that I don't mean I plagiarize — consciously, at least. But I do feel, as many writers do, that I am a vehicle, a channel for something that writes through me — badly sometimes, better at others. I cannot write if 'it' does not write me.

Or, as Robert Bringhurst has noted, you can walk the path where seizings have been known to occur, but you can't *make* poetry happen to you.

This does not mean that what P.K. called verse is without its pleasures. It can be witty and amusing, it can be impressive, intellectually engaging, and affecting by turns. But it won't break your heart or make you shout for joy. It will never knock your socks off — that is, leave you barefoot on the earth. Only writing that is rooted in the real has that power — the power to move us, because it is itself always in motion.

THE ART OF DISCERNMENT

> *Sometimes, we go into a man's study and find his books and papers all over the place, and can say without hesitation: "What a mess! We really must clear this room up." Yet, at other times, we may go into a room which looks very like the first; but after looking round we decide that we must leave it just as it is, recognizing that, in this case,* even the dust has its place.
>
> — Ludwig Wittgenstein

But how *do* we do it? In difficult cases, how do we form the right gestalt? The problem occurs on archaeological digs and in physicians' consulting rooms as well as in eighteenth-century German schoolrooms and twenty-first-century poetry workshops. When we are confronted with apparent chaos, even if we sense that it means *something*, how do we know *what*? The problem for us post-Enlightenment types is that there is no recipe. Trying to specify necessary and sufficient conditions for detecting true gestalts is like trying to model a live cat with a Meccano set. Yet it is a fact that there are brilliant historians, brilliant diagnosticians who, like brilliant mathematicians, repeatedly get it right where others fail. There are also brilliant readers, and they, too, repeatedly get it right about what difficult poems mean. But because there aren't any recipes, the suggestion that we can 'get it right' about poetry tends to spark objections. I'd like to spend some time with a few of these.

There is no one thing a poem means!
One of the most common objections is that there is no one thing a poem means. Great poems are great because they offer something to each and every one of us, and so — it is said — there's no possibility of 'getting it right.' If this is meant to affirm that great poems are iridescent, I agree: intelligence refracts off them differently in different contexts. If it is meant to affirm that great poems are often ambiguous, that they say two or more things simultaneously, and that these things are often in tension, sometimes downright contradictory, I agree again. If, though, it means that meaning doesn't really exist, that we always project rather than perceive coherence, then I disagree. The name philosophers give to this position is *skepticism*. Skepticism in all its forms — about mean-

ing, about moral and aesthetic truths, about the existence of a mind-independent world — is one intelligible consequence of the collision of rationality with experience. But it is not the only one. Where it is not simply a kind of adolescent vandalism, skepticism is, in fact, the expression of a preference for the dictatorship of rationality. It is worth pausing a moment to consider the motives behind such a preference.

Skepticism about meaning, in its most common forms, builds on a platform that resembles the fact-value distinction: there's a world of brute facts, it says, which exists independently of the human mind, but any meaning we impute to these facts is a projection. Meaning, the skeptic claims, is an *interpretation* of the facts; it is therefore open to challenge. It is a fact that the lilies in your garden are pink, another that they are five feet tall, another that they smell like cloves; it is an interpretation of these facts that they are beautiful. Some people hate lilies! Similarly, it is a fact that Shakespeare's 116th sonnet has fourteen lines, it is a fact that the first of these is "Let me not to the marriage of true minds," and it is a fact that the rhyme scheme is ABABCDCDEFEFGG; but it is open to doubt that the poem is a testament to the power of true love. Maybe it's meant to be ironic. Maybe it's just a kind of self-serving display. Who can tell? Indeed. And who can tell if we have the poem in the version Shakespeare intended. Maybe the first line was supposed to be "One cannot to the marriage of true minds" (more obvious iambic pentameter). Or what if Shakespeare wasn't Shakespeare? What if all of 'Shakespeare' is a hoax, invented by some eighteenth-century scam artist? Come to that, how do we know the past 'exists,' that it actually occurred? How do I know that I'm not now dreaming, not just about this sonnet, but about everything? Maybe I'm a brain in a vat. It's possible that nothing — nothing — exists except this present momentary experience.

Yup, it's possible. Do you want to live there? It's a world in which the concept 'knowledge' makes no sense and, as Wittgenstein pointed out, in which doubt doesn't really make any sense either. Doubt is possible only against a background that is held to be indubitable. Consider: your friend apparently just got hit by a bus; it is a fact that she is lying in the middle of the road, clutching her leg and howling. Do you doubt that she's in pain? Only if you *know* that she's an amazing actress and that she had warned you, earlier in the day, that she wanted to play a practical joke on some third party who also happens to be there; and you saw that the bus driver was actually her sister (who you *know* is not a bus driver); et cetera. Absent these or other fantastical conditions, you *know* she's in pain. You're a moral monster, or lying there bleeding yourself, if you don't try to do something about it.

Of course there are difficult cases. Of course we will sometimes judge incorrectly. Poems, and other literary artifacts, are often complex and ambiguous; they are sometimes obscure. This doesn't mean they don't have meaning. What it means is that understanding them takes skill, that what we come to understand may be multiple, and that we must be prepared to revise our understandings as we become more experienced and more informed about the experience of others. Here, then, are some of the things that motivate a preference for the dictatorship of rationality: laziness, impatience, a lack of confidence, a lack of flexibility, and, most important, terror of being wrong. Skepticism insulates its adherent against making mistakes — it eliminates the background of the real against which mistakes are judged, a background necessary for the *concept* 'mistake' to be formulated. If reality is eliminated, mistakes become impossible.

Although its superficial forms are multiple, all genuine skepticisms ultimately reduce to skepticism about the existence of a mind-independent world. For, as we saw, once rationality starts demanding *criteria* of truth — sets up a court of appeal with dockets, and warrants, and evidence and arguments, demanding the impossibility of doubt — there's no stable place for the skeptic to dig in her heels. To be consistent, the skeptic must deny not only the knowability of meaning, but also the knowability of the physical world, of cultural institutions, and the existence of other human beings. She must become a solipsist, and a brief one at that, since she cannot know that 'she' is anything other than the ground of present experience. An inconsistent skeptic is a cheat: someone who wants the *frisson* of the abyss while wearing a safety harness. And the rationality to which she's sold her soul will eventually catch up with her. The consistent skeptic, on the other hand, is in epistemological, ontological, social, moral, and semiotic free fall; but what she thereby gains is the inviolability of her 'own experience.' Nothing touches it. This trade-off is, I believe, the ultimate one: security *vs.* meaning. One's choice in this matter is one of the deepest facets of characterological style.

What the author intends is not necessarily what the poem means!
Another common objection to the idea that we can 'get it right' about a poem is that it confuses authorial intention with the end product. What the author intends is not necessarily what the poem means. This is true: poems — especially good ones — are often much bigger than their authors; they can mean more, and more deeply, than those authors can consciously say, know, or perceive. But from this it does not follow that authorial intention is irrelevant. For authorial intention includes not only conscious design — though this is often, surprisingly often, absent — it includes, it *is* mostly, a commitment to hew closely to the source or sources of inspiration, to attend, to stay with it or them, to admit when the poem has strayed off course, beguiled by a nifty bit of rhetoric or a flashy simile. Great poems are hard to write because they demand so much of us — not by way of invention, but by way of honest perception. This honesty includes being able to get out of the way: being able to recognize when an awkwardness should not be smoothed over, when a leap should not be prepared for, when a jarringness should not be resolved. The resonant gestalts in the world to which artists try to respond push back: they shove the words of the poet as well as the feet of the dancer around. The result *cannot* be something intended in advance, and it is often not fully comprehended once it's finished. The intention *to attend* and to respond *accurately* is, however, essential.

You can't paraphrase a good poem!
Some opponents of the idea that we can 'get it right' have been victims of bad teaching. One way of teaching poetry badly involves offering a paraphrase of 'the meaning' and ramming it down students' throats. Intelligent students can tell that this wrecks the poem. But the fact that such paraphrases should (mostly) be eschewed doesn't entail that meanings can't be discerned and subsequently communicated. Teaching poetry, like teaching medical students how to read symptoms, is an attempt to assist others in the perception of gestalts. How do we do this? Curiously, it turns out that teaching a poem is in many respects like writing one: you start with that old workshop adage, 'Show, don't tell.'

Every writer knows it's (roughly, usually) true: we can hear, immediately, the difference between "She was really frustrated" and "'No!' she yelled at the skewed textbox on the screen, hitting command–z so hard she sprained her thumb." And we intuitively recognize that in many contexts the second will constitute better, 'more effective' writing. But *why* is it (usually) better? What is it that showing does that telling doesn't do?

When we 'show,' we are setting details side by side and allowing the mind of the reader to form a gestalt — we are goosing intelligence into activity, insisting that it come alive. "Oh, I get what's happening!" When you tell someone something, on the other hand, you invite passivity: you turn the mind into a bucket for facts, or maybe a data processor. You deny it the excitement of being an animal, the *experience* of understanding.

The same goes for teaching. If you tell a potential reader what a poem is about, she won't have the experience of *finding the gestalt*. But if you help her focus her attention on crucial details, her mind can become active in sensing the resonance among them. "She uses the word 'disc' in line two, not 'coin' or 'plate.' Now take a look at line four — does anything spring out?" No request for an explanation, no need for a précis, just, "Oh! Yes. 'Rays'!" (And of course the variations here are as manifold as the resources on which poetry draws — we can help people notice connections of sound, of history, of connotation, of etymology, and we can help people notice absences: "'Snarling' is an obvious choice at the end of line 17 — it would sustain the alliterative structure. Try substituting it. What happens?")

The mind-enlivening effect of gestalt formation appears to have been at least part of what W.H. Auden and John Garrett had in mind when they defined poetry as "memorable speech." Poetry "must move our emotions, or excite our intellect," they say, "for only that which is moving or exciting is memorable," and they go on to describe the "power of suggestion and incantation" inherent in poetic speech. In other words, the words themselves are not our exclusive focus; it is the comprehension to which they give rise that draws our attention. Often enough, of course, we do remember the words themselves, for they continue to stimulate insight each time we return to them.

What a poem means to me *is all that matters!*
The final objection I want to discuss is one whose most potent voicing occurred in the question period after a lecture I gave on similarities be-

36   The Experience of Meaning

tween poems and mathematical proofs. A woman at the back of the hall actually stood up and howled, "You're taking away my freedom! Whatever a poem means to *me* is all that matters!" The depths of her dismay were astonishing, but it was clear she'd seen to the heart of the matter: if poems were like mathematical proofs, it meant that they were *true*. (It should be noted that not all mathematicians would agree with a robust version of this assessment. Some would urge that mathematical proofs are indeed like poems and what follows from this — they say — is that proofs have no objective, mind-independent validity.) It could be that my interlocutor had garden-variety math fear, but I don't think so. There being a fact (or facts) of the matter, she was claiming, ruined her experience of being moved. Versions of this objection are not uncommon, though they are rarely so dramatic, and they all urge the same thing: a poem is a projection test; it cannot, it must not, mean anything in and of itself.

I can only guess at the schoolroom or life traumas that result in this view. I am very sorry they have occurred. And I agree that *some* poems *are* nothing more than projection tests: they are designed to be so. But it is incontrovertible that others — Shakespeare's 116th sonnet, for example — are not. Note that the objection is not skeptical: meaning exists, alright; it's just that it's *personal*. This may be the key. If what my distressed interlocutor wanted to insist is that poems can speak to us directly, intimately, that they can affect us profoundly and make us change our lives in ways we can't rationally explain, and that this can seem like a kind of magic, especially when it is set against technocracy's idea of how to make sense, then I agree with her completely. Poems can indeed do this. (Mathematical proofs can do it, too.) All that I am saying, in that case, is that we don't have to assume that we are projecting in order to explain this power. Telling the truth, showing it, can have the same overwhelming effect.

ə♥

It's true: neither as readers nor as writers can we be certain, in a difficult case, that we've got the right gestalt. Our doubts as writers can spring from our doubts as readers. From an early age, things called poems are put in front of us that we don't entirely understand. We try to understand them, just as we try, in the pitch dark, to see. And, if my hypothesis is right, we try to form gestalts even when there's no coherence to discern. We get that faux poetic sugar high: a buzz whose effects are not sustained. We start fooling around, making similar linguistic objects: ontologically vacant constructs that allow the mind to experience itself forming gestalts. More sugar highs. We feel vaguely dissatisfied; in moments alone we aren't sure why we're getting credit for something that doesn't make sense. But then someone else publicly insists there's an emperor under the bedizened robes, and we doubt our own doubts. Often, the doubts eventually fall away: we develop a taste for ontological disconnect. We call it fun.

But haven't I claimed that there's no recipe for discernment, either in the perception or the communication of real gestalts? And if we can't, as writers, guarantee our readers secure access, if we can't, as teachers, guarantee apprentice readers they'll never get it wrong again, then doesn't it follow that 'anything goes' is the appropriate attitude — that poetry is, ultimately, about nothing more than the reader's pleasure in forming gestalts, empty or otherwise?

No. That we can't guarantee the poem will precipitate the right gestalt for everyone, or even for anyone, does not mean that there is no right gestalt to precipitate. It does not mean that there is no point in trying to tell the truth, or in trying to listen to it being told. It means only that there is no formula for success, no series of steps that can assure insight.

Skilled writers can assist readers in various ways: they can show rather than tell; they can try to respond accurately to the resonance they perceive; they can eliminate distractions; they can control for tone. Especially, they can control for tone. Emotional tone is a crucial sub-gestalt of the large complex gestalt of the poem. Consider the differences among "No, goddammit!", "I'd rather you didn't," and "Well, could you ask Sybil first?". What we register in each case is an emotional attitude. Our comprehension is not the result of careful reflection on constituent parts which we then add together: the emotional tone doesn't have any parts; it permeates the whole utterance. Picking up the tone of an utterance is fundamental to perceiving its meaning, as fundamental as our knowledge of the lexicon. (It is how we tell the difference between irony and testimony, for example.) As we look through the poem to the world, its tone determines our posture and therefore what we see. That what we perceive shifts with shifts in our perception of tone shows how similar tone is to light. And that we can be mistaken in our impression of nuance has an exact parallel in the case of vision: if we make a mistake in visual perception, the solution isn't to theorize that it's impossible to see accurately, it's to look again, from a different standpoint. Rereading a great poem can be a lesson in abandoning our first impressions; it can also be a complex confirmation of them.

Although skilled writers can amplify our ability to see what they are pointing to, in the end, we see it or we don't: the penny drops, our vision shifts, the gestalt forms, or it doesn't. Recognition of this fact can produce humility or a sense of tolerance in both writers and readers — forgiveness, openness, an undefended curiosity, a willingness to learn. In other cases, difficulty in conveying or registering meaning seems to act as a lightning rod for insecurity and aggression, a need to *make* people see things as we do (or to make sure they don't see things we don't). Although we are a species that often responds to aggression — at least, male aggression — with admiration and approval, this is not an effective way to assist the perception of gestalts. Perceiving gestalts frequently depends on circumstances beyond our control — mood, talent, the light falling just so, the phone not ringing. Yelling usually doesn't help. Simone Weil remarked that in the interior life, the virtue that most facilitates discernment is patience: "In sense perception, if one is not sure of what one sees, one shifts one's perspective, and what is real appears. In the inner life, time serves as space. With time, one is changed, and if, in the course of such change, one keeps one's vision oriented towards the same thing, in the end illusion is dissipated and the real appears." This, it seems to me, is true of all forms of discernment.

FREE VERSE AND ITS VICISSITUDES

> *We must not insist on knowing where verse ends and prose (or verseless composition) begins, for they pass into one another ...*
> — Gerard Manley Hopkins

The exercise I began by contemplating — cut-up technique — wouldn't work in a culture where poems are expected to fulfill certain overt formal constraints. This has led some people to think that the problem is free verse, and that a return to formal verse is the solution to the present glut of meaningless poetry. It may be that the prevalence of free verse in the last century has contributed to the impression that you can put anything down on the page and call it a poem. But there have been reams of material laid out in rhyming quatrains that weren't real poems either. And it's unlikely that the pool of raw lyric talent is smaller than it was in the past. Why, then, do many readers point to free verse and complain that they've become confused about what poetry is? At least part of the problem may be that we — writers as well as readers — don't fully understand our tools.

What is free verse?

The easy answer is that it's not formal verse: it doesn't follow a regular prosodic pattern. (In English, 'formal verse' is sometimes construed as poetry that has not only a metrical scheme but also a rhyme scheme. The fundamental role of blank verse in English literary history shows that the crucial feature is prosody.) Like many easy answers, this one is not very helpful. 'Not formal verse' casts too wide a net and hauls in newspaper editorials, grade school arithmetic quizzes, and public service announcements as well as *Leaves of Grass*. Narrowing the definition further, though, always seems to leave out some canonical example — or at least something that someone thinks should be a canonical example.

While I concur with Northrop Frye that it is better to expand literary taste than to restrict it, I nonetheless think there are uses of language that, in certain contexts, are not poetic — the user agreement that one must accept in order to log on to a new network, for example. This is not to deny that some of the phrases and sentences in the user agreement could show up verbatim in a composition that I would recognize as a poem. But that poem would be recognizable *as* a poem in part because of the context of its presentation: it wouldn't be *indistinguishable* from clauses four through nine of the user agreement. To put this differently: our intuitions that not everything is a poem deserve respect. They shouldn't be used to build walls around our imaginations, but nor should they be tossed on the cultural scrapheap as (just so many more) baseless prejudices. To insist that some collections of words in some contexts are not poems is, once again, to resist skepticism — that is, to choose the often painful world of potentially mistaken experience

40   The Experience of Meaning

over the oblivious, self-insulating world of incorrigible opinion. Trying to think about free verse is part of the project of acknowledging that meaning exists.

ॐ

It is tempting to think that we can refine the concept of free verse by adding a second exclusion 'from the other side,' as it were — to say that not only is free verse not formal verse, it is also not prose. The problem is that some of what routinely gets identified as free verse *is* prose: if you read it out loud, a person who can't see the page you're reading from will misidentify it. Well: but isn't this just bad free verse? Not always. Does this mean then that free verse is nothing more than good prose? What is prose, anyway?

This may be the key question. The concept 'prose' appears to be every bit as problematic as the concept 'free verse,' and, because the two overlap, it is very hard to draw a bead on either.

Some people imagine that prose is just what humans use on a daily basis to communicate — that prose is 'ordinary speech.' But anyone who has carried a recording device onto a bus, or into a coffee shop, a playground, or a suburban kitchen knows that the transcription is hard to decipher: ordinary speech is elliptical, broken, often ungrammatical, and rarely continuous in the voice of a single speaker for more than a few quasi-sentences. When prose is spoken out loud, it's usually in the form of a lecture, a sermon, a public announcement, or a reading from a book. That is: prose nearly always begins life written down, and when it is spoken extempore, the purpose — usually a lecture of some kind — is frequently to produce a transcript. Having recognized that prose is not 'ordinary speech,' however, many still think that learning to compose good prose is simply a matter of organizing what you want to say and not making any grammatical mistakes. This is like imagining that, handed a paint roller, anyone can produce a Rothko.

What distinguishes a Rothko from what I myself might achieve by spreading paint around in two swatches on a large canvas? This question has no precise answer because Rothkos themselves were not produced according to necessary and sufficient criteria. Texture, we might say. Balance. Rhythm and luminosity. What sort of texture? What sort of balance? Look and see. These phenomena cannot be usefully captured by analysis. They're gestalts.

Good and bad prose are also distinguished by their texture, their balance, their rhythm and luminosity. What makes a particular prose texture 'good' or admirable will depend on context — what a speaker wants to say and to whom she wants to say it. Once our attention is called to it, many of us can immediately recognize turgid prose, spritely prose, indifferent prose, elegant prose, and through exposure we can cultivate various aspects of style. These characteristics, however, are like faces or moral qualities — the more we are pressed to break them down into articulated elements or machine-readable routines, the less good we get at recognizing and deploying them.

T.S. Eliot refused to draw the distinction between prose and poetry in prosodic terms; instead, he drew it with reference to the flow and structure of ideas. Poetry, he suggested, was informed by a "logic of the imagination," prose by a "logic of concepts." This does not mean that prose is unimaginative or that concepts never occur in poetry. What Eliot wants us to notice is that thinking, in a poem, proceeds by association of images — 'rose,' connoting voluptuousness, intensity, sweetness, and velvetiness, can stir memories of erotic love. (Are memories images? Yes, often, though not always visual, and sometimes in motion.) The pain of lost, unrequited, rejected, or jealous erotic love can be extreme, and hence we are brought by imagistic association to reflect on the rose's thorns. Et cetera. Where thinking does not proceed in this way — where it proceeds by conceptual connections as in legal argument or computer programming, or by causal-conceptual connections as in science or engineering — we have, Eliot suggests, the inner form of prose.

This is a striking claim, and gets us a long way towards understanding phenomena as disparate as Roo Borson's prose poetry and Pope's *Essay on Man*. Pope's *Essay* deploys many striking images but its overarching plan is clearly that of argumentative prose. Borson's work is laid out in prose paragraphs, but it thinks associatively, lyrically. And we can go further. While Eliot is on to something when he says that prose and poetry are to be distinguished by their logics, I believe there is also an *aural dimension* to each of those logics. The language of imagistic logic is by nature more resonant than the language of conceptual logic. Poets may choose to mute linguistic resonance for just the reasons that composers

42   The Experience of Meaning

of non-verbal music may choose to mute the instruments their compositions are scored for: to signal a restriction, sometimes amounting to a chokehold, on emotional expressiveness — which is not the same thing as putting a chokehold on emotion itself. When a free verse poet damps down the verbal music that usually characterizes imagistic thought, one result can be what some postwar European poets labelled 'anti-poetry': rhetorically flat writing — a political refusal of beauty — laid out in discrete lines. (The lines allow what Dennis Lee has called 'pointing' — a kind of visual emphasis that does not have an aural counterpart.) Or, if the material is not lineated, the result can be a prose anti-poem.

But I've got ahead of myself. In what does 'aural resonance' consist? And why does it standardly characterize what Eliot identifies as the logic of images?

Verbal music, like non-verbal music, both stirs and sculpts emotion. It is made up of resonant sound connections among words, whose unfolding is also rhythmic. Verbal music also includes enactive connections between the sounds of words, lines, or phrases and their meanings. Sound connections range from standard rhyme through frame rhyme, slant rhyme, assonance, and alliteration to subtle relations between emotional tone and vowel colour. Rhythm includes tempo or pace, rhetorical period or cadence, anaphora, and, in English, the accentual systems of Anglo-Saxon verse and other patterns of stressed and unstressed syllables. (If you listen for the main stresses in many good English free verse lines, you'll hear there are usually three or four, regardless of the number of feet. This is the ghost of *Beowulf.*) In languages like ancient Greek and Arabic, whose verse patterns are quantitative, rhythm includes pace, period, cadence, and patterns of long and short syllables. In so-called metrical verse, the patterns are regular (think Strauss waltzes); in what might be called 'free prosody', the patterns are irregular (think Béla Bartók and the Hungarian folksongs on which he drew). Prosodic feet — iambs, trochees, dactyls, anapests, spondees, pyrrhics, choriambs — exist in free prosody, but you can (up to a point) combine them in any way you like (that is, as pitch, tone, vowel colour, and pace require); and you can (up to a point) pile on any number in a line.

The reason that imagistic logic, when it takes linguistic form, is verbally resonant is that imagistic thought is itself resonant in structure. It doesn't proceed in causal or conceptual sequences; it proceeds by analogy and association. These function cumulatively, as well as moment to moment; and this means that a resonant thought structure — a lyric poem or a Mozart string quartet — has a synchronic, rather than a diachronic, nature. The mind moves back and forth among its aspects or facets, bringing them into focus as a whole. Thinking, in resonant structures, proceeds by way of sensing sympathetic vibrations — the quickening of perceptions, images, motifs and ideas that are structurally and tonally related to other perceptions, images, motifs and ideas. Or, to put this another way, imagistic perception picks up on the force fields of larger gestalts that inform individual things. The composer of a resonant thought structure is, first, *struck* by an individual being or moment; she becomes suddenly aware, often in a way that she can't begin to articulate, that it is a facet of some resonant whole. Imagistic *thinking* is the discernment of that whole; it allows the whole, as a whole, to ring in the mind while not losing awareness of the particulars in which it resounds.

The linguistic embodiment of imagistic thinking naturally seeks resonant form because, unless it is purposefully being made to resist its nature, it is an attempt to sing along with reality, to respond in kind, to co-respond; and thus it, too, traces and awakens sympathetic vibrations.

What Eliot calls the logic of concepts — the interior form of prose — does not attend to the force fields of larger gestalts that inform individual things. It focuses, rather, on individuals as discrete objects that can be manipulated or controlled. Language that tracks conceptual logic becomes a tool of analysis, a means of dividing things off from one another and of preventing the thinker from being swept up by 'irrelevant' tonal and structural similarities. (What are the similarities irrelevant to? — To perceiving things as objects that can be used without caring about them. Meaningful poetry, as Blake understood, is structurally immune to the agendas of technocracy.) Prose, especially bad prose, tolerates linguistic noise — lack of concision, clumsiness, jargon — because the fact that noise obscures resonance is not of paramount concern. It is possible, of course, for prose thought to avail itself of linguistic music, as it does in courtroom argument, sermons, and other forms of oratory. Persuasion — as advertisers and turf-conscious philosophers know — is an emotional business. But stirring oratory is often said to 'rise to the heights of poetry.' This is no accident. (In complementary fashion, imagistic thought may deliberately eschew heightened linguistic music when it wants to critique mindless, jingoistic sentimentality.)

How are these observations relevant to characterizing free verse? One thing they suggest is that, Eliot notwithstanding, there *is* something we mean when we say something sounds prose-y; and that there is also a heightened musical quality to language-use that we intuitively identify as poetry. Another thing they suggest is that formal verse is not the standard, the 'essence,' of resonant language. Rather, formal verse *formalizes* linguistic resonance, in much the way that codes of etiquette formalize spontaneous gestures of gratitude and respect. Once established, social codes are often imposed; their forced observance can supplant natural feeling and distort it. Something similar can happen to imagistic thought in cultures that rigidly impose formal verse structures on poetic insight. Wordsworth's significance, for example, is not that he failed in his attempt to write poetry in the 'ordinary language' his poetics enjoin, but that he succeeded in avoiding many formalisms that clogged English verse — thus opening it to become a vehicle of spontaneous ontological insight.

The 'free prosody' of much free verse is neither accidental nor unimportant: free verse that is not prose-y stands to poetry much as folk song and chant stand to music. In them, we hear a species of spontaneous natural response to experience of the world. These natural responses can be, and often are, refined to great effect. But their power, their appeal, lies in their unfettered immediacy, their *proximity* to a situation in which some human animal, paying attention to something, is informed by its resonant structure.

Prose *is also* a way for human beings to tell the truth about the world. But it's a different truth, a truth about the distinctness of individuals rather than their connectedness. This is why the gesture of presenting prose-y language *as* poetry can be potent. If something in the writing or the context cues readers that the tension is deliberate, that it's part of what we're supposed to notice, then the gesture can be meaningful in any number of ways: it can be ironic, elegiac, sneering, or humorous; it can embody critique, or political resistance, or experimental curiosity (at least the first time). Where the tension is not experienced — where either the poet does not cue it effectively or her readers fail to pick up —

Poetry and Meaninglessness   45

then the gesture of lineating prose-y language is meaningless. Well! Even meaninglessness can be meaningful as a kind of vandalism. But, in my experience, the intent of lineating prose-y language is rarely to vandalize. And that's the problem: the composition sounds like prose, but that sound is not intended.

How does this happen? Television, video, the persecution of silence, relentless exposure to bad writing in the media, formless speech from politicians and CEOs, the speed with which we consume print, and advertising, advertising, advertising have made us numb. We have become insensitive to linguistic music, because no one teaches us how to listen to it; and we've become suspicious of its effects because, owing to our inexperience with it, it can be, and is, used to manipulate us. We can't hear the difference between free prosody and prosiness. Or, better, we can hear it, but we don't pay attention to it, we don't know *how* to pay attention to it. We don't register the possibilities of meaning offered by alert prosody, and so we misuse or neglect them. One result is the idea that any chunk of language declared to be a poem is a poem. It's not true; we know it's not true; but we don't understand why, so we can't begin to rectify the situation. Prosodic meaninglessness proliferates.

Let me underline: I am not suggesting that imagistic thought voiced in the muted prosody natural to prose cannot be a poem. I am arguing that if it is to be meaningful, the writer must have *chosen* muted prosody. The choice need not be conscious, but it must be an active part of the poem's gesture of address. And for this to be possible, we as readers and listeners must be able to pick up on various aspects of linguistic music. We must be capable of registering the prosodic gestures a writer has made.

Which brings us to what, among poets, is called 'the line.' What is it? For formal verse, the answer is easy: it's a string of a certain number of feet or syllables. But in free prosody, counting won't help — there are neither rules nor limits. Yet again, it looks like there's no aural distinction between taut, imagistic prose and the best free verse. Maybe the line is simply a typographic conceit, a vestigial literary organ that, at most, can be used to make readers read your fine imagistic prose more slowly?

Yes: in some cases that is what it has become. But in the case of free prosody, the line remains prosodically significant. It is, as musicians might say, a musical phrase — a 'horizontal' unit of melodic sense. The

46   The Experience of Meaning

root of the musical phrase is (as the Black Mountaineers kept telling us) the breath — what you can comfortably sing before you need to stop, even if only for a fraction of a second, and gulp some more air.

"This is useless as a metric," someone might object. "People have different lung capacities." True. But like heartbeats, lung capacities fall within a certain range. And within that range, there's a narrower range that's comfortable for most healthy human adults. That narrower range is the foundation of the line in free prosody.

The play of the musical phrase in, against, over, and through the sentence is what creates the amazingly complex texture of good poetry, whether free or formal. When the phrasal units match the grammatically clausal units of the sentence, you get end-stopped lines: thinking holds hands with singing. (Example: the hymn.) When the grammatical clauses lie athwart the phrase, singing pulls against thought, and you get enjambment. Enjambed passages in lyric poems often seem to be saying several things simultaneously. That's because they are. The phrase — the free or formal line — says, "These words/sounds/accentual patterns/images together form a meaningful gesture"; the enjambed sentence says, "And grammar tells you this distinct clausal or sentential gesture is being made simultaneously." When these claims are true, and the meanings, though in tension, are resonant, the poem embodies Herakleitos' back-stretched connection.

Phrase marks in written Western classical music are long arcing lines drawn in by the composer (or music teacher) above the notes. They often — but by no means always — indicate that the performer should produce all the notes under the line in one breath if they're a singer or a wind player, or in one bow if they're a string player. But sometimes the phrase marks are too long to make this physically possible. Other times they are over notes that the composer has marked staccato, each one requiring a sharp separation from the next. And what about pianists or guitar players? Neither breath nor bow length constrains physical performance for them, so what's the point of phrase marks? In all these cases, you must perform the music *as if* a single breath sustained and shaped the notes under the mark. In other words, the fundamental effort is imaginative and involves the creation of a gestalt: the individual notes must be placed beside one another so that the continuous unbroken gesture of the phrase becomes audible. The notes must be played as *aspects* of that whole. In a language like English, with a lot of consonants and a dearth of default feminine rhymes, rendering a fine free prosodic line is not unlike playing long phrases on the piano. The instrument doesn't make it easy; but it can be, and is, done brilliantly.

The line as phrase is characteristic of what I've been calling free prosody — the linguistic music towards which imagistic thought naturally inclines. However, the appearance of the line, though not its musical substance, can be retained in poems that use the voice of prose. Lineation then functions as a kind of clausal punctuation, or simply as an indicator that the words are to be read as carefully as though they *were* poetry.

There are, then, at least three intersecting continua against which various species of free verse, formal verse, and prose must be plotted:

(1) an epistemological continuum — the extent to which the thought in a given composition is structured resonantly or in linear causal/conceptual sequences;
(2) a musical continuum — the extent to which a composition is characterized by the presence or absence of overt linguistic music;
(3) a typographical continuum — the extent to which a composition is laid out in discrete lines or in a continuous unlineated block.

Free verse, as it is currently written in North America, consists (on the whole) of imagistic language laid out in discrete lines that may or may not be characterized by heightened linguistic music. The fact that such music may be absent is, I believe, the source of a good deal of contemporary confusion about 'what poetry is.' Good linguistic music — like good vocal or instrumental music — is inherently appealing. But we are taught almost nothing about how to listen for it, or for its absence. And our natural proclivities are frequently exploited — that is, abused — by public media, advertising, and Hollywood. Many novice writers, and even some experienced ones, have difficulty hearing the difference between a densely stressed line and a sparsely stressed one. Yet hearing this, and responding to other physical aspects of the language of which a poem is made, is crucial to grasping the voice, the tone, and thereby the meaning of any good poem. Free verse is no single thing, and the strategies that make one poem excellent may be completely absent in another.

WHY MEANING MATTERS

> *At the burial of an epoch*
> *no psalm is heard at the tomb.*
> *Soon nettles and thistles*
> *will decorate the spot.*
> *The only busy hands are those*
> *of the gravediggers. Faster! Faster!*
> *And it's quiet, Lord, so quiet*
> *you can hear time passing.*
>
> — Anna Akhmatova,
> translated by Stanley Kunitz
> with Max Hayward

"'Meaningless' poetry. It's a tempest in a teapot! — Who cares? Poetry is a non-market genre."

Poetry may be a non-market genre. But meaning isn't. Meaning is not a genre at all. It's the iridescent, flowing substance of any life worth living. Our experience of meaning is not fundamentally linguistic either in structure or in content: it is a quasi-perceptual gestalt phenomenon. Because it is a gestalt phenomenon, the intellectual capacities involved in the experience of meaning can be disrupted if we try to analyze or describe them. This, it seems to me, has important consequences for a culture that values analysis and description as core features of intelligence. It also has consequences for our understanding of the natural world: the present planetary crisis is in large measure a result of our neglect of meaning. If, as either readers or writers, we abet this neglect, our practice is complicit.

৯

τὸ γὰρ αὐτὸ νοεῖν ἐστίν τε καὶ εἶναι, said Father Parmenides. What is for meaning is for being, too. Or: the experience of meaning will, if you

Poetry and Meaninglessness   49

let it, tell you something about the nature of the world. The experience of meaning is the experience of a gestalt — either a shift to coherence out of chaos, or a shift from one coherent arrangement to another, the perception of their resonant relation. That this experience is ubiquitous, that it is deeply pleasurable, and that the form of thought that underlies it is fundamental to accurate perception and to problem-solving of many kinds are good reasons for thinking that it is evolutionarily adaptive.

There is hot debate about the details of evolutionary theory, but there is little doubt that most of the capacities a living being frequently displays are a reflection of what — given some initial constraints like having legs instead of roots — it needs to do in order to survive: respond to light, for example, or grab hold of things it wants to eat; sense the gravitational pull of the moon; pick up on the polarity of the earth's magnetic field. If gestalt comprehension is evolutionarily adaptive, it follows that resonant structures, wholes that hang together, are out there, just like light, graspable things to eat, the moon, and the earth's magnetic field. It follows that the world itself is made up, at least in part, of non-piecemeal resonant structures. In some respects, yes, it's built like a machine, because that's another way of understanding it that appears to be evolutionarily adaptive. But the world is also built like a web of analogies. It is as much a piece of music as it is a pile of lumber.

A culture that denies or derogates gestalt comprehension will thus be missing out on an important way the world is. Its members won't just scoff at the notion of causality that underlies the *I Ching*, or the possibility of navigating by songlines; their susceptibility to the beauty of ecological wholes will be denigrated. People in such a culture will be encouraged to regard aspects of ecologies as facts; but they won't be encouraged to pick up on how or that those facts *matter*. The meaning of the facts will be obscured.

For the experience of natural beauty is yet another gestalt experience deeply allied with meaning. Pick any of the notions that Enlightenment philosophy has been unable to crack, but which, equally, it hasn't been able to make go away — meaning, certainly, and beauty; but also goodness, identity, being — and you'll find that it's an idea or an experience that depends on gestalt rather than on piecemeal thinking. I know next to nothing about quantum superposition and entanglement, or about Rupert Sheldrake's morphic fields; but it seems to me remarkable that these allegedly inexplicable phenomena appear to be characterized by the same interdetermination of parts and wholes that characterizes gestalts.

Perhaps we find these phenomena mysterious (or specious) because we're trying to cram them into an epistemic box into which they won't fit: maybe their apparent parts aren't like independent billiard balls, maybe they're structurally connected *aspects* of complex wholes. The exercise of cramming everything into the piecemeal-thinking box is, however, an enterprise to which this culture is profoundly dedicated. The reasons for this dedication are many, but at least one of them may have to do with the evolution of ways of knowing. Piecemeal parts and their interactions are just what Indo-European languages and their writing systems seem designed to pick out and describe, and just what analyses are supposed to reveal. As students of both metaphysics and linguistics have noticed, the categories into which the world seems to parse itself bear a striking resemblance to grammatical structures in the language the parser speaks.

And the area of the human brain that controls speech production is overwhelmingly located in the hemisphere that controls the dextrous hand — the one that grasps things and manipulates them. This is not, I believe, an evolutionary accident. Language, too, can be used to divide the world into graspable chunks and to keep these chunks distinct from one another; it helps us hold the chunks still so that we can analyze them, figure out standard cause-and-effect relationships among them, and then manipulate them — to feed ourselves, to keep ourselves safe, and warm, and dry. Used in this way, language is both the servant and the foundation of technology. It is the mental avatar of the grasping hand.

ॐ

One of the striking features of gestalts is that they're hard to undermine. Unlike many of the results of calculative intelligence, they have a gravity that can pull unrelated details into orbit around them, a gravity that resists the disintegrating effects of counter-evidence. Can they nonetheless be mistaken? Indeed. The *phi* phenomenon, like the little pop in your mind when you read a compilation of randomly chosen words and phrases, shows that gestalt comprehension can be profoundly mistaken. Isn't this grounds for distrusting it wherever it occurs?

Poetry and Meaninglessness 51

Not unless it's also grounds for distrusting every form of reasoning. Most of us make mistakes in addition and subtraction, and some of us make them repeatedly. Does this lead us to give up on calculation? On the contrary. It leads us to double-check. When I was a kid, someone told me that 96 percent of all once-accepted scientific claims have been proven wrong. I don't know where the figure 96 came from, but the true percentage has to be fairly high: earth-centred universes in astronomy (or sun-centred universes with circular planetary orbits); occult forces in medieval physics and the collapse of Newtonian mechanics at sub-atomic levels; phlogiston in chemistry and humours in biology — the list of faulty paradigms, let alone sloppy measurements and mistaken taxonomies, is long. Yet we have no trouble believing in science. Bridges collapse, tailings ponds collapse, space shuttles explode, deep-sea oil wells explode. Yet we have no trouble trusting engineers. Gestalts — of which scientific paradigms are actually good examples — are no less trustworthy than other kinds of human knowledge. And the safeguard is the same as it is elsewhere: double-check. Or triple-check. Get someone else to check. Wait and check again. Shifting our position in time as well as in space can offer a salutary new perspective.

How can we be certain? *Absolutely* certain? We can't. This question is one of the oldest in philosophy, perhaps because the anxiety that underlies it runs deep. If we're to speak to that anxiety, we need to remind ourselves that the logic of mistakes is a version of the logic of doubt: mistakes are not possible except against a background that is deemed reliable. "But surely," someone will ask, "if I've been mistaken before, I could be mistaken now. Or tomorrow. Or next Tuesday." Of course. But this does not license the exhilarating thought that maybe we're *always* mistaken. If we're mistaken *all* the time, we *aren't* mistaken all the time; we can't be. As I argued earlier, the impulse to insulate ourselves against the possibility of mistakes leads to skepticism, the idea that there's no mind-independent reality, nothing against which to measure what we think and seem to perceive. Is it possible this is actually our situation? Yes, it's possible. It's possible that nothing exists but this second or two of experience. But retreating to such a metaphysics strikes me as a boring, brute, and ultimately cowardly way to deal with the tensions we discover in existence.

A mistake is a mistake only in relation to a network of truths we hold secure. Could that background network be wrong? Yes. I would argue that it *has* been wrong, and in many ways still is wrong, in the case of securely held beliefs about the nature of human beings of tribes or races not familiar to the believer, about the nature of female human beings, about the nature of nonhuman beings, just as it was wrong about the position of the earth relative to the sun. How do we come to entertain doubts about some deep-rooted cultural orthodoxy? By checking beliefs our culture invites us to hold against a background we hold to be even more secure: our direct experience — what happens when we pay attention to human beings of other races or genders, what happens when we pay attention to nonhuman beings, what happens when we pay attention to what we're seeing through a telescope. But can't direct experience be coloured by racist, sexist, anthropocentric, or terracentric prejudice? Yes. And so we must struggle to be honest with ourselves. Paying attention is hard work. It takes courage — in some cases, to see what's there, in some cases to admit we've been wrong. It takes time. It takes patience.

Knowledge — of any sort — is never just about facts; it is always a function of the interpenetration of facts and character. In other words, real knowledge is always a kind of wisdom. To understand reality, we not only have to search it out; we must refine, strengthen, and clarify the instrument with which we search. This is what practice is for.

Two features of practice seem worth mentioning here. First, although talent helps, anyone can improve. Second, and crucially, becoming skilled at anything requires technique. A few folks are lucky — for them, technique develops so easily that it seems innate. For the rest of us, the acquisition of technique often involves at least some analysis: focused reflection on what this tool does, what that hand position is good for, sometimes the definition of a concept, or confirmation of a guess through calculation. What has been made precise in this way is then taken up again into the practice as a whole. Part of what we practise in such cases is the interaction between analytic and gestalt intelligence.

In addition to encouraging people to practise gestalt comprehension if they want to get better at it, we can also say something about the *effect* of perceiving complex gestalts. The perception of complex resonant structure in the world changes us. This change is the litmus of the real. It is by attending to whether we've been changed by what we claim to know that we learn to distinguish between significant and insignificant gestalts. It is as though we ourselves have been realigned — as though our place in the shape of the whole has shifted. Often, even in difficult cases and when we can't say how or why, we can tell immediately that a change has taken place. Other times recognition takes years. In rare instances, we may never know for sure.

And sometimes, not all the time but sometimes, we make mistakes.

Putting up with uncertainty is the price we pay for making ourselves available to meaning.

ঌ

Understanding, I've suggested, is a function of the interpenetration of facts and character. Character, too, as Aristotle might have said, is a gestalt concept — a complex integrated whole that is not a mere assemblage of parts. A person's character is not a recipe — two parts vanity, three parts determination, and a dash of grumpiness, say. It's not something we acquire the way we acquire a closet full of clothes or a set of crockery. And our comprehension of another person's character has many of the subsidiary features of gestalt comprehension: it happens in a flash — we don't add it up. Also, it's hard to revise (think of the importance we attach to first impressions); and there's no method for teaching someone to be a good judge of character. The interdetermination of aspects of character is nothing static, and this is why we say good portraiture, portraiture that captures character, lives. Even though the painting or the photograph is still, it reveals dynamic interconnectedness: how, if that shifts, this must shift, too. It points to inner life.

Gerard Manley Hopkins called character *inscape*. It's a very suggestive word, the way it conjures 'interior landscape' — its emphasis on the nonhuman and its sense of space, of vistas; complexities that shift with perspective; attunements that invite contemplation. Landscapes are not simply assemblages of trees, rocks, and water; they hang together in ways that are hard to analyze. Hopkins describes a line of fir trees as "melodious" and the long shoulder of a hill as a "slow tune." Melodies are

Dorothea Lange: *Migrant Mother*   Diego Velázquez: *Portrait of Juan de Pareja*

where gestalt epistemology started; they are paradigmatic examples of gestalts. Here, the metaphors are especially telling: they speak of visual perception sung to by what it sees.

Hopkins himself provides no abstract definition of inscape. Here is how W.H. Gardner, quoting W.A.M. Peters, S.J., summarizes it: "that unified complex of characteristics which constitute[s] 'the outward reflection of the inner nature of a thing.'" Hopkins also coined the word *instress* for the force or energy that sustains an inscape. Gardner elaborates:

> But *instress* is not only the unifying force *in* the object; it connotes also that impulse *from* the 'inscape' which acts on the senses.... Instress, then, is often the *sensation* of inscape — [an] ... illumination, a sudden perception of that deeper pattern, order, and unity which gives meaning to external forms....

The connection with gestalt perception is both striking and obvious. Note that inscape and instress are explicitly identified as the source of meaning.

But this is the voice of a commentator, not Hopkins himself. How does Hopkins talk about inscape?

Poetry and Meaninglessness   55

Walked down to the Rhone glacier. It has three stages — first a smoothly-moulded bed in a pan or theatre of thorny peaks, swells of ice rising through the snow-sheet and the snow itself tossing and fretting into the sides of the rock walls in spray-like points:... it is like bright-plucked water swaying in a pail—; second ... was a ruck of horned waves steep and narrow in the gut ... a descending limb which was like the rude and knotty bossings of a strombus shell—; third the foot, a broad limb opening out and reaching the plain shaped like the fan-fin of a dolphin or a great bivalve shell turned on its face, the flutings in either case being suggested by the crevasses and the ribs by the risings between them, these being swerved and inscaped strictly to the motion of the mass.

Here the word 'inscape' occurs as a verb, and it means the sculpting of an aspect by the action of the whole.

The passage also presents us with a puzzle, for it is surely a description. Don't attempts to describe insight block or suppress gestalt comprehension? That's what the evidence indicates. So, we need to notice three things.

First, this is not a description of Hopkins's thought processes, his attempts to perceive or understand the glacier; it is a description of the glacier. Elsewhere, Hopkins says it's better to be alone if you want to pick up on inscape; and in yet another journal entry he says, "with a companion the eye and the ear are for the most part shut and instress cannot come." Why? Perhaps because attending to social dynamics saps energy required for attending to the world. However, it might be because social engagement usually requires conversation — the use of language. One of the reasons you might want to be alone when attending to complex gestalts is so that you won't have to talk.

Another thing to notice is that this description is not being produced during the encounter with the glacier, it is being written later as Hopkins sits at his desk, remembering.

The third thing to notice is that it is no ordinary description.

It is not an analysis, nor does it appeal to quantitative measurement; it makes no use of technical terms; no attempt is being made to isolate parts of the glacier for utilitarian or laboratory examination. It is, rather, an *appreciation*. Hopkins's language is shot through with, taken over by, the tumbling, shocking impact, the rush and sway of what he perceives: *tossing and fretting; like bright-plucked water swaying in a pail; a ruck of horned waves; knotty bossings of a strombus; the fan-fin of a dolphin.* His account understands the world with metaphors, those exemplars of gestalt shifts; and it is made literally resonant — echoing the resonance Hopkins perceived — with rhyme, rhythm, and alliteration. This is not the language of the grasping hand, language trying to hold experience still so we can figure out how to use it. This is language overtaken by integrated comprehension, charged, torqued, smelted by the need to mean.

Hopkins's work is full of this kind of attention to the natural world: kestrels, oak trees, ash trees, poplars, bluebells, the moon, pigeons, snow, clouds, the sea. The poems, even passages in the journals, can be difficult because the language is so bent, stretched, pressured. But there is no question that it is meaningful. Reading a Hopkins poem doesn't give you a little pop in the mind. It takes the top of your head off — and lets the world in.

Hopkins shows us the meanings of the things he attends to; he shows us *that* they mean. But it is just this — the fact that the natural world has meaning — that the culture of technocracy denies. A technocracy is defined not by the quantity of its gadgets but by its refusal to regard gestalt comprehension as legitimate. In such a culture, the arts are thought of as entertainments; visual thinking in mathematics and the sciences is derogated; indigenous wisdom is dismissed as superstition; moral issues are treated as problems in cost-benefit analysis; the purpose of education is to get a job.

In such a culture, the beings that populate natural ecologies are regarded as resources, parts of a kind of biological machine. Developers and restoration specialists ask: "If we give you just as many trees, and just as many ponds, bugs and birds, what's your problem?" Our problem is that violence is being done to reality; meaning is being abused. But we are powerless to say this, often powerless even to recognize it, because the way of thinking on which it depends is not acknowledged as genuine. Our ability to experience things *as the gestalts they are* is dismissed and undermined.

Here is Hopkins again:

The ashtree growing in the corner of the garden was felled. It was lopped first: I heard the sound and looking out and seeing it maimed there came at that moment a great pang and I wished to die and not see the inscapes of the world destroyed any more

The inscapes of the world *are* being destroyed — at a geological pace just shy of a meteor impact. Meaning is not something we can ignore or make fun of in these circumstances. It is not something we should feel free to confuse with 'personal interpretation.' We should not be satisfied with 'little pops in the mind' when we need insight into reality. Poetry, along with the other arts, is now called, as it has been in other serious circumstances, to bear witness.

This does not mean that environmental catastrophe and the political, moral, and economic tyrannies that drive it are the only worthy themes. It means that human work and human thinking must be attuned to the real, extra-human world, rather than to possibilities of fame, or fun, or capturing the market. It also does not mean there is no joy. There is always — always — light in the dark. It is part of our responsibility as artists to be alert to that light, to respond to it, and to name it truly.

Our responsibility as readers is also great. Our inner ear gives life to the music of the human mind. In this, there is also joy and remarkable beauty. We must not think of ourselves as consumers. Good literature delights and satisfies, but it is not commercial entertainment: its purpose is not to drug, nor to distract, nor to sell, and we should not measure it by those standards. We must not be afraid to cultivate reading as an art, a skill that we practise with delight certainly, but also with the diligence and patience that make true delight possible.

Simplicity and the Experience of Meaning

Simplicity is frequently touted as an ideal in art, mathematics, and the sciences, although truth overrides it in the sciences, and 'expressiveness' or 'interest' or 'pleasingness' often override it in art. In many cases, truth, expressiveness, and pleasingness are nonetheless felt to be *bound up* with simplicity of presentation or conception. Why should this be so? I'd like to begin an approach to this question by way of a poem rather than a proof.

In "Archaic Torso of Apollo," Rilke describes his encounter with a headless Greek sculpture:

> We can't know that fabulous head
> where eyes like apples ripened. But
> his torso glows still like a candelabra
> in which his gazing, though it's shrouded,
>
> rivets us and gleams. Otherwise, the prow
> of his breast could not blind you, and no smile
> would ripple down the slight twist of the loins,
> there, to the core, which held his sex.
>
> Otherwise this stone would stand defaced, cut off
> under the shoulders' diaphanous plunge,
> and wouldn't shimmer like the pelt of some wild beast;
>
> and wouldn't burst from all its boundaries
> like a star: for there is no place
> that does not see you. You must change your life.

The poem is a testament to the power of art. It is also an extraordinarily vivid description of the experience of meaning wherever we encounter it, and it captures that experience in a startling image. Although the statue is headless, what we see is its gaze — a gaze that remains present, tangible, in the eyeless marble of the torso. The radiance of this gaze informs the fragment, and it informs us, too. It reaches right into us and demands a response.

Whence the mystique of simplicity? My proposal is that in many cases it's not simplicity itself that we're after — at least not simplicity in any quantitative sense. What we're after is the phenomenon described in Rilke's poem. Once the question of truth is settled, and often prior to it, what we value in a proof or conjecture is what we value in a work of lyric art: potency of meaning. There is something *like* quantitative simplicity that matters here, namely an absence of clutter: lyric artifacts possess a resonant clarity that allows their meaning to break on our inner eye like light. But this absence of clutter is not tantamount to 'being simple' and it has nothing to do with minimum numbers of components, axioms, or procedures: consider Eliot's *Four Quartets*, for instance, or Mozart's late symphonies. Many truths are complex, and they are simpl*ified* at the cost of distortion, at the cost of ceasing to be truths. Why, then, do we valorize quantitative simplicity? Because getting rid of clutter — an action that facilitates potency of meaning — can involve tossing items out. But getting rid of clutter can also involve rearranging the items that one has without throwing any of them away. And it is crucial to notice that the clearest or most compelling arrangement is not always the one whose components have been most strictly reduced.

The case that springs to mind is our present model of the solar system. Attempts to explain apparent planetary motion with *one* focus — the centre of a circle — generated clutter; attempts to explain it with *two* foci precipitated an experience of meaning so powerful that it changed the intellectual life of Europe. It is that experience we seek — the flash of insight, the sense we've seen into the heart of things. At its core is a phenomenon that has gone by a number of names in the history of human thought — Wittgenstein called it *Sehen als*, Gerard Manley Hopkins called it the sensation of inscape, Plato described it as κατ᾽ εἶδος λεγόμενον, the old Taoists called it awareness of *zìrán* (自然). What each points to is the arrival of gestalt insight.

60   The Experience of Meaning

Why or how could an absence of clutter matter to this process?

That it matters, at least in some cases, is clear. Here is Ben Shahn, talking about making visual art. It is important to remember that his work is richly textured, and in no way minimalist:

> [F]orm is not just the intention of content; it is the embodiment of content. Form is based, first, upon a supposition, a theme. Form is, second, a marshalling of materials, the inert matter in which the theme is to be cast. Form is, third, a setting of boundaries, of limits, the whole extent of idea, *but no more*, an outer shape of idea. Form is, next, the relating of inner shapes to the outer limits, the initial establishing of harmonies. Form is, further, the abolishing of excessive content, of content that falls outside the true limits of the theme. It is the abolishing of excessive materials, whatever material is extraneous to inner harmony, to the order of shapes now established.

Among lyric poets — lyric writers in general — *less is more* is one of the few near-universal precepts. It served Mies van der Rohe as a motto; and Wittgenstein's *Tractatus* embodies it. The phrase appears famously in Robert Browning's "Andrea del Sarto"; but the thought is as old as Hesiod.

Why should this be so? How *could* less be more?

Towards the end of *War and Peace*, Tolstoy's protagonist, Pierre Bezukhov, is captured by the French, imprisoned in a rudimentary camp for a month, and then forced to march west with the French as they retreat. It is October. He has no shoes. On the first evening of the march, Pierre moves off by himself and settles on the frozen ground by a cart wheel to think. He is motionless for over an hour, and then suddenly bursts into a huge happy laugh. It's so loud that people around the campfires turn in astonishment, and someone comes to investigate. Pierre moves farther away.

> The enormous, endless bivouac, noisy earlier with the crackling of campfires and the talking of men, was growing still; the red

Simplicity and the Experience of Meaning

flames of the campfires were dying out and turning pale. The full moon stood high in the bright sky. Forests and fields, invisible earlier beyond the territory of the camp, now opened out in the distance. And further beyond these forests and fields could be seen the bright, wavering, endless distance calling one to itself. Pierre looked into the sky, into the depths of the retreating, twinkling stars. "And all this is mine, and all this is in me, and all this is me!" thought Pierre. "And all this they've caught and put in a shed and boarded it up!" He smiled and went to his comrades to lie down and sleep.

This is the moment of Pierre's inner transformation, the effects of which will play out over the remainder of his life. Tolstoy describes the transformation abstractly in this way:

In captivity, in the shed, Pierre had learned, not with his mind, but with his whole being, his life, that man is created for happiness, that happiness is within him, in the satisfying of natural human needs, and that all unhappiness comes not from lack, but from superfluity....

Months later, rescued, recovered from a serious illness, Pierre appears, Tolstoy tells us, "almost unchanged in his external ways": he looks the same, he's still absent-minded, kind, and distracted. His servants, however, notice that he has become "much simpler"; and he has ceased being a talker and become an exceptional listener. Before his experience in the war, he had appeared unhappy, whereas now he seemed always to be smiling:

Formerly he had been unable to see the great, the unfathomable and infinite, in anything. He had only sensed that it must be somewhere and had sought for it.... He had armed himself with a mental spyglass and gazed into the distance.... Now he had learned to see [it] in everything, and ... joyfully contemplated the ever-changing, ever-great, unfathomable, and infinite life around him.

There is a great deal going on here; *War and Peace* is a big novel. But one way of summarizing Tolstoy's insight is this: Paring life to its basics

62   The Experience of Meaning

allows one to see its ontological core, which is that the world is a resonant whole.

The American poet Robert Hass, discussing the minimalist imagism of haiku, says something eerily reminiscent of Pierre's changed experience of seeing:

> Often enough, when a thing is seen clearly, there is a sense of absence about it ... as if, the more palpable it is, the more some immense subterranean displacement seems to be working in it; as if at the point of truest observation the visible and invisible exerted enormous counterpressure.

To put this in gestalt terms: the whole is experienced through the particular, which is a part of it. This is possible only if every part is internally related to every other part: if it is the nature of the whole that determines the nature of each part.

Visualize a geodesic sphere. Because its nodes are dimensionless points, each exists only as a set of angles. Now imagine the sphere's lines are elastic, so that any or all of the nodes can move. If any one of them does move, this will affect the angles that define it: some will contract, some will expand. *As will the constituting angles of every other node.* Now, put the whole thing in motion. Each node will be in interdefined dynamic relation with every other node; and each will, necessarily, reflect the state of the whole at every moment.

It is in some such way, Tolstoy is claiming, that Pierre came to experience the world, or something unnamably large, through its individual beings.

And it is a striking fact about the imagination that we can easily hold the image of this dancing geodesic sphere before the mind's eye even as we appreciate the extraordinary complexity of any mathematical description of it. Here, an observation from Arne Næss, the environmental philosopher and scholar of Spinoza, is crucial. Næss points out that ecosystems theory draws a distinction between complexity and complicatedness. What is *complicated* is disunified, chaotic — Næss gives the example of trying to find your way through a huge unfamiliar city without a map. What is *complex*, by contrast, may be intricate, but it is not chaotic; it has a unifying gestalt — Næss's example, of course, is an ecosystem. By definition, a complex thing cannot be simple in the sense of

Simplicity and the Experience of Meaning 63

having no parts or divisions. It will have multiple aspects, and there are often many different relations among these aspects. But complexity is uncluttered. Everything fits. Clutter, then, may be defined as that which does not belong to a gestalt, that which has no internal relation to other aspects of an array. On this view, one way to describe Pierre's transformation is to say that he ceased to experience the world as complicated and came to experience it as complex.

The geodesic sphere, talk of 'arrays' — these are visual images. Ben Shahn, you'll recall, spoke of "abolishing ... whatever material is extraneous to inner harmony." His image was aural. It suggests that in powerful gestalts, we experience the presence of internal relations as the mutual attunement of parts or aspects. Because of this attunement, the gestalt as a whole is resonant: when one part sounds, other parts sound as well. Clutter is anything that damps down or muffles this resonance. The etymological root of 'clarity' means *to shout, to resound*; and resonance requires space. Complexity can accommodate space; complicatedness often cannot. Think of a harp; think of the parts of the harp separated and piled in a structureless heap. Mies van der Rohe, he who often said *less is more*, also often said *God is in the details*. And Wittgenstein claimed that the following stanza from Longfellow's "The Builders" could serve him as a motto:

> In the elder days of Art,
> Builders wrought with greatest care
> Each minute and unseen part;
> For the gods see everywhere.

What they were pointing to is the way the meaning of a well-wrought whole arises from the resonant attunement of its parts.

Willa Cather has put this point in a way that foregrounds the experience of the audience for a composition:

> [V]ery nearly the whole of the higher artistic process [is] finding what conventions of form and what detail one can do without and yet preserve the spirit of the whole — so that all that one has suppressed and cut away is there to the reader's consciousness as much as if it were in type on the page.

I'm not sure about the image of type on the page, which suggests that the meaning of what one hasn't said can be as clear as if one had said it. For reasons I'll review shortly, I think that the meaning of what one hasn't said can be *clearer* than verbally articulated meaning. But the central claim, that an artist can enhance the experience of meaning by saying as little as possible, echoes Shahn's view precisely.

"All that one has suppressed or cut away": that is, what we have not made explicit, or what we have not represented focally; what we have shown, but not told. Imagine the effect of presenting the two articulated squares in the visual proof of the Pythagorean theorem on page 14 and saying simply "Behold!", not providing any accompanying algebraic statement of the theorem. Some beholders might not see what we want them to see; but a person who does see it, who has not been taught the theorem, will be electrified.

Robert Hass, discussing a poem by Buson, shows how this lack of explicitness can work to goad the mind into action:

January 16 was a holiday in the Japan of the Tokugawa Shogunate. Apprentices who had been sent from home to learn a trade were given a day off to visit their families. The day also had associations with kite-flying. Buson gives us one kid on his way home:

> Apprentice's holiday:
> hops over kite string,
>   keeps going.

That easy leap is like William Carlos Williams, but it is when you start thinking about the kite tugging in the wind that the poem opens up.

Buson does not say that the kite is tugging in the wind, but it's there, because the apprentice hops over the string. If we listen to the poem, sense its resonant imagistic structure, we see the taut string, and then the kite in the sky, and then feel it tugging — ah! it's still on a string but it is also aloft; its image enacts the one-day holiday — and we know it's sunny and windy, and chilly and invigorating; and then we register what the social situation must be that the apprentice hops over the taut string instead of walking around the person flying the kite; and what is packed into the phrase "keeps going" — all of this and more is what Hass means when he says the poem "opens up." Would you get the same effect if you spelled it all out? No. This is why Hass simply told us to look. Although I have now spelled out a good deal, it is, luckily, such a great poem that it can reclaim the silent spaces in which its meaning moves. Reading it again, we experience its brilliant, resonant particularity.

છ

I said at the outset that what we prize in mathematical demonstrations is what we prize in works of art: the ability to precipitate an experience of meaning. Marjorie Wikler Senechal puts it this way:

> Paul Erdős, the great twentieth-century mathematician who loved only numbers, an atheist, claimed that God has a book in which the best proof of every theorem is written. Erdős never listed the criteria a proof must satisfy to be inscribed in God's book: he didn't need to. Though no one has seen the book or ever will, all mathematicians know that Euclid's proof of the infinitude of primes is in it, and no mathematician doubts that computer-generated proofs, the kind that methodically check case after case, are not. The proofs in God's book are elegant. They surprise. In other words, they are light, quick, exact, and visible.

In other words, the proofs in God's book involve gestalt shifts: they are potent with meaning. They may be complex, but they are not complicated: there is no clutter. They do not tediously spell everything out; they invite us to *see* what they are saying. Arthur Koestler describes his own experience with Euclid's proof of the infinitude of primes this way (he was, at the time, in a Spanish prison, anticipating execution at any moment):

> Since I had become acquainted with Euclid's proof at school, it had always filled me with a deep satisfaction that was aesthetic rather than intellectual. Now, as I recalled the method and scratched the symbols on the wall, I felt the same enchantment.

66   The Experience of Meaning

And then, for the first time, I suddenly understood the reason for this enchantment: the scribbled symbols on the wall represented one of the rare cases where a meaningful and comprehensive statement about the infinite is arrived at by precise and finite means. The infinite is a mystical mass shrouded in a haze; and yet it was possible to gain some knowledge of it without losing oneself in treacly ambiguities. The significance of this swept over me like a wave. The wave had originated in an articulate verbal insight; but this evaporated at once, leaving in its wake only a wordless essence, a fragrance of eternity, a quiver of the arrow in the blue. [Buson's kite.] I must have stood there for some minutes entranced, with a wordless awareness that 'this is perfect — perfect'; until I noticed some slight mental discomfort nagging at the back of my mind — some trivial circumstance that marred the perfection of the moment. Then I remembered the nature of that irrelevant annoyance: I was, of course, in prison and might be shot. But this was immediately answered by a feeling whose verbal translation would be: "So what? is that all? have you got nothing more serious to worry about?" — an answer so spontaneous, fresh and amused as if the intruding annoyance had been the loss of a collar-stud.

I have quoted at length because the echoes of Pierre's experience are so striking.

Mathematical demonstrations like Euclid's proof involve the crystallization of certain internal relationships: we *see* that the theorem has to be so. They are like haiku: single images through which the resonance of something much larger sounds. Other demonstrations — like Gauss's insight that there's a simple way to obtain the sum of any continuous sequence of integers — involve gestalt shifts. We see things first one way, and then we see them — the same things! — another way. This is the essence not of haiku, but of metaphor: x is not y; and yet it is. It is the dawning of the second gestalt, in relation to the first, that is the experience of meaning.

In either case — whether the gestalt crystallizes or shifts — if there are pieces left over, details that don't fit, we may, as Ptolemy, and subsequently Copernicus, did, ignore them — tuck them away into eccentrics and epicycles. We don't see them as details that don't fit. Sometimes, though, they start to bother us; and once that happens, we've become aware of them *as* clutter; we want to clear them up; what was once a gestalt — something we *saw* — now strikes us as merely a model, an *interpretation* of the data. That model may still have the weight of cultural authority behind it, but it doesn't ring with its own authority. We keep revisiting the clutter — as Kepler did Tycho's observations of Mars — until the penny drops. We don't like messy or complicated models in science or images in poems because, even when they save the phenomena, they don't precipitate an experience of meaning.

So we come to understand that a gestalt is false, that an alleged proof is in error, because we acknowledge the existence of perceptions or data that don't fit; we experience irresoluble clutter that blocks a satisfying experience of meaning. But now: what is the ontological status of that clutter? How, on the Gestalt account, if parts are not spontaneously perceived but are perceived subsequent to wholes — how do we become aware of this recalcitrant data in the first place? Come to that, how is it that we can perceive aspects, details, parts — whatever we want to call them — at all? We may be spontaneously aware of faces as wholes, but we can certainly attend to their eyes and noses, and experience them spontaneously *as* eyes and noses, too. Indeed, it appears that we perceive those eyes and noses as integrated wholes themselves — we recognize them without being able to draw or accurately specify *their* 'elemental' building blocks either. When we focus on them, ignoring their context, we perceive them as though they were gestalts. That's because they *are* gestalts.

A nose, an eye, a motif in a melody, an individual triangle in a visual proof — anything we see or understand as a *thing* — has shape, is a whole whose own aspects are internally related. And it works the other way as well: a face can become an aspect of a photograph, or a painting, or a crowd; a melody can become an aspect of the first subject of a movement in a sonata which, in turn, can become an aspect of the movement as a whole. When the wholes discerned by gestalt comprehension are events rather than physical beings, we often refer to 'what's going on' or 'what happened.' Events, too, are capable of analysis into other, briefer, events; and they may be subsumed into larger histories. The world, in other words, is an immense complex of what Næss called subordinate

68   The Experience of Meaning

and superordinate gestalts. To paraphrase the homespun philosopher, it's gestalts all the way down. And up, too.

It's also gestalts sideways. What is the ontological status of clutter? Clutter consists of what we might call con- or peri-ordinate gestalts — things that don't fit; facts we say we don't understand, but wish we did; recalcitrant data. It consists of gestalts that don't seem to belong to a superordinate gestalt; or, to put it another way, of gestalts that don't seem to have internal relations to other gestalts. Their perception therefore does not precipitate an experience of meaning. This failure to precipitate an experience of meaning is the hallmark of conordinate gestalts. I believe this is what Richard Feynman had in mind when he claimed that nobody understands quantum mechanics. Why not? Because, according to Feynman, nothing in our experience is analogous to the behaviour of electrons and photons. At the core of the Gestalt theory of learning is the view that to *understand* something just is to perceive its relevant structural similarity to some other thing or situation. The perception of telling similarity is the litmus that understanding has occurred. Where such perception is absent, we may have 'the facts' but we have no superordinate gestalt; we don't see *why* they are the facts; we don't know what they *mean*. So we keep looking at them this way, that way, hoping we can sense connections.

Our world is meaningful to the extent that it consists of sub- and superordinate gestalts; there are immense numbers of complex interactions among them in all things, beings, artifacts, contexts, ecologies, and cultures. Is there a limit to what, within a given whole, can be discriminated as a part? This is asking if there are atoms — genuine ontological uncuttables — in the experienceable world. I don't know. Is there a largest superordinate gestalt — either a limit to what the mind can comprehend or to the coherence of the universe? I don't know.

The fact of false gestalts — the tangled history of European views of planetary motion, for example — raises another issue about the relation between meaning and simplicity. A desire for truth, for accuracy, is part of the picture, but it's not the only part. Tycho, who made the observations on which Kepler's view is founded, was himself a geocentrist. And Kepler made a number of mistakes in the calculations he based on Tycho's data. But he refused to believe that the cosmological picture

Simplicity and the Experience of Meaning 69

could be geometrically complicated. So, he kept returning to Tycho's observations and at last, after years of effort, they precipitated a beautiful uncluttered ellipse for the orbit of Mars. (Indeed it may have been a concern with cosmological clutter that made Copernicus reluctant to publish his own increasingly epicycle-ridden view.) We ourselves look at Kepler's three laws and marvel at their simplicity. "Ah!" we say, sweeping the epicycles off the table, "of course."

What, though, is the foundation of that "of course"? Why keep plugging away at Tycho's observations? Why keep trying to 'understand' quantum mechanics? Aristotle said it was simply what humans do, that by nature we want to grasp the similarities that unify our experience and make it whole. I think Aristotle was right: it's a raw fact about our intelligence: we prefer less complicated gestalts to more complicated ones. Max Wertheimer and others characterized our preference in terms of the so-called Law of *Prägnanz*, a word that might be translated as 'concision' or 'pithiness.' They further specified aspects of the Law of *Prägnanz* — features possessed by subordinate gestalts that will make them tend to hang together: the 'good curve,' proximity, unified movement, and the like. Gestalt theorists were not, however, able to specify rigorous formulæ for the emergence of gestalts; the 'factors' remained tendencies, not laws.

The thing is: it isn't just any arrangement of multiple aspects or features that does genuinely 'hang together'; it isn't, as Poincaré notes, any odd or bizarre combination of facts or objects that will be mathematically fertile; and it isn't any juxtaposition of images in a poem or painting, nor any harmonic sequence in a string quartet, that will strike us as profound. To deny this is to fail to be responsible to our experience. I do not think we have explanations of the tendencies the Gestalt theorists identified. This does not mean we should think the tendencies don't exist.

Much of what we perceive — light, air, water, plants, rocks, other animals — is perceived by other beings: that's what we perceive them doing — perceiving the same world we do. As long as you're not a skeptic — as long as you believe that light, air, water, plants, rocks, and other animals exist independently of your own mind — it's overwhelmingly unlikely that all of us, including those other perceiving beings, have it entirely wrong about the nature and disposition of our shared environment. There is, however, overwhelming evidence that our own species is, in gestalt terms, a bad idea. We have been unable to sustain stable internal relations to many other aspects of the biosphere, and we are set to take big chunks of it with us when we go. Why? What's wrong with us? My guess is that it has something to do with a lack of respect for, and denial of, human gestalt capacities. Those capacities tell us we're just one among many internally related aspects of the world. This is an inconvenient perception if you purpose dominion and control.

ॐ

Great physicists and philosophers have argued that the big cosmological picture has to be simple. They have good reason. There is a remarkable fit between a number of clear, simple geometrical figures (spheres, ellipses, cubes, spirals, parabolas, pentagons, for example) and a good deal of what goes on in the visible universe (planets, their orbits, pyrite, the construction of many biological organisms, gravitational field strength, quasi-crystals, for example). There are also remarkably clear, simple algebraic expressions for the geometrical relationships involved.

And yet there is not a similarly good fit between geometry, on the one hand, and arithmetic, on the other. Some of the relationships we grasp — so immediately, so concretely — turn out not to have finitely calculable arithmetical values. The diagonal of any given square is incommensurable with its sides; the golden section, like π, cannot be expressed as a ratio of integers. At the very heart of European cosmological pictures for the last 2,400 years is a less than perfect fit between rational numbers and geometry. We can form no 'good gestalt' of their relationship. Why is this? We don't know. But it complicates the demand for simplicity in a culture that privileges calculative results above results of other kinds.

The puzzle, I believe, is generated by that privileging: by the idea that only calculative results matter, that only they are really 'real.' This is not, however, what the evidence suggests. The evidence suggests that gestalt thinking and perception constitute one kind of intelligence, and calculation constitutes another; and that neither comprehends the other, neither can fully translate the other into its own terms. I know of no concerted efforts to document this claim. But Jonathan Schooler's work in experimental psychology documents a related claim: that gestalt comprehension and language-use are somehow at odds.

Schooler and his associates have shown that the ability to recognize previously seen faces or previously heard segments of music, to perform gestalt shifts of the Necker cube variety, to perceive analogies, and to solve insight problems are impaired by attempts to describe the face, figure, or thought processes involved. He also points out that cognitive psychology has not been keen to embrace this fact. In one of his earliest papers, Schooler cites mid-twentieth-century studies that demonstrated the effect, but whose results were subsequently overlooked. He lists later twentieth-century studies in which the effect shows up, but whose authors *wave away their own results*. They conclude not that verbalization interferes with our ability to think in certain ways, but that it uses up time that might otherwise be devoted to 'visual encoding'; or that presenting subjects with schematic sentences caused them to focus on schematic aspects of pictures; or that the negative effects observed were anomalous; or that training may need to be more intensive if it is to produce results. As Schooler says, "verbal processing has been assumed to be the 'deepest' and most memorable form of processing.... [T]he present Zeitgeist emphasizing the value of verbal processing has caused ... researchers to generally overlook or simply disregard its potential to produce interference." This zeitgeist has also caused most Western intellectuals to ignore or to reject the importance of gestalt comprehension, and thereby to avoid serious contemplation of the experience of meaning.

Without such contemplation, however, I do not think we can come to an accurate appreciation of why we prefer some mathematical and scientific theories to others. We turn to theories for insight, for a shift from what seems to be a complicated situation — one that consists of a bunch of conordinate gestalts or, sometimes, just a mass of inchoate impressions — to a complex one, in which parts and wholes are interdefined. Insight does not require reducing the number of aspects to a minimum; nor does it require limiting the types or amounts of interdefinition. It requires the absence of things that don't fit.

There are, notoriously, no criteria in the arts or sciences for achieving or executing integrated wholes. But the absence of such criteria need not mean that the wholes themselves are suspect; it could mean, and I think it does, that the demand for criteria is, sometimes, misplaced. Computers cannot replicate the process (if that's what it is) of insight because computational structures, of their essence, consist of discrete, non-interdefined elements arranged in rule-governed sequences: this is exactly what a gestalt is not. Perhaps — perhaps — as we come to understand more about how brains work, we will be able to formulate reductionist biophysical laws that underlie gestalt thinking and perception. Or perhaps we will come to appreciate that we are looking for a kind of representation of gestalt thinking that we cannot have, that gestalt thinking will always *underlie* any 'satisfactory' biophysical laws we formulate, and that the deep mystery will remain. The deep answer starts to look like Plato's: *being* consists of gestalts. What *is* is shape. Except that it's shape in motion — there's nothing changeless or eternal about it. The view of Herakleitos, then, the riddler, who saw change and unity and dynamic interdefinition as the fundamental features of the cosmos, and was quite content to allow the strain on language, in the form of repeated and multiple paradoxes, to stand unresolved. Who asserted that this bending and breaking of linguistic intelligence was the price of understanding.

Schooler and his colleagues have explicitly tied the lab-tested phenomena of 'verbal overshadowing' to classic discussions of insight and creativity — things that, as a culture, we claim to value — but there is little evidence that we are paying attention. In North American philosophy, for example, computational models of learning have linked hands with logico-linguistic analysis and penetrated deeply into the idea of what epistemology *is*. Analogical thinking is dismissed as weak or inferior. The idea that there might be philosophically significant thought that occurs without words is still a kind of heresy. The idea that meaning itself might be a non-verbal phenomenon is not even on the radar.

But I am convinced it is the truth. The famous anecdotes from the history of science, mathematics, and the arts, the repeated lab experiments with hundreds of unremarkable undergraduates, confirm it: insight is not verbal. If you try to make it verbal, you shut it down. By demanding that people think verbally, we are depriving them of the experience of meaning. They will know, increasingly, *what* is the case, but less and less will they have a sense that they understand why.

Simplicity and the Experience of Meaning   73

Yet a sense that we understand why is one of the things human beings most deeply desire. It's what we want from mathematics, science, and the arts; I think it's even what we want from philosophy: the revelation of meaning. We want to experience gestalts so powerful they make us change our lives. I do not know why we want this. One possibility is that that's what being itself is: the resonance of gestalts. When we experience meaning, we are, to a greater or lesser degree, filled with resonance ourselves. And if being is resonance, then, in such moments, we more completely are.

ꙮ Plato and Gestalt, or Why There Is No Theory of Forms

Plato is famous for having developed the so-called theory of forms: the idea that there is a universe of non-tangible, imperishable entities whose being lends some measure of reality to human experience of the mutable world. Yet there is nothing like a theory to this effect in any of Plato's dialogues. A letter attributed to Plato explains why:

> There is not, nor will there be, a treatise on this subject by me. For it is not possible to speak of it as other kinds of studies are spoken of; rather, out of long abiding and living with the issue itself, suddenly, as when a spark leaps from a fire and kindles a light, [this sort of understanding] arises in the soul and, once it does, it sustains itself thereafter.

This passage echoes both the claims and the situation of Gestalt theory on a number of points: like Plato, Gestalt theorists were not able to provide a compelling systematic theory of what gestalts are and how we grasp them; gestalt insights often appear suddenly after a period of sustained intellectual struggle with an issue; when gestalt insight occurs, the effect is that of a light bulb going on in the mind; and, once they strike a person, gestalts are there to stay — they're very hard to dislodge. Other passages from Plato's dialogues reinforce these echoes; and yet other passages establish further points of connection.

There is one very obvious point on which Plato and the Gestalt theorists do not appear to concur: Plato claimed explicitly that forms have mind-independent existence in a realm distinct from the world in which we live, a realm to which the soul has access after death. I know of no one associated with the Gestalt school who explicitly connects gestalt insight with the immortality of the soul, nor anyone who argues that insights, as entities, exist in a special realm of their own. Some, like Wolfgang Köhler, argued that the structures of electrical events in the brain directly mirror the structures of perceptual experience. Others, like Wolfgang Metzger, argued for a position with both physicalist and Idealist elements — gestalts, Metzger claimed, are in part determined by the activity of human minds, but they are also determined in part by things and events in a physical, mind-independent world. Yet others, like Max Wertheimer, were silent on metaphysical issues.

I propose to be silent, too. We can begin to attend to what goes on when we and those around us experience understanding without first committing ourselves to views about the nature of apparently physical 'stuff' or its relations to apparently mental 'ideas.' We can, then — and I shall — set most of Plato's metaphysics aside and focus on his epistemological observations: what he says about what it's like to think. When we do this, we find the echoes that I've mentioned. The emergence of roughly the same view in two distinct civilizations, in both cases athwart mainstream intellectual opinion and standard teaching practices, should give us pause. It suggests that there may be epistemological phenomena that our own intellectual culture ought to be quite curious about.

ॐ

First, I want to look in greater detail at the evidence that Plato's forms are something like gestalts. There are several points of correspondence.

What Thinking Is

One of Max Wertheimer's preoccupations was how to encourage people to think like Gauss — how, that is, to teach them to make the kinds of gestalt shifts necessary to what he termed 'productive thinking.' He explicitly divided the problem into two parts. The first part was negative: productive thinking, he claimed, is not bound by habit, it does not merely regurgitate facts or procedures taught by rote in schools, and it does not proceed mechanically. We must rid ourselves of these influences so that we may approach issues "freely, open-mindedly." The second, 'positive' part then involved trying to perceive the "inner relation" between a problematic situation — one in which things are not arrayed in a satisfactory or comprehensible way — and a situation in which difficulties, tensions, or incoherencies have been cleared away. Wertheimer described this as "illuminating and making transparent essential structural features ... in spite of ... difficulties."

Wertheimer's descriptions of how he proceeded with actual subjects suggest that he often simply blocked the habitual path: "Solve the problem without counting." And, if that alone didn't precipitate insight, he then offered cases for comparison: similar but simpler versions of the problem, or of problems that contained an aspect of the main problem; or he asked leading questions. Often, Wertheimer noted, young children who had not been thoroughly schooled were better able to 'think productively' than intelligent, well-educated adults. He describes many such children trying one approach or another, halting, puzzling, trying again, halting, puzzling, and then suddenly brightening as the solution came. Köhler in "What Is Thinking?" uses illustrations drawn from the history of science and mathematics, and emphasizes how brilliant individuals often wrestle intensely with problems before new gestalts dawn.

Plato, too, was preoccupied with getting people to really think. He believed the process involved two stages. The first stage he called *elenkhos*, or refutation. It was negative, an attempt to disabuse people of mere opinions, prejudices that they espoused in a knee-jerk way out of habit or fashion, and which prevented them from feeling the desire to know the truth. The second, positive, stage Plato called *dialektikē*, or dialectic. Sometimes he characterized it casually as the activity of friendly non-disputatious enquiry, question-and-answer discussion between an older, experienced individual and a younger, less experienced one. At other times, he identified dialectic with the so-called method of collection and division.

Plato defined the method of collection and division as an intellectual process that itself had two parts: "first, seeing and gathering together into one form that which is scattered about, making distinct the thing one wishes to explain [and then] cutting up each form along its joints, according to its natural pattern, and trying *not* to shatter any part, assailing it in the manner of a bad butcher" (*Phaidros* 265d–e). That is: apparently you *intuit* that x is best understood as part of some whole, y; and then you develop more precise insight into both x's and y's respective natures through a delineation of y's internal structure. Intuition — or perhaps a kind of inexplicit know-how, cultivated through practice — also seems to be involved in this delineation, in making good divisions

Plato and Gestalt   77

that don't 'shatter' parts. Plato does provide some examples. But aside from these, there is no discussion of what is involved in either process.

Konrad Lorenz, however, is more vocal. In the introduction to his essay "Gestalt Perception as a Source of Scientific Knowledge," he offers an explicit discussion of the role of intuition in gestalt thinking:

> Of myself ... it is simply not true that my first step in approaching any phenomenon I have observed consists in creating a rather random hypothesis and subsequently trying to find fault with it.... I strongly suspect that, at the time when a set of phenomena seriously begins to fascinate me, my Gestalt perception has already achieved its crucial function and 'suspected' an interesting lawfulness in that particular bunch of sensory data.... [I]ncreased observation accelerates the input of sensory data until, when sufficient redundancy is achieved, the consciously perceived lawfulness detaches itself from the background of accidentals, an event which is accompanied by a very characteristic experience of relief ..., the sigh: "Aha!" ... [I]f our conscious effort at cognition really had to start at the level of miscellaneous, unprocessed sensory data ... [i]nductive procedure would, I think, really be impossible.... Gestalt perception, on the other hand, when based on a sufficient wealth of unbiassed observation, has a way of being *right*, and if one is familiar with its occasional trick of being altogether wrong and knows when to discount its assertions, it is an invaluable and quite indispensable guide.

Plato shows the method of collection and division in action on the concepts of angling, sophistry, and statecraft, as well as madness; and he also gives an abstract summary of the method that includes brief examples of its application to the concepts of literacy and music. The examples make clear that the method is anything but mechanical. It aims at clear conceptual hierarchies, but there don't seem to be any rules; and there are indications that the hierarchies can be remade. It is worth noting that there is a direct line of intellectual transmission from collection and division as it appears in Plato to the taxonomies used by biologists today. It's also worth noting that biologists actively involved in developing taxonomies say that the process is an art as well as a science; and that as we learn more, earlier taxonomies are taken apart and reconstructed.

In Plato's dialogues, the character in charge of the discussion (usually Socrates, but occasionally some other older philosopher) frequently offers analogies and asks leading questions in an attempt to assist her or his interlocutor to think through an issue. These assists appear in both the elenktic and dialectical stages. Plato shows dramatically that both stages are difficult; and his characters complain explicitly about the difficulty of the second, positive, stage: it requires exceptional effort. Sometimes, it appears that understanding is reached; but often 'true knowledge' is not vouchsafed in the dialogue and some alleged sketch or analogy is offered instead.

In the thirty-some dialogues Plato wrote, characters of many different kinds are shown struggling with the challenge of real thought. Only three come in for praise. They are all young.

There are clearly aspects of Plato's account that have no counterpart in the Gestalt account. But they seem minor by comparison with the aspects that are shared:

- thinking, in both, is a two-stage process: a clearing-out of what's been accepted without real thinking, followed by a good-willed investigation into the deep interior structure of a concept or situation;
- 'penetrating' to this interior structure may, in the gestalt case, precipitate insight, or a solution to the problem; in Plato's case, rehearsal of the structure is aimed at grasping a form;
- the process of collection and division, in Plato, appears to involve the kind of intuition Lorenz associates with gestalt processes in contemporary scientific theorizing;
- in both, there is an absence of clearly defined procedural rules;
- in both, instead, teaching employs analogies and leading questions;
- both Köhler and Plato stress that the second stage can involve extraordinary effort.

Arbitrary Components and Necessary Parts

In a dialogue called *Politikos*, Plato sets his characters the task of revealing the nature of the true statesman. The dialogue is the third in a series; the two earlier dialogues investigate the nature of knowledge and the nature of the sophist, respectively. By the time we get to *Politikos*, we've been exposed to many examples of collection and division, but have not been offered a principled account. Early in *Politikos*, there is a methodological digression. Young Socrates — old Socrates' namesake — has just attempted to 'divide' a conceptual genus in a way that his older interlocutor, a stranger from Elea, doesn't like. Young Socrates grasps that he's made a mistake, but asks for clarification about what he did wrong. The Eleatic Stranger gives him some examples that make the same mistake — dividing the genus 'human race' into Greeks and everyone else; dividing the genus 'number' into the number 10,000 and all other numbers. The correct binomial divisions, the Stranger says, are 'female and male' in the case of 'human race' and 'odd and even' in the case of number. In other words, Young Socrates has mistaken an arbitrary part — a *meros* — for a real class — a *genos*.

"You're absolutely right," says Young Socrates, "but that's just the trouble, Stranger: I don't understand how to tell the difference between a mere part and a real class. How do you do it?"

Those of us who have read the three linked dialogues to this point are now on the edge of our collective seat. This is exactly the question we ourselves have been dying to ask.

"Ah, Socrates, you most excellent young man!" the Stranger exclaims. "But we've strayed from our subject and now you want us to stray further. So let's leave that question for now and return to it in a while." We can imagine a slight pause. "However, there is one thing you must take great care not to do, and that is to suppose that you have ever heard from me a plain account of the matter."

"What matter?" asks Young Socrates.

"That class and part are different from each other."

"Well, what then shall I say I've heard from you?"

"That whenever there is a class of something, it is necessarily also a part of that thing; but it is not at all necessary that a part be a class."

I'm still amazed every time I read this passage. We are brought right to the threshold of what we need to know about division, the key question has been asked — and Plato forces us to march right by the door, insisting that we stare at it over our shoulders as we do so. Was there to have been a fourth dialogue as some speculate, *Philosopher*, in which this question was to have been front and centre? Perhaps. In the extant works, however, it is never mentioned again.

Leap to the twentieth century. In 1933, Max Wertheimer published a brief essay called "Zu dem Problem der Unterscheidung von Einzelinhalt und Teil," which appeared in English translation in 1959 under the title "On the Problem of the Distinction Between Arbitrary Component and Necessary Part." It consists entirely of examples. In a footnote, the translator, Michael Wertheimer, explains the essay's importance: "the paper is frequently referred to in [other essays by Max Wertheimer] as including examples demonstrating that what may be an arbitrary component in one whole may be a structural, intrinsic part in another."

Although the distinction is crucial to the very idea of gestalt shifts, and hence to productive thinking, Wertheimer nowhere gives a principled account of how the distinction is made. In a paper on the formation of numerical concepts in Indigenous societies, published in 1912, he offers a number of tantalizing observations, but does not specify criteria. (The essay as a whole is sharply critical of the stultifying effects of Western European abstract thought.)

> The conditions and functions already discussed apply not only to the formation of quantitative structures [in the thought of some Indigenous peoples] but also to *operations* upon and with such structures. This is shown in progressions towards larger structures analogous to those attained by [Western European] abstract methods of addition and multiplication. Thus several specific structures combined together yield specific (not arbitrary) larger structures. Similarly with division. The parts of a larger structure are not abstract in arrangement and organization of material and the material itself is divisible only in such a way as to conform with its natural properties and with natural requirements. Certain arrangements predetermine through their form *certain* divisions.... Identity of parts is not the universally decisive factor in division.
>
> Instead [what is decisive] is, on the one hand, predetermination [by] the gestalt of the whole (e.g., the cleavage plane of crystalline structures) and, on the other, the tendency (not necessarily conscious) to maintain — even after ... division — certain naturally unified wholes (*Gestalten*).... It is but a psychological fiction to assume that all divisions are arbitrary and hence on the same footing with one another. Instead we find that objects themselves imply certain specific divisions. It is possible to divide objects without

regard for these factors, but such divisions belong in the class of operations which are 'remote from reality' [*wirklichkeitsabstrakt*].

The last sentence (minus the Germanic inflection) could easily have occurred in one of Plato's dialogues.

Again, in a paper published in 1923, Wertheimer describes and illustrates a number of factors that influence how the multiple aspects of a situation may be grouped, or be left ungrouped; but he does not specify how these factors interact with one another in complex, real world situations.

Although the distinction between arbitrary component and necessary part is real, it also appears to be radically context-dependent both in Gestalt theory and in Plato's dialectic method.

Incorrigibility

One of Wertheimer's earliest significant publications was his report, in 1912, on his research into apparent motion. In it, Gestalt concepts are only nascent; but the paper laid the foundation for his later work. Apparent motion occurs when we perceive continuous movement where there is none: 'motion pictures' are a good example. Wertheimer conducted various experiments with various pieces of equipment, but his main investigations used a tachistoscope to expose subjects to two stationary images in succession. He found that when the interval between exposures was around 60 milliseconds, viewers did not perceive two distinct images in succession, but instead saw a single object moving continuously back and forth between two positions — the so-called *phi* phenomenon. (The exposure interval required to achieve this effect varied with the viewers' distances from the images; but even at a fixed distance, significant variation in the exposure interval still produced the perception of apparent motion.)

The fact of such illusory continuous motion was well known. "The Nickelodeon" opened its doors in Pittsburgh in 1905 and the Babelsberg Film Studio was founded near Berlin in 1912. Apparent motion had been described in the scientific literature by Sigmund Exner, one of Wertheimer's teachers, as early as 1875. Wertheimer's achievement consisted in experiments sufficiently well designed and measurements precise enough to show that none of the extant explanations for the phenomenon were acceptable. Wertheimer's discussion mentions the potential relevance of von Ehrenfels's notion of 'gestalt quality'; he shows that peripheral sense perception — what's going on in the eyes — cannot begin to account for his experimental results; and he speculates that holistic, integrative processes in the cortex must be involved.

The point I want to focus on is that the gestalt of apparent motion, even when it's known to be in error, is incorrigible. Subjects can be told what they are perceiving — two distinct images; they can be shown the apparatus; they can strive to see that what they have been shown is there — and still what they experience is the continuous movement of a single object rather than two distinct images. The incorrigibility of gestalts is known outside the laboratory, too: Kepler's sudden vision, while teaching, of the polyhedral organization of the position of planetary orbits is a striking example. Konrad Lorenz also mentions the "fundamental incorrigibility" of Gestalt perception and reports on an experiment described by Alexander Bavelas in which subjects — in this case, engineers — were asked to find the principle behind what was, in fact, a completely random series of stimuli. The majority of the engineers believed they had discerned an organizational principle and refused to believe that there wasn't one when the nature of the experiment was revealed to them. One man came to Bavelas some time afterward with notes he had made during the experiment to prove that the apparatus providing the random distribution had failed.

Does this mean that gestalt insight can't be trusted? Indeed. But it doesn't mean that it's any less trustworthy than any other kind of thinking or perception. As Lorenz says, what's required is that we be aware of the way in which it can be mistaken — that a shape can suggest itself on insufficient data — and that we look, and look, and look again, as Kepler did. The point I wish to reinforce is the *sense* of certainty that accompanies gestalt comprehension. Mistakes in calculative or deductive reasoning are extremely common; but we react very differently to the prospect of error. Regarding arithmetic or long chains of deduction in a complicated proof, we are very open to doubt. We're open to doubt even when we're right.

The evidence for a similar incorrigibility attaching to the perception of forms in Plato's work is weaker, and it is indirect. One indication comes from the passage from *Letter VII* that I mentioned in my overview: the claim appears to be that once a form is perceived, that insight sustains itself. This is consistent with the picture Plato paints of the foundation of "immortal discourse" in *Phaidros* and *Symposium*. It also dovetails with the definition of ἐπιστήμη (*epistēmē*) — a term Plato often uses for comprehension of forms. In a book of definitions attributed to the school of Plato, ἐπιστήμη is defined as "conception of the soul which cannot be dislodged by reasoning; ability to conceive one or more things which cannot be dislodged by reasoning; true argument which cannot be dislodged by thinking." In *Timaios*, it is νόησις (*noēsis*) that is identified with knowledge of the forms and said to be "immovable by persuasion." (The handbook of definitions defines νόησις as "the starting point of knowledge.")

There is, finally, the indirect evidence of Plato's *Lecture on the Good*, a notorious occasion on which Plato is reported to have bewildered and annoyed his audience by talking almost entirely about mathematics. Why he did this has been a puzzle to commentators. The secondhand report that we have says he used mathematical material to argue that the Good was 'one' — but this could mean almost anything, from Pythagorean number mysticism to a sophisticated logical argument about the indivisibility, and therefore the imperishability, of forms. My proposal is that it had, at least in part, to do with what I believe was the wellspring of Plato's project: the phenomenological similarity between the experience of necessary truth in geometry and the experience of moral beauty manifest in Socrates' character. One of the reasons Plato's dialogues have remained in the canon over the centuries is the *faith* they express in the power of moral insight to change human lives from the inside: moral beauty compels us the way necessary truth does. Also, at certain critical points in the dialogues, Socrates is made to stress the importance of asking not what is *likely*, but what is conceptually *necessary*. Both this last exegetical point and the larger picture suggest that the experience of incorrigibility figured in Plato's understanding of the nature of forms.

Sudden Insight After Much Hard Work

A summary statement of the way in which gestalts seem to precipitate themselves out of nowhere after a period of sustained but apparently fruitless labour is given by Wolfgang Köhler. In the final paragraph of "What Is Thinking?" he says:

> Only the *result* of the organizing process is usually experienced.... [The] most important intellectual achievements ... are often made possible by an abrupt reorganization of given materials, a revolution, the result of which suddenly appears ready-made on the mental scene. From where does it come?... [T]he brain, which seems, better than the active self, able to do precisely such things — but ... only when the crucial material has first been thoroughly examined and made ready in active mental work.

Earlier in the essay, Köhler has provided stories from the lives of scientists known to him — including Otto Loewi — which illustrate these observations. We could add Kepler, Kekulé, and Poincaré to his list. The echo of the passage from *Letter VII* is strong: one grasps the form "suddenly" only after long "abiding and living with the issue itself." Both aspects are reinforced later in *Letter VII* by another famous passage:

> Only with much hard toil — by means of much threshing and kneading of each of these things, one with another — names and definitions, what is seen and what is experienced in sense perception — in well-meaning debate, questioning, sifting and separating without envy, at the extremity of effort — does the light of intelligence and understanding burst forth regarding any issue.

The need for hard work of the kind the letter describes is also the subject of the second part of *Parmenides*, and of the 'ladder of love' in *Symposium*. It is implied in the introductions to both *Sophist* and *Politikos*.

In his general characterizations of productive thinking, Wertheimer, unlike Köhler, mentions neither the need for preparatory work nor suddenness; but the suddenness with which gestalt insight dawns is widely attested in his discussion of actual cases.

> [The young boy] asked, not too well pleased, "Should I count them?" "No," I answered. Suddenly smiling, he [produced the solution].... Told not to do it by counting step by step, [another

boy] said slowly: "The numbers ascend consistently ..." And then, suddenly happy, "Oh, I have an idea!"

Confronting a different problem involving a geometrical figure drawn on paper, a very young girl was at first puzzled:

> "I certainly don't know how to do *that*."... Hesitatingly she said: "I could make it right here ... but ..." Suddenly she cried out, "May I have a pair of scissors?" [and demonstrated how to solve the problem].

Although in the dialogues Plato prefers to describe and illustrate the hard preparatory work, in one passage he also mentions the suddenness with which insight is occasionally achieved. It occurs at the climax of Diotima's speech in *Symposium*. She has previously adumbrated at some length the labours the aspiring student of *eros* must undergo. Now she says:

> When someone has reached this point in his study of erotics, observing beautiful things one after another in the correct order, as he nears his goal, suddenly he will behold something astounding, beautiful in its nature, and this, Socrates, is the point of all his earlier labours.

Language and Its Discontents

There is something about comprehending forms that doesn't want to be talked about and something about gestalt comprehension that doesn't want to be talked about either. But what, exactly? And is it the same in the two cases? These questions return us to the passage from *Letter VII* with which this discussion began.

The letter is attributed to Plato, but there is scholarly debate about whether it is genuine. I side with those who find its attribution dubious. The Greek lacks the beauty, wit, and tensile strength of the dialogues. However, there is no room for doubt that whoever wrote it was almost as familiar with Plato's life and teaching as Plato was with Socrates.' It is as good a bet that we are being offered a reasonably faithful representation of Plato's views in *Letter VII* as that we are being offered a faithful representation of Socrates' trial in *Apology*. Not a bet for the nervous, but one I'm inclined to take.

The key sentence begins: ῥητὸν γὰρ οὐδαμῶς ἐστιν ὡς ἄλλα μαθήματα.... The first word, ῥητόν (*rhēton*), is the third person present indicative of ῥέω (*rheō*), 'to flow or gush,' whence the French *rheum*, a runny nose, and the English *rhetoric*, a flow of words. The only other passage in Plato in which I have found the word occurs in *Theaitētos*. ῥέω occurs there twice. H.N. Fowler translates it both times as 'expressible'; M.J. Levett and Miles Burnyeat translate its positive occurrence as 'capable of being expressed' and its negative form as 'unaccountable.' Francis Cornford offers 'inexplicable' and 'incapable of explanation.'

I have translated the passage in *Letter VII* in the blandest form the text will tolerate: "it is not possible to speak of this subject as other kinds of studies are spoken of." Glenn Morrow is a bit less cautious: "this knowledge is not something that can be put into words like other sciences." R.G. Bury goes even further: "it does not at all admit of verbal expression like other studies."

The Greek, then, is ambiguous. The author could be saying, "You can't lay it out the way you can lay out other systematic branches of learning" — that is, it has no specifiable method; or even, perhaps, given the larger context of the passage, that if you try to give it a systematic representation, you will distort it and leave it open to attack. Or, the author could be saying something much stronger: "This knowledge is ineffable. Words can't touch it." The denial of a specifiable method echoes the remarkable passage in *Politikos* in which the Eleatic Stranger declines to explain how to distinguish genuine sub-classes from arbitrary parts. The suggestion that a systematic statement will distort the author's views and leave them open to attack allows for a plausible reading of the otherwise incomprehensible last section of *Parmenides*. But the claim that knowledge of the forms is strictly ineffable, completely untouchable by language, is not supported by any passage in the dialogues with which I am familiar. (At 509b in *Republic*, Socrates' claim is that the Good is 'beyond' being, not beyond words. And he wishes to be excused from speaking of it because he lacks knowledge of it rather than because he knows what it is and knows it to be ineffable. At least, that's what he says.)

Plato and Gestalt 87

With gestalt thinking, the situation is a little clearer. There's a century of accumulated evidence, ranging from anecdotes about Einstein to laboratory research conducted by platoons of psychologists, that shows that the processes involved in at least some kinds of gestalt comprehension cannot be easily articulated. There's no describable series of steps, as there is with problems that require analysis alone. To try to articulate the thought processes involved is to undermine them.

"Wait a minute," someone might object, "what about the method of collection and division? — all that question-and-answer talk, kneading names and definitions together, making and remaking the conceptual hierarchies? Isn't Plato advocating just the kind of verbal activity that Jonathan Schooler says *blocks* gestalt understanding?" A good question. But the answer is no. Plato's conceptual hierarchies are not series of logical deductions. This is why the exchange between Young Socrates and the Eleatic Stranger in *Politikos* is so important: the crucial information about how to make species from genera in the right way is never stated; the procedure is illustrated through examples. What Plato appears to be advocating, then, is not systematic analysis but *practice* in forming specific gestalts, gestalts that are, as Arne Næss would say, subordinate to a generic gestalt. The way in which forms combine with one another through the special offices of the Like and the Unlike is itself remarkably suggestive of the netlike structures of our current understanding of both very large-scale mega-evolutionary and small-scale micro-evolutionary biology. Good taxonomists, in both philosophy and biology, have an eye for family resemblance just as good musicians have an ear for melodic similarity.

Eros and Directedness

Socrates is famous for insisting that he knows only that he does not know. The dialogues are replete with his protestations of ignorance. The one field of inquiry in which he professes expertise is erotics: he knows how to love. We are given a portrait of his initial lessons in *Symposium*, where he is shown also to be well known as a 'lover of boys.' This aspect of his portrait is also prominent in *Phaidros* and in the opening exchanges of *Protagoras*. We have independent confirmation of his interest in *eros* and erotics from Xenophon.

88   The Experience of Meaning

What does Socrates' proficiency in love have to do with his dedication to philosophy? There seem to be two ways in which they are connected. The first is that his appetite for love is surpassed only by his self-restraint: the two together give his life its characteristic philosophical *tonos*. (For Xenophon, his self-restraint is the reason that he is universally thought to be a good man, indeed, the best. In Plato's dialogues, his self-restraint is used to promote the idea that the soul is distinct from the body and that philosophers should act as though the body is of no account.)

The second way *eros* and philosophy are connected in Plato's work is through Socrates' passionate attraction to the ground of philosophical insight, the forms of Beauty, Self-Possession, Knowledge, Justice, and the Good. This attraction combines steadfast, single-minded pursuit with awe. In *Phaidros*, Socrates represents erotic love as the vehicle through which we are reminded of our disembodied vision of the forms. What we love when we're embodied — the characterological traits of others that attract us, and the force with which we are attracted — are direct indicators of what and how much our souls saw at the rim of heaven.

In other words, it is *eros* that keeps Socrates *on track* as a philosopher: it keeps him on the scent; it sustains him when the conceptual going gets rough. Plato's whole corpus suggests that *eros* is the source of the intuitions that drive the method of collection and division. In the absence of *eros*, there is no *interest* in truth — we get a shrug: whatever. Where there is *eros* but it is misdirected — unfocused, or focused on conquest rather than truth — we find excited puppyish play with concepts or, worse, conceptual gamesmanship, the sophistry that is the target of much of Plato's work.

In the Gestalt theorists, the phenomenon that echoes *eros* is called 'directedness.' It appears in Wertheimer's early paper on apparent motion as "a place toward which the attention is attracted"; he stresses that it's a fundamental feature in Einstein's productive thinking; and he argues that it constitutes the moral foundation of all scientific activity. Wertheimer's essay "The Famous Story of Young Gauss" concludes with a paragraph that evokes Plato's portrait of Socrates:

Just as a task, a problem situation in productive thinking, is not something closed within itself, but tends toward its solution, its structural completion, so even a task with its solution is often not a thing by itself. It again may function as a part that points beyond itself, striving to envisage, to clarify a broader field. Often such a process takes a long time; it is a drama with setbacks and struggles. There are fine cases in which the process proceeds irresistibly, through months, through years, never losing sight of the deeper issue, never getting lost in petty details, in detours, bypaths.

Köhler, in a slightly different vein, concludes "What Is Thinking?" with this observation:

> Why do such revolutions which occur in certain brains tend to be the right revolutions? This is the same question we asked ourselves before: why do brain processes tend to produce perceptual organizations of remarkable clearness of structure? At least this part of nature, the human brain, seems to operate in a most selective fashion. It is the *direction* of its operations which is truly remarkable.

Is there any reason that an interest in gestalt thinking should be coupled with a passionate desire for truth?

Truth is often understood as a correspondence between what is said or thought and states of affairs in the world. But it can also be understood as a kind of coherence. This view of truth has a long and distinguished philosophical lineage and is reflected in the English verb 'to true,' which means to bring something into alignment with other things. It is also reflected in the idea that we trust people of integrity. On this way of understanding it, truth connotes wholeness. To grasp truth means to see how things hang together. Being able to see how things hang together, though, just is to comprehend a gestalt. A person with a talent for perceiving gestalt phenomena, then, might easily develop a passionate appetite for truth. She might feel chronic discomfort if she becomes aware of details that don't fit. She will be much less able than many of us to ignore facts that don't cohere with the larger picture.

Wertheimer, in his essay on truth, speaks of "that relationship to the things themselves that means to do them justice." Justice, too, is a notion with more than one sense. Right now, in North American philosophy, the most prominent conception is one developed by John Rawls: justice as fairness. This notion focuses on a fair distribution of resources among

90   The Experience of Meaning

humans and fair access to the services provided by human community. But it is hard to see how to apply the idea of a fair distribution to the "things themselves" — perhaps the idea is that we give a fair share of attention to each one of them. There is, however, another notion of justice — Plato's — that dovetails with the notion of truth as integrity. Plato argued that justice was achieved — first in the soul, and then in the state — when the parts of some entity, its interior faculties, achieved harmony. Understood this way, justice aims to realize the same state of affairs that truth does: an integrated whole. To 'do justice' to the things themselves, then, would be to understand how they fit together.

Strange Ontological Status

The ontological status of forms is a long-standing source of puzzlement and occasional hostility among philosophers. Forms are real — they're the realest things there are — yet you can't see them with your physical eyes or touch them or smell them. But you can perceive them 'in' physical objects: beautiful human beings, good human beings, just human beings.

As I mentioned at the outset, Plato is usually credited with a 'two realms' doctrine: forms exist in the same place the immortal soul goes when it dies. A two-realms doctrine appears to be necessary because Plato also acknowledges the reality of physical objects (they're not *as* real as forms, but they do exist) and it appears that forms don't exist *merely* in individual minds. One of the cardinal functions of forms is to explain how two human beings — whose experience of the world is by definition unique — can carry on a conversation in which they understand one another. Such understanding requires, Plato reasonably suggests, that they mean the same things by (most of) their words. How are they able to do this? (If the answer seems obvious, think again. The history of Western European philosophy can be regarded as a series of attempts to address this question, none of which has received universal assent.) Some imagine that Aristotle escaped the implausibility of claiming that forms have a mind-independent non-material existence by suggesting that they are something like the 'defining functions' of material things. His view, however, is notorious for leaving the hard questions unanswered. Plato, it begins to seem, was not engaging in flights of fancy

Plato and Gestalt   91

when he concluded that forms are *things* with outright and independent existence apart from substance. He was attempting to confront, head on, the challenge of explaining our experience of meaning; and he was willing to bite the ontological bullet, as it were, rather than let go of the power and reality of that experience. Western European languages don't have a term for entities that are *like* ideas yet exist independently of any mind. 'Angel' may be the closest they get. But to claim forms are like angels is, these days, to ask for trouble rather than to solve it.

We might say that gestalts are what we pick out with the English word 'thing' and its cognates in other languages. But what is a thing? Listing answers to that question is another way of describing the history of both Eastern and Western philosophy.

When I first did an internet search for indexed articles that discussed the relationship of Plato's forms to gestalts, I got exactly one hit: a grumpy essay from 1929 arguing that Gestalt theory should be dismissed. It's obvious, the author states, that the central claim is wrong: of course we perceive parts of wholes! Parts are what wholes are made of! (He offers the example of a car accident about which one might well remember, above all else, the pooling blood.) And besides, he says, the theory's key term is vague and ill-defined. "The Gestalt ... is assumed to be of non-empirical origin, existing with the first experience and not a product of experience, and hence, of the same abstract and phantom-like nature attributable to ... Platonic Forms"!

After a fashion, I agree.

ᴈ❧

The case for the claim that Plato's forms are fourth-century Athenian versions of twentieth-century German gestalts is circumstantial. This is as it must be, given that we have little information about Plato's thought apart from the dialogues. The dialogues themselves present great challenges to anyone who tries to form a good gestalt of their aims and purposes: they contradict one another; they are ambiguous; they are vague. They are also dramatic fictions; there are major discontinuities between the cultural context in which they were created and those in which they are now being read; we don't even know the order in which they were composed. For all these reasons, an attempt to provide a unified account of Plato's notion of forms will face stiff objections, starting with the objection that no unified account of *any* aspect of his philosophy is possible. I grant the concern and take the objections as read. The exercise of comparing Plato's views with those of Gestalt theory is, of course, itself an exercise in Gestalt comprehension. Plato's views are like an out-of-focus picture. If you set Gestalt theory beside that picture, certain aspects suddenly stand out and an intelligible whole appears to be visible. "But what about that dark streak there?" a viewer with different concerns asks. "Couldn't that be a dog's tail? And if it is, doesn't that make nonsense of the claim that the picture is a head-and-shoulders portrait?" Certainly. But what's the irrefutable evidence that the dark streak *is* a dog's tail? There is none.

ه

Earlier I mentioned that for both gestalts and forms, the distinction between necessary part and arbitrary component is radically context-dependent. This is one reason that we might expect Plato's corpus to appear disunified: the way a form looks or doesn't look, whether it appears at all, is often a function of its conceptual environment. Gestalt comprehension doesn't follow a recipe. There are no rules beyond the most general: think outside the box; try hard; don't give up; develop intellectual muscle by practising on examples; follow your nose; and don't try to analyze what you're doing. — It's the advice one would give any aspiring artist.

Let me be absolutely clear: I am not claiming that human perception and understanding invent the world. I am claiming that, although there is a mind-independent world, many of its truths are not comprehended by human beings. They are like the figure 4 in the two-shape line drawing. The 4 is there whether anyone sees it or not. It's harder to perceive when its environment consists of other sets of irregular closed figures with lines through them, and it's easier to perceive when its environment consists of 4s of roughly the same size and shape.

The grasp of gestalts is, however, also a function of the willingness and the ability of the perceiver to perceive. This is why Plato wrote dialogues rather than tracts: what one sees, the way in which one sees, how much one is capable of seeing, depends on character. (It will depend, too, on the "innumerable, multi-directional" nuances of the relationship between the parties to the discussion.) Again, this does not mean that 'human being is the measure of all things.' It means that in order to see beyond one's own preoccupations, one must know what those preoccupations are: one must know oneself. Either that, or be lucky enough to have a teacher who can discern one's strengths and weaknesses, and then offer appropriate guidance. Doctrine, except of the vaguest sort, is not useful in such a situation. Enabling gestalt comprehension calls for astuteness, perceptiveness, and imagination on the part of the teacher — the ability to provoke, soothe, encourage, forbid, frustrate, or inspire as necessary. What Socrates says and the way he says it will, at any given moment, depend very much on whom he's talking to. Plato was more interested in the process of how individual souls might be led to understanding than he was in setting out theses and arguing for them. Why, then, did he write at all? I suspect the dialogues were at least in part teaching aids: opportunities for students to watch others grapple with their own particular blindnesses, hopes, and prejudices. I believe they were also in part a documentary record of how a similar interest in enabling real thinking had got Socrates into trouble when he tried it on the good old boys of the Athenian imperium.

To summarize: Gestalts themselves are radically context-dependent. How something is situated, how it is framed, what other things surround it — all these will affect whether and how readily it is seen. And the process depends further on the character of the perceiver — her openness, her prejudices, the flexibility of her mind, and in some cases her expertise. Finally, analysis of what has happened in a given case of successful gestalt comprehension is not usually useful. It won't help in developing a recipe; and the activity undermines the faculty of gestalt comprehension itself.

Is Plato the only Western thinker before von Ehrenfels to have been alert to the role of gestalt comprehension in human understanding? No. Herakleitos and Spinoza are obvious candidates; perhaps Lichtenberg; Goethe almost certainly. And Aristotle. We see it in the faculty of synthetic imagination in Kant and in Berkeley's discussion of abstract ideas. But the impact of Aristotle's development of syllogistic logic — his codification of procedures for good thinking — cannot be overestimated. And since Aristotle, the idea that philosophy should aim to secure thinking from error has come to seem more important than the idea that it should cultivate our ability to perceive the truth. Many professionals now believe the two aims are identical. What the Gestalt theorists attempted to demonstrate, and what Plato knew, is that they aren't.

Why are we so deeply susceptible to the charms of epistemological security? Partly because as a species we enjoy the exercise of power for its own sake; we have a penchant for controlling things. Explicit methods, in any area of endeavour, can be policed. However, and in tension with this first reason, we're also interested in epistemological security because a failure or refusal to think accurately can have disastrous consequences. The mechanistic thinking that Wertheimer so loathed is connected not only to the Enlightenment's celebration of technology but also to the idea that political institutions should be justified before the court of reason. One aim of that thinking — at least in the eighteenth century — was to save us from excesses of cruelty, racism, and sexism.

Our attraction to 'rules of thought' thus balances our proclivity to accept unexamined gestalts. It aims to secure us against prejudice, superstition, and whim. But to imagine that this, and this alone, is what thinking is for is to deprive ourselves of its most significant dimension. The first and fundamental aim of thinking is to understand, to discern the lineaments of reality. The correction of mistakes accompanies this discernment; it is not achieved by shackling thought to ensure that mistakes are never made.

There is no series of steps we can implement to precipitate gestalts in all audiences. Real thinking does not always occur in words; it can decay under analysis; its processes are not always reportable. This means that real thinking is in some sense wild: it cannot be corralled or regulated. But it is also the only access humans have to the experience of insight, to moral and mathematical beauty, to ontological vision.

Where the danger lies, there too lies meaningful life.

❧ "Show, Don't Tell"

Show, don't tell is a maxim basic to literary craft. It means, roughly, *Avoid dull, abstract or cliché-ridden summaries and provide rich, specific, vividly rendered details.* Anyone who has attended the first two weeks of an introductory creative writing course will have encountered it. Practised literary writers, whether they've taken a creative writing course or not, know it's true. I've heard novelists dispute it for practical reasons. "Showing takes too long," they'll say. "You have to compress the narrative in places and save the showing for the crucial episodes." But even this caveat acknowledges that showing makes a deeper impression than telling. Poets occasionally tell for summary emphasis: "Beauty is truth, truth beauty, — that is all / Ye know on earth, and all ye need to know." But even then, we often feel that we're being shown something beyond what's told — as though what appears to be an instance of telling is nonetheless some kind of showing.

Why is showing so fundamental to good literature? Why is it more effective than telling? To say that showing is vivid is simply to repeat the fact: details, the *right* details, arrest our attention; they make an impression. Often the details themselves are not vivid. I think of Marie Howe's extraordinary poems about being raped by her father — the reportage is bare, third-person, stripped of adverbs; there are no virtuoso linguistic effects. "The Mother," for example, consists of simple images, most of them aural: the mother standing at the bottom of the stairs listening to her daughter's waking voice, the sound of "the first slap," the scrape of her son's chair suddenly pushed back from his desk, "and again the girl's voice, now quietly weeping, and the creak of her bed." What is shown is not just rape, but the mother's complicity, the brother's powerlessness, the fact that it's a repeated, habitual violation (this information conveyed by the single adjective 'first'). To say, "I was repeatedly raped by my father; the violence was habitual; my mother was complicit; my brother couldn't help" — these abstractions evoke horror and arouse pity. But that's not what Howe wants, the kind of horror that arouses pity. It's too easy. She wants something more visceral. She wants the kind of horror that leaves the rational mind speechless, that puts a roaring in the space where the mind used to be, an empty shaft in the gut. These are the marks that you've grasped the truth and that she has conveyed it.

What conveys truth here, and conveys it in myriad other cases ranging from outrage to ecstasy, is a constellation of verbally unadorned but precisely chosen details. It is in these constellated details that the genius of showing lies. Their connections are not made explicit. Facets of a larger shape are placed before the reader's mind, and discernment of that shape requires simultaneous integration of multiple, superficially discontinuous aspects. When we are being shown something, it is as though the mind holds its breath; attention is focused, the experience of time is suspended. We wait for all the pieces 'to fall into place'; and when they do, insight flashes on the mind's eye.

Of course, the maxim *show, don't tell* applies to all good writing, not just to poetry. And this might seem to produce some terminological sheer. For aren't stories things we *tell*? They are indeed. And great storytellers are precisely those who know how to show. They avoid filling in all the gaps; they present events in juxtaposition rather than in metronomic sequence; they crystallize settings with the use of telling [!] details. Howe's poem is a fine example of just such storytelling. The word 'tell,' then, has a number of distinct meanings, not all of which conflict with what is meant by 'show.' Telling of the problematic kind involves an airless explicitness; it doesn't just connect the dots, it obliterates them with a felt marker.

The flash of insight occasioned by good writing, on the other hand, has the lineaments of the Eureka effect, the "Aha!" of sudden discovery in mathematics and the sciences. I believe that grasping what is being shown in a literary context is indeed related to insight in theoretical fields. Telling the reader 'what happened' makes the mind's eye glaze over in just the way that it glazes over when it's forced to memorize formulae that it doesn't understand. Showing is like offering an elegant proof — one that allows the student to *see* what is the case. In both contexts, the

"Show, Don't Tell"   97

mind is active, it reaches to understand what's going on. When it succeeds, it feels the satisfaction of having grasped meaning.

ə◆

We show — and grasp what is being shown — not just as writers and readers of literature. Sensitivity to how details are informed by the whole to which they belong is the foundation of medical diagnosis. As Carlo Ginzburg has pointed out, it is also the foundation of connoisseurship. (Think of wine experts who must identify not only the grape, but the terroir and the vintage.) Sensitivity to 'informed' detail is essential to detection of many sorts: finding mushrooms, tracking wild animals, solving crimes. We are also 'reading the signs' when we suddenly realize — at a party, say, and without being able to say exactly why — that one of our acquaintances is having an affair with another of our acquaintances, not their spouse. It's what Newton was doing when he sat "in contemplative mood," having seen an apple fall perpendicularly from its branch to the ground in his mother's garden.

The literary writer's ability to show is, thus, developed in response to a more widespread capacity, one that humans share with many other species: the ability to read. We, all of us mid-to-large-size animals, read tracks, weather, and terrain; vocal tones in our own and other species; postures and facial expressions; the moon and the stars. Plants also read gravitational forces, the texture, intensity, and direction of light, aromas, the presence of barriers and supports. When as artist or thinker we *show*, we are activating the desire to respond intelligently to the world. The ability to understand — to read the signs accurately — has been honed by evolution. Reading in this wide sense is what the mind is for. It is how we survive and how we remain integrated with our environment. When we 'get it,' when we see how things fit, there is a release of psychic tension. This is one definition of pleasure.

Ginzburg argues that the kind of comprehension involved in 'reading the signs' occurs in non-repeatable situations and depends on non-generalizable individuals. For this reason, he says, it is not scientific; good science requires repeated measurement of repeatable phenomena. But repeated measurements are only one aspect of scientific inquiry. Paradigm-shifting *insight* like Newton's depends on the same sensitivity to detail that characterizes forensic, medical, hunting, and literary insight.

And there are regularities that inform 'reading the signs.' Planting clues and understanding them involve what Gestalt theorists called the factors of closure and good continuation.

Given:

we see a broken circle, not five unconnected slightly curved segments.

Given:

we see a branch with a sprout attached to it, rather than

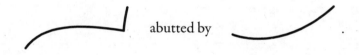

Given:

we see a rectangle occluding the intersection point of a pair of crossed lines. Unless the circumstances are very unusual, it doesn't occur to us that the lines under the rectangle might be hooked or bent:

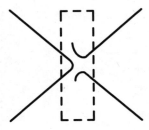

nor to imagine that they do not continue at all:

(Though this is precisely how Bishop Berkeley invites us to see the whole world.)

And these same perceptual tendencies toward closure and good continuity are operating when we 'put together' the events in Marie Howe's poem.

Here is another example, an excerpt from Robert Gray's long poem "Under the Summer Leaves":

> But first, each day, we'd have to pass
> a last great complicated trunkless mangrove,
> sprouting myriad-limbed off the earth,
> and every time, a man would be standing in there,
> amid its crooked mesh of shadows.
> He remained very still, his back to the path
> on which a few people walked –
> the young boardriders, reluctantly returning,
> lugging a short board against the hip,
> their broad faces with a white stripe, sullen and stolid
> like dripping steers; the shrill girls

keeping to their own groups, brown as a baker's shop, and
    carrying
radios long as suitcases, wispy salt afloat
above their shoulders, and on the foreshores of their chests;
and sometimes older people, going outwards,
unemployed fishermen, pensioners, wearing floral hats
and towels like astrakhan collars,
in their seaweed idleness.
That man was leaned slightly against a thick branch,
one hand propped along it, never glancing
as we came by. Although he was shaded with a lattice,
you could see he was an Aboriginal
by the hand from a sleeve, and the igneous bones
of the last quarter of his face.
There were bottles everywhere about his feet
but never any foodscraps or paper, nor signs of a camp.
An aurora of immense, pure, colourless light
would be vaulting upwards ahead of us
within an absolute shade of blueness; vaulting on itself
and upon itself
like the felt streamings of a gas flame,
from beyond the sandhills, and their grandstand view.

When Gray shows us the surfers, the pensioners, the Aboriginal, the bottles, the "great complicated trunkless" mangrove and the vaulting light, we don't experience a list of unconnected images; we perceive the large, fraught, tragic, complex colonial situation of which the human things are aspects, and the stunning natural beauty that even now contains them. Reading the situation, we grasp not just that it exists, but also how it is filled with multiple and contrasting tensions.

ॐ

So far, I've focused on the most obvious way in which literature can show: by placing various events or things side by side, inviting us to see the larger shape that informs them. Reading such literature involves a skill like 'seeing the face in the leaves' — we must discern the unifying gestalt in what, at first, may not appear to be coherent. There is, however, another category of gestalt comprehension, the gestalt shift. This is usually what occurs in visual proofs in mathematics: one clear and distinct way of seeing things alternates with another, equally clear and distinct.

Theorem: π, the ratio of a circle's circumference to its diameter, is greater than 3.

Proof:

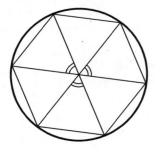

To grasp the proof, one must first see that the sides of the hexagon are sides of equilateral triangles, equal in length to the circle's radius. (This depends on knowing that a circle comprises 360°, and thus that the angle of each triangle whose apex is the centre of the circle is 60°. One must also know that the angles of a triangle sum to 180° and that angles opposite sides equal in length are themselves equal [Euclid, Book I, Proposition 5].) Thus one perceives that the ratio of the hexagon's perimeter to its diagonal is 3. But that diagonal is also the circle's diameter; and the circle's circumference is greater than the hexagon's perimeter. The proof turns on seeing the relationship between the hexagon's perimeter and the circle's radius; the hexagon and the circle share crucial structural aspects.

Is there a kind of literary showing that depends on a shift *between* established gestalts rather than a shift *to* a gestalt from what does not appear to be unified? Indeed. It is called metaphor. (I take similes, analogies of any sort, to be members of the same basic class.)

> I do not know much about gods; but I think that the river
> Is a strong brown god — sullen, untamed and intractable,
> — T.S. Eliot, "The Dry Salvages"

> But, soft! what light through yonder window breaks?
> It is the east, and Juliet is the sun!
> > — Shakespeare, *Romeo and Juliet*, II.ii

Or this:

> ... A narrow hotel room.
> View on an alley.
> One lamppost shines on the asphalt.
> Experience, its beautiful slag.
> > — from "Elegy" by Tomas Tranströmer,
> > translated by Robert Bly

In this last example, the gestalt action is complex. We are first asked to exercise closure: to grasp the emotional tone of the scene shown by the first three of the four short sentences. Then we are offered an extraordinary metaphor — a metaphor in which neither the 'is' nor one of the terms, 'memory,' is made explicit — which simultaneously extends and complicates the tone. That slag should be said to be beautiful is a paradox; yet we have no difficulty comprehending what Tranströmer means.

Emily McGiffin's "Hanging Gardens" offers yet another example of a gestalt shift in a literary context. The figure on which the poem turns is called extended metaphor. It functions very like the gestalt shift required to grasp a visual proof. Again, as in a visual proof, the 'is' is not explicit.

The poem is part of a sequence called "Nine Meditations on Edward Burtynsky." Each is annotated with the name of one of Burtynsky's photographs of industrial devastation. In this case, the photograph is *Feng Jie #4, Three Gorges Dam Project, Yangtze River, 2002.*

HANGING GARDENS

> I destroyed the city
> and its houses, from foundation to parapet.
> I devastated and I burned them.
>
> I tore out the bricks
> and earth of its walls, of its temples,

of the ziggurat — all that there was
I hove into the Euphrates. I dug canals

through that city, I drowned it.
I made its very foundations disappear.

I destroyed it more completely
than a devastating flood.

So that the city, its temples and gods,
would not be remembered, I blotted it out
with water. I made of it an inundated land.

And with the labourers I took, my spoil,
I raised up the palace a Kuyunjik. I cut
a canal through the arduous Mount Tas
to bring the waters of the Khosr, I watered

the meadows of the Tigris and planted gardens,
orchards with seeds gathered in the lands
I had conquered: pines, cypresses, junipers, almonds,

dates, ebony, ash, rosewood, olive, tamarisk, walnut,
terebinth, fir, oak, pomegranate, pear, quince, grapevine,
fig. All that the gods had bestowed upon the earth

I arrayed in my palace without rival, amid streams
numerous as the stars of heaven. I gave it order, grace,
grandeur as befitted me, guardian of honour, lover
of justice, pious and charitable, with all humankind
submissive at my feet.

By choosing to tell Stephanie Dalley's version of the story — according to which the famous hanging gardens were not of Babylon, but of Nineveh, constructed during the rule of Sennacherib, who was responsible for the *destruction* of Babylon — McGiffin is able to suggest a striking and complex political argument. The poem invites us to see echoes

104   The Experience of Meaning

not only between the flooded rubble of Babylon and the flooded rubble of Fengjie County. *Because* we see those similarities, we feel the force of the poem's suggestion that the motivations in the two cases are also the same: brutal and morally blind self-aggrandizement. The suggestion is not explicit but it is utterly clear. And because we are not passively absorbing an explicit denunciation of the Three Gorges Dam, bolstered by expert figures and projections, our minds are forced to become active in comprehending the suggestion of similarity. The effect, as in Marie Howe's poem, is visceral.

That effect can also be insidious. Innuendo that relies either on our tendency to see parallel gestalts or to pursue gestalt closure from scanty evidence has destroyed reputations and brought down governments. This is because gestalt apprehension is also much more powerful, much less easy to dislodge, than the products of reason and calculation.

The gestalt factor operating in local and extended metaphors is, of course, similarity. One of the deeply interesting things about metaphor is that it doesn't invite us to see a larger shape that informs the entities or situations it identifies. In metaphor, gestalts shimmer over and under one another but do not dissolve into parts of a superordinate gestalt. There is no thing to which they point other than themselves. 'The similarity,' if explicitly articulated, is an abstraction, just as 'elements' are.

ॐ

Exercise: Return to the excerpt from Tranströmer's "Elegy." State explicitly what is conveyed in these four lines. Be exact. Leave nothing out, but do not add anything either.

Question: Why doesn't explicit statement work here? How could making things explicit get in the way of full comprehension?

What we are seeking when we ask this question is a *gestalt* of exact, non-imagistic, fully explicit reportage; we want to *understand* what it is, what it does, and why it sometimes fails. The indications are, however, that we won't be able to convey such a gestalt *through* exact, non-imagistic, fully explicit reportage. We are confronted, now in a literary context, with what Einstein reported about his own thought processes

"Show, Don't Tell"   105

in physics, what Lorenz reported about recognizing distant birds in flight, what Jonathan Schooler has established in the lab: the experience of gestalt insight is compromised if you ask people to talk about it. There is also recent evidence that Freud, in his 1895 "Project for a Scientific Psychology," was right: a neural network that corresponds to a phenomenological sense of self has been shown to inhibit 'cross-talk' among other areas of the brain; activity in this neural network is associated with linear, linguistic thinking. There is further evidence that although both hemispheres of the brain are involved in nearly everything we do, think, and experience, each has a fundamentally different style: one hemisphere is more closely involved with the senses and the physical body; it is more active when we perceive wholes, emotional cues, and non-verbal meaning; activity in the other hemisphere predominates when we are taken up with analysis, with isolating details, and with rendering thought into speech.

There is nothing in the foregoing that amounts to a coherent constellation of aspects, let alone a proof. But here is one thing that it might be showing: perhaps the abstract, sometimes cliché-ridden summaries that constitute explicit reportage are artifacts of inhibited patterns of thought. Maybe, when we show, we are activating less-inhibited, less rigidly structured 'cross-talk' and this cross-talk precipitates gestalt comprehension. Maybe such comprehension intensifies activity in the 'wholistic' hemisphere, the one more deeply and broadly involved with the body, which is why showing affects us viscerally in a way that explicit reportage often doesn't.

Is it possible that the inhibiting activity of the ego evolved as a way to check up on and, as necessary, to correct gestalt thinking's occasional mistakes? This seems likely. I suspect that we share both styles of thought with other species. But the fact that members of technocratic cultures rarely value or cultivate gestalt capacities suggests that the correction may have gone too far. Explicit reportage, on the other hand, especially its digitized version, is held up as the standard to which we all should aspire. The increasing speed, and with it the increasing brevity, of electronic communications exacerbates the situation. It erodes not only our capacity to perceive the nuance on which robust gestalt comprehension depends, it erodes our capacity for procedural rigour, which is the prime virtue of linguistic intelligence. Is there a way to restore coordination and balance? I do not know.

ֆֆ

"Beauty is truth, truth beauty, — that is all / Ye know on earth, and all ye need to know." Earlier, I suggested that even when poets offer us summary abstractions, we can feel we are being shown something beyond what is told. How? Why? The answer often involves the music of language. In this case, the music of the words echoes and reinforces the overt 'content': 'truth' is an assonantal rhyme of 'beauty'; and then there's that wonderful spondee **truth beaut**-y, driving the point home. There is a rhyme not just between the words but also between the so-called content and the so-called form: that rhyme, the meta-rhyme, is what these lines show. The wholeness of Keats's literary vision.

Is it true, what he tells us? "Beauty is truth, truth beauty"? The words are in quotation marks in the poem as well. They are spoken by a Grecian urn, a closed, smoothly continuous, balanced, radially symmetrical, timeless, *silent* form. The urn, according to the poem, is the emblem of beauty, beauty's synecdoche. But it is also the epitome of the 'good gestalt.' Thus *that it is true* is what gestalt thinking — silently, timelessly — knows about itself. It corresponds to reality.

What is it to be true? According to the word's etymology, it is to be faithful, to be as *reliable as a tree*. But how reliable is that? The intelligence of the ego has learned that sometimes we leap too soon, or too far, or in the wrong direction: gestalts, even beautiful ones, can be false. The ego is on the defensive; it wants assurance not that gestalts are more or less reliable, but that they are *correct* — that they *set us straight*.

How does gestalt thinking comprehend this kind of 'correcting' thought? One of Keats's letters gives us a brief characterization: it is an "irritable reaching after fact and reason." Doesn't gestalt thinking also reach after facts? Indeed, it depends on them. But it doesn't simply collect information — it reaches *through* 'the facts' to what, as an ensemble, they mean. Doesn't Keats also imply that in the absence of "irritable reaching after fact and reason" we're left in "uncertainties, Mysteries, doubts"? Yes. But those are not the products of gestalt reflection. They are the condition we must tolerate if we want to put ourselves in the way of gestalt insight. The conviction that there is a universal force attracting the centres of all masses toward one another, or that the transformations that define Fuchsian functions are identical to those of non-Euclidean geometry, or that truth is beauty — all arise out of "contemplative mood." Ego-inhibited thinking is impatient. Narrow. It lacks vision. It has no ear. At its worst, it is a rule-bound fussbudget. At its best, it is an efficient secretary-cum-accountant.

To trust gestalt thinking is to risk faith. Can the tree break? Yes, in a bad enough storm. But to live instead by the abstraction of the straight line is to refuse to go outdoors. It is to refuse the joy and pleasure of insight, and the wisdom that Keats calls "a friend to man." It denies the heart of intelligence.

❧ Music

I

> *It is impossible for me to say in my book one word about all that music has meant in my life. How then can I hope to be understood?*
>
> — Ludwig Wittgenstein

The view that there is something ineffable about music's meaning is widely shared. Philosophers as disparate as Suzanne Langer, Vladimir Jankélévitch, and Roger Scruton have attempted to explain it; Albert Einstein felt it, as did Victor Hugo. This is not a minor curiosity; its ineffability is not the result of scholarly or literary neglect. Music has tremendous power. It affects us so deeply that we desire intensely to communicate to others the importance of our experience — and, by our own lights, fail.

*

My personal experience confirms this view: attempts to delineate theories of musical significance fall flat in much the way that attempts to describe visual proofs in geometry fall flat. The profound or startling experience of music's meaning goes missing.

*

I will assume that the widely acknowledged sense of music's ineffability points to something real about the world. It is not possible in prose — even the flexible and imagistic prose of Wittgenstein's meditations — to capture many experiences of music's meaning. Why?

*

Music is pre-eminently a gestalt phenomenon.

It is not a coincidence that Gestalt epistemology began with attempts to make sense of the human capacity for comprehending melody. Nor that Max Wertheimer, the chief exponent of the Berlin school, was deeply involved with music. Nor that Wittgenstein, who often thinks about gestalt phenomena without calling them that, was also deeply involved with music. Nor that Arne Næss, who has championed gestalt epistemology as the prerequisite for an adequate understanding of ecological relationships, trained into adulthood as a classical pianist.

Or, rather, it *is* a coincidence: sensitivity — availability — to music and a heightened awareness of other gestalt phenomena often coincide.

*

What happens when two-year-olds, who are just learning to talk, faultlessly transpose a melody they have just learned to another key?

> CLAIRE F. MICHAELS AND CLAUDIA CARELLO: Invariant patterns over time refer to constant patterns of change — that is, manners or styles of change.... A melody is a simple example.... One invariant for a melody happens to be a set of ratios of times and fundamental frequencies; as an example, given some arbitrary initial frequency, F, the second and third notes of the children's song *Three Blind Mice* will be .891 F and .794 F, with the third note lasting twice as long as the first two, which are of equal duration. What we have done in specifying the ratios of frequencies and durations is to describe a pattern over time. In whatever key and tempo the song is played, the first three notes will always bear these relationships.

But no one supposes two-year-old children are calculating these relationships. Calculative intelligence can get no purchase on how prenumerate children apprehend melodies.

*

Gestalt insight has repeatedly been demonstrated to resist articulation.

*

For some philosophers, the puzzle about music's meaning stems from the fact that, although music is language-like, its basic components — tones — do not refer. Music appears to have a syntax (Schenker; Lerdahl and Jackendoff); but it has no lexicon.

*

How can music precipitate the experience of meaning if it has no lexicon? Perhaps it refers to feelings or emotions (Raffman). Perhaps it expresses feeling (Langer) or emotions (Kivy). Perhaps its meaning is its form (Hanslick). Perhaps it is an unmediated representation of the Will (Schopenhauer). Perhaps any given work refers to the predicates that describe it (Goodman). Perhaps any given work of art refers only to itself (Croce).

*

The experience of grasping a referent is indeed one paradigmatic experience of meaning. But another paradigmatic experience of meaning — one that subsumes the grasping of referents as a species of a much wider genus — is the dawning of a gestalt or the perception of a gestalt shift.

*

It is the comprehension of powerful and complex gestalts and the relations among them that underlies intense experiences of meaning in music.

II

> "I have found a paper of mine among some others," said Goethe today, "in which I call architecture 'petrified music.' Really there is something in this; the tone of mind produced by architecture approaches the effect of music."
> — Johann Peter Eckermann

Music occurs in aural space.

*

Aural space is space as it is perceived by beings that can hear. It is the auditory analogue of visual space.

*

There are several modes of space: auditory, visual, kinaesthetic, tactile. These modes correspond roughly to distinct modes of perception. (It is not clear that all the canonical senses establish modes of space. Olfactory space? Arguably. Gustatory space? Less obvious.)

Any given experience may involve a number of modes: we see and hear the wind in the leaves, and we feel that same wind on our skin.

*

Aural space is as real and mind-independent as visual space. Like things in visual space, things in aural space may also be experienced in the absence of physical stimulation. Aural images may be heard in the mind's ear as visual images are seen in the mind's eye.

*

Silence is the substrate of aural space, as light is the substrate of visual space.

*

Tonal music occurs not only in aural space but also in tonal space.

*

Tonal space is a species of aural space.

*

A tonal space is defined by a musical scale or a family of scales.

A tone is a point in a musical scale at which one increment of the scale gives way to another. A tone is not the same thing as a pitch — a particular physical frequency — because a given scale (say, the Western European harmonic minor scale or the Javanese pelog scale) can begin on any physical frequency. But when music is played, performed, sung, or otherwise made physically real, tones are instantiated by pitches.

The concepts tone and scale are wholly interdefined.

*

So-called atonal music is what is left when tonal relationships have been removed from tonal music. It is a kind of ghost. Its space is defined by differences in pitch frequency.

112   The Experience of Meaning

*

A great deal of music is also organized rhythmically. Rhythms do not require tones for their specification. They can be instantiated without pitch.

Rhythm is perceived aurally, kinaesthetically, and proprioceptively.

*

A very small proportion of human beings with otherwise normal hearing cannot perceive tonal relationships — they are unable to discriminate among pitches and cannot recognize pitch intervals. The rest of us, whether we receive musical training or not, absorb our culture's preferred organizations of tones — its scales — through exposure to music, just as we absorb linguistic grammar through exposure to language.

All known human scales span an octave, although there are significant differences, culture to culture, among the standard sequences of tones that fall between an octave's outer limits.

*

Tonal space is experienced whenever we experience tones, for example, when we play, dance to, or listen to music. Like other forms of aural space, it may also be experienced through aural images in the absence of physically sounding tones.

*

Tonal space, when it is perceived, is perceived by the imagination. It is perceived, not invented or made up.

To hear, physically, a pitch of a certain frequency is not the same thing as understanding (either intuitively or through study) the relationships among tones that constitute a tonal structure. Understanding tonal relationships requires engagement with images in tonal space.

*

We perceive movement among tones. This movement is the foundation of our experience of tonal space. It is understood through the action of metaphor.

*

Movement among tones is governed by the syntax of a given scale.

Music   113

The structure of a given scale or family of scales determines how musical tension is built up and released.

Movement occurs away from and towards the tonic, the tone that determines the octave that forms the outer limits of a scale.

*

Unlike the organization of kinaesthetic space and some species of visual space, the fundamental organization of aural space is not determined by gravity. Gravity, however, becomes the central metaphor that organizes tonal space.

The centres of gravity in any tonal space are the tonics of the scales in play.

*

Compositions in tonal space are aural architectures.

Tonally organized music makes gestures in tonal space.

III

> *Seiji Ozawa soon raised an arm.*
>
> *"Very good. You know the music," he said, nodding to Takaseki [the student conductor].... But to me, Bartók is ..." He ended his sentence with a movement of his arm and body that was difficult to describe. "In words you can describe eight kinds of sadness," he would say later. "In music, so many more."*
>
> — Helen Epstein

To understand a gesture is to comprehend a gestalt.

*

In the concept 'gesture,' I include facial expression, posture, and many movements of parts of the body other than the hands. (We elbow people out of the way; we wrinkle our noses when we are disgusted; we leap for joy.)

*

Musical works in the Western tonal tradition — and in most other traditions as well — are geometries of feeling.

They reveal tonal contours that are projective transformations of the contours of expressive gestures.

This is one aspect of music's connection to dance.

*

Imagine a series of stop-action photos of a human wrist and hand as it extends and turns to reach for something deeply loved (or fiercely desired, or undeserved, or that belonged to someone else, now gone). Imagine that series abstracted and mapped as the simultaneous changes in position of certain key points: the tips of the fingers, their knuckles, the outside edge of the hand — a sequence of complex spline curves. Put that abstract series in motion. Then imagine a geometry that projected those moving curves in a complex way, collapsing some dimensions, expanding others. And finally imagine another complex projective function that mapped the result into a nonvisual medium. (Suzanne Langer might have had something like this in mind when she claimed that musical works share the logical form of feelings.)

> GUNNAR JOHANSSON: Flashlight bulbs [or, subsequently, reflective patches] were ... attached to the main joints of an assistant dressed in tight-fitting dark clothes [who was filmed in the dark].... The actor walked in a normal style over the scene from the left to the right and back, in a direction fronto-parallel to the camera lens.... The [resulting] motion pattern has been shown [to viewers] in many class demonstrations as well as under more strict experimental conditions. It always evokes the same spontaneous response after the first one or two steps: this is a walking human being!... When the motion is stopped, the set of elements is never interpreted as representing a human body....
>
> Far more complex geometrically is the general case where the distal track [of the assistant] can represent any angle between 0 and 90 degrees to an observer's fronto-parallel plane. Under these conditions of projection, the distally constant distances between couples of joints will be represented ... by continuously changing

distances between the [flashlight bulbs] representing these joints.... [In these experiments] all observers immediately reported seeing a person walking toward them. Furthermore, the perceived direction of motion track roughly corresponds to the recorded one.

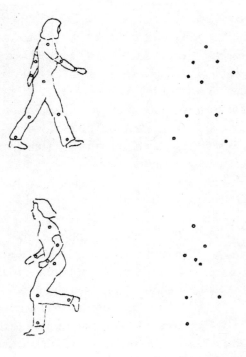

Fig. 7   Outline contours of a walking and a running subject and the corresponding light-reflecting point configurations.

These results were found without any exception. Every observer immediately reported the correct motion pattern. Also, in this case, the degree of perceptual vividness appears to be very high for all observers....

Human walking is also readily recognized when the number of recorded elements in the stimulus pattern is reduced.... [A] number of other demonstration patterns have also been produced and studied. These patterns include running in different directions and also in a circular track, cycling, climbing, dancing in couples, various types of gymnastic motion, etc. In all these cases, spontaneous and correct identification of the types of activity has been made without exception.

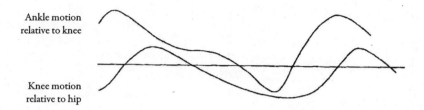

Fig. 8 *The relative pendulum motion components of knee and ankle of a walking person. The two motions are plotted against their common time axis, and therefore the diagram also illustrates typical phase relations between the two motions.*

*

The expressive gestures tracked by music may be human or nonhuman. They may include the movements of plants or of water, of light and shadow, and may include the contours of landscapes.

*

It is my guess that comprehension of unfolding tonal shapes in music has its foundation in the neurophysiology required for comprehension of visually perceivable gestures made by animals. That is: If it is eventually established that humans possess so-called mirror neurons, I believe these will be found to be active in the perception of tonal music. And that the neurophysiology of musical perception will be found to be linked to the comprehension of landscape and architecture.

*

A geometry of feeling reveals relations of identity in difference among abstract tonal contours and the contours of physical gestures.

A melody, motif, or phrase, a harmonic sequence, has a shape discernible by tonal imagination in just the way that a contour traced by the tilt of a head has a shape discernible by visual perception.

IV

This brief sketch ... suffices to suggest how intimately the issues about internal relations are bound up with a whole range of other philosophical problems — problems about the notions of substance, of essence, and of 'bare particulars,' about 'real' versus 'nominal' definitions, about nominalism versus realism, about the way in which we refer to and identify particulars, and about the nature of necessary truth. It is perhaps not too much to say that a philosopher's views on internal relations are themselves internally related to all his other philosophical views.

— Richard Rorty

The role of imagination and metaphor in the comprehension of tonal music has caused much philosophical confusion.

*

Roger Scruton, for example, is contemptuous of the idea that tonal shapes are real. He is equally contemptuous of those who imagine that music expresses emotion.

Sound exists in space, he agrees, but tones — constituents of scales that have harmonic meaning only in relation to other constituents of the same scale — exist only in the rational imagination, that is, in the imaginations of humans and gods. ("Hearing sound involves the exercise of the ear: it displays an *acoustic* capacity.... Animals also [have this capacity] and respond to sounds and to the information contained in sounds. But to hear music we need capacities that only rational beings have.") Tones *cannot* move, he thinks, because they are not the sort of thing that can change physical position in physical space. Thus, tones can be said to move merely metaphorically. It is also merely metaphorically that the metaphorical movements of tones conjure emotions. ("There are no metaphorical facts, since all metaphors are false.... Nevertheless, there are contexts in which metaphors seem indispensable ... because we are using them to describe something other than the material world; in particular because we are attempting to describe how the world *seems....*")

*

118   The Experience of Meaning

Scruton is correct that metaphors can "seem indispensable" when we're trying to describe the relationship between a given passage of music and an emotion. He is not correct when he claims that such relationships therefore have no mind-independent reality.

*

Metaphors are rhetorical strategies in the service of ontological truth. A metaphor points to resonance among the internal structural relations that make one thing what it is and those that make another thing what it is.

> T.S. ELIOT: The important difference [between major and minor poets] is whether a knowledge of the whole, or at least of a very large part, of a poet's work, makes one enjoy more, because it makes one understand better, any one of his poems. That implies a significant unity in his whole work. One can't put his increased understanding altogether into words: I could not say just why I think I understand and enjoy *Comus* better for having read *Paradise Lost*, or *Paradise Lost* better for having read *Samson Agonistes*, but I am convinced that this is so.

*

In pointing to resonance among internal structural relations, a metaphor not only heightens our awareness of the echoes between things but, by drawing attention to the internal structural relations that make things what they are, it also heightens our awareness of the things themselves. We experience more profoundly what each thing is.

*

By 'metaphor,' I mean the linguistic expression of the result of focused analogical thinking.

*

The truth of metaphors is context-dependent: things change.

Just as what is literally true of a thing alters with time, what is metaphorically true of it alters as well.

*

Emotions move. They are, in a way, events.

*

Although music is archetypally lyric — that is, resonantly coherent — much of it is also inherently dramatic. Dramatic music is best described by metaphors that involve motion: tension, release, complication, resolution, suspension, cadence.

(All metaphors are *in* motion — gestalts flash back and forth across the hinge of what is common — but not all metaphors are *about* movement from one theme or motif to another, one harmonic structure to another.)

*

Metaphors are informative in direct proportion to their depth, that is, in proportion to the ontological significance *for* a thing of the internal structural relations that are highlighted by the metaphor.

A metaphor is significant to the degree that the internal structural relations brought to the fore in saying that A is B *matter* to A's being what it is.

"Comparing peaches and mangoes is comparing apples and oranges!" is a weak metaphorical claim; it tells us little of substance. "The rain is Art Blakey / with the arms of Indra" tells us a great deal about a particular rainstorm.

*

Internal structural relations cannot be discerned other than through gestalt comprehension. And only gestalt comprehension discerns the ontological significance of any given set of internal relations.

*

Our capacity to discern internal structural relations and their ontological significance also varies with time. It is a function of complex interactions among many factors: our experience; our training; our cultural, intellectual, physical, and emotional perspectives; our state of health; our social context; whether or not we've had a good night's sleep.

*

Music both expresses and conjures feeling because there are structural echoes between the complex contours traced in aural space by sequences of tones and the complex contours traced by emotionally expressive gestures in physical space.

In 'sequences of tone' I include sequences of harmonic structures — movements among chords.

Music expresses feeling in just the way that gestures express feeling. It conjures feeling in us in just the way that the gestures of others conjure feeling in us.

*

The intuitive recognition of connections among the shapes of musical ideas and the shapes of expressive gestures appears in all accounts of music's meaning, either as their foundation or as a foundational puzzle that must be solved.

This is true also of Scruton's account. Indeed, I agree with many things Scruton says: his grasp of the importance of Gestalt theory, his view that music can educate our emotions, and especially his appreciation that musical comprehension is metaphorical, rooted in our ability to hear musical structures as gestures.

Scruton's anthropocentrism has, however, led him to seize on the inaccurate view that there is no sense to the expression 'genuine metaphorical relationship.' He believes that metaphors are mere human confections; it follows that they can never reflect accurate perception of aspects of a mind-independent world. This vitiates the significance of his account of music's meaning.

*

The refusal to understand metaphorical thought as something capable of detecting real structural resonance across distinct domains — this failure has repeatedly sabotaged Western European discussions of meaning in general.

V

Blossoms at night,
and the faces of people
moved by music.

— Issa, translated by Robert Hass

I remember the first time I played under Yannick Nézet-Séguin. It was early in his career and he was not yet well known. The orchestra instantly adored him. This was partly because he was friendly and respectful (uncommon traits in a conductor in the old days). But it was mostly because he was extraordinarily easy to play for: we knew exactly what he wanted and exactly when he wanted it. And he responded to what we gave him.

His technique was superb, his beat crystal clear, and his cues precise. This alone, however, would have produced an accurate, not a stirring performance. (And even accuracy can be compromised when a conductor fails to communicate — musicians, like everyone else, get sloppy when they're bored.) Nézet-Séguin is never boring. He communicates constantly, compellingly, with his eyes, his face, his whole body, as well as with his hands. What does he communicate? Feeling: resolution, determination, tenderness, sorrow, triumph, erotic passion, fury, excitement, anxiety, wonder, pain, joy, delight, playfulness, astonishment, anticipation, coldness, reflectiveness, bliss, ease, lilt, ecstasy, agitation, optimism, mania, dreaminess, desire, urgency, confidence, aggression, sassiness. For example.

In videotaped performances with close-ups, you will see that musicians watch Nézet-Séguin more than they watch many other conductors. This isn't because they're afraid of losing the beat or missing a cue. They watch because Nézet-Séguin *means*: he means with his whole being. The intensity of his meaning makes musicians want to mean, too. This is why Nézet-Séguin has become one of the world's most sought-after conductors. When he conducts, nobody phones it in.

Anyone who remains unsure that gestures alone can communicate feeling very precisely should view still photographs of Nézet-Séguin conducting, or view a performance with the sound turned off.

*

Does the fact that still pictures of Nézet-Séguin are highly communicative belie Gunnar Johansson's research?

No, it shows how good humans are at reading movement in still representations of animate beings.

*

Feeling informs tempo and rhythm; it shapes phrases, motifs, and subjects in both stark and subtle ways. Feeling also calls forth tone colour: harshness, brilliance, silkiness, ethereality, warmth.

*

Am I denying that there are 'purely musical' gestures, sequences of tones that are about nothing more than tonal and rhythmic relationships? Not at all. I am denying the claim, not uncommon in scholarly literature on music, that music *never* communicates feeling, that it communicates *only* tonal and rhythmic structures.

*

It is clear that works of music possess tonal and rhythmic structure and that these structures are often enjoyed — and analyzed — independently of any feeling the music might arouse. They are distinguishable aspects of the work.

However, phrasing, tempo, tone quality, colour, where a musician sits in the beat are, in a good deal of music, determined by feeling. Ignoring these aspects is like ignoring the way tones of voice convey meaning in linguistic contexts.

*

The concept 'feeling' includes emotion and also phenomena we often consider physical: respiration, heartbeat, body temperature — things of which we are mostly unaware but to which our attention can be drawn. It includes phenomena we often consider cerebral — attentiveness, concentration, curiosity, perplexity, and certainty, for example. It includes the notion of taste, as in a taste for simple furnishings. It includes things of which we say we have a 'sense' — a sense of beauty, a sense of decorum, a sense of outrage.

Music   123

Under the rubric 'feeling' I wish to include most aspects of experience that are not predominantly calculative or deductive or taxonomic. (There is no clear boundary here. Feelings often accompany calculation, deductive reasoning, and dialectic sorting.)

*

Feelings are essential to the perception of many if not all gestalts. They are one of the ways in which we learn about the world and the things in it.

> WILLIAM BLAKE: What it will be Questiond When the Sun rises do you not see a round Disk of fire somewhat like a Guinea O no no I see an Innumerable company of the Heavenly host crying Holy Holy Holy is the Lord God Almighty I question not my Corporeal or Vegetative Eye any more than I would Question a Window concerning a Sight I look thro it & not with it.

*

Feelings are themselves gestalts of processes and perceptions that we are often not directly aware of: complex networks of physical sensations, thoughts or images, and memories.

*

When we habitually experience certain emotions in certain situations, they often become aspects of our gestalts of those situations. This creates an epistemologically complex situation in which truth can be obscured. Or illuminated. (Aristotle in *Nichomachean Ethics* is particularly insistent that an excellent character, which involves habituated feeling, will allow us to perceive at least some things more correctly than we otherwise would.)

It is true that often, especially as we mature, we are able to distinguish what we perceive from what we feel about what we perceive. But being able to draw the distinction does not mean emotion has nothing to do with perception, nor that it is not fundamental to accurate perception.

We are adept at distinguishing the colour of a thing from that thing, the sound of a thing from that thing, and similarly its taste, smell, and texture. Becoming adept at distinguishing the emotions a thing arouses from the thing itself gives us greater freedom of action. It does not challenge the epistemological importance of emotion in perception.

*

How are music and feeling connected? The way gesture and feeling are connected. Gestures show feeling; they reveal feeling; they express feeling. They rarely represent or describe it.

VI

> *No, I don't think I would get on with Hegel. Hegel seems to me to be always wanting to say that things which look different are really the same. Whereas my interest is in showing that things which look the same are really different. I was thinking of using as a motto for my book a quotation from* King Lear: *"I'll teach you differences." [Then laughing:] The remark "You'd be surprised" wouldn't be a bad motto either.*
> — Ludwig Wittgenstein

Many treatises on music by philosophers, musicologists and ethnomusicologists, anthropologists, archaeologists, neurophysiologists, critics, sociologists, and psychologists speak of music as though it were a unitary phenomenon. It isn't. Not even music in the narrow subtradition that Wittgenstein loved is a monolith.

*

Different works in different traditions interest us for different reasons. Their interest derives from different atavistic roots. A partial list of reasons that a piece of music might interest us could include:

- It intrigues us by developing fascinating or intricate or arresting tonal or rhythmic patterns.
- It intrigues those of us educated in the tradition by pushing the boundaries of tonal or rhythmic expectation.
- It offers an education of the emotions.
- It facilitates reflection, meditation, or contemplation.
- It induces a feeling we find pleasant or exciting.

- It refuses to challenge us emotionally and reassures us with emotional commonplaces (the musical equivalent of Hallmark verse).
- It stirs erotic longing, lending credence to Charles Darwin's view that the capacity for music is a sexually selected trait.
- It affects us physically or emotionally through the use of striking sonorities or timbres.
- It is loud, rhythmic, and perhaps also choral, lending credence to Joseph Jordania's view that loud rhythmic singing and drumming were core elements of early hominin intimidation displays.
- It induces entrainment — synchronized movement — among audience members, lending credence to the view, espoused by scholars like Steven Mithen and Ian Cross, that music was evolutionarily selected because of its capacity to produce social cohesion. (The classic example of entrainment is the synchronization over time of pendulum clocks that have been placed on a common support; the coördination of work gang movements with singing is another. Any piece of music with a lively rhythm will produce a degree of entrainment among listeners, even if, owing to the inhibitions encouraged by nineteenth- and twentieth-century Western European concert etiquette, this is expressed only through invisible toe-tapping inside shoes.)
- It consists of displays of bravura technique on the part of a soloist, which excite and impress the way athletic prowess impresses. (Musicians are, in fact, micro-athletes.)
- It does several of the foregoing things at the same time.

*

How does music educate emotion? If the work is profound or insightful it will enable us to feel emotions characteristic of mature or enlightened persons: serenity in the face of tragedy; joy in the face of evanescence; resolution in the face of loss; acceptance in the face of realization; the importance of a sense of humour; the omnipresence of dark in the light, and light in the dark.

Music promotes rehearsals of mature emotional responses by walking or carrying us through insightful sequences of tonal gestural gestalts. A given gesture may be harmonized with another; or may be balanced by another, creating a kind of emotional stability through symmetry; or one gesture may resolve — sometimes suddenly, sometimes imperceptibly — into another.

*

The structure of music's rehearsals of mature emotional responses is metaphoric and it also elapses in time: because of resonant internal structural relations, a given gestalt is enabled to *become* another.

*

Music and myth — in which narratively distinct events are understood to be metaphorically connected — are different embodiments of the same way of knowing. Their logic is, in this respect, the logic of dream.

*

When music is well constructed, the transformation of one gestalt into another can carry the conviction of mathematical proof.

*

"He raised his eyebrow disdainfully." Many of us can make this gesture and those of us who can't nonetheless recognize it instantly. Yet in many cases where we sense disdain, we will be unable to identify what clued us in. We 'just know.' And even when we can say "It was the way he raised his eyebrow," we will then demonstrate (if we can), rather than attempt to give a description of the movements that constituted the disdainful nature of the raising.

*

In the same way, we hear the plaint in a plaintive melody. This ability is exactly as mysterious as — no less, no more than — our ability to discern meaning in gestures.

*

Gestural meaning and tone of voice are the fundamental or default meanings when they are coupled with language.

Where gesture and tone of voice complement the semantic-syntactic parsing of words, we feel an augmentation of linguistic meaning. Where either gesture or tone of voice contradicts semantic-syntactic parsing — "Oh, he *said* he couldn't care less, but I could tell he was really hoping I would" — the meaning conveyed by gesture or tone of voice wins.

(The case in which gesture and tone of voice contradict one another is one in which we are made anxiously confused or deeply suspicious, often both.)

*

Because explicit criteria can rarely be provided to defend our discernment of subtle gestural meaning, in technocratic culture such discernment is often dismissed.

*

The fact that correct discernment of tonal meaning usually lacks specifiable criteria as back-up means neither that such discernment is a fiction nor that it is infallible. What it means is that we discover mistakes in tonal discernment by a different process than calculation or analysis of gestural components.

*

Music presents not only metaphors for feelings but also metaphors for qualities of feelings: fleeting ecstasy, sustained ecstasy, tumultuous grief, deadening grief, incredulous serenity, confident serenity — "the thousand ways of smiling, of getting up from one's chair, of taking a baby in one's arms, feelings that are not reducible to classic categorical affects but that colour them in a sensitive way," as Michel Imberty remarks.

*

Guy Davenport has described Mozart's D major string quartet, K. 499, as "a polyhedral fragrance of light." Fragrance: that most memorable of sensed qualities and the one most difficult to articulate. Light: the world's ontological metaphor for love.

*

128   The Experience of Meaning

And matters are more complex still.

ARNE NÆSS: Take the example of Beethoven's *Sonate Pathétique*, which has three movements.... Many people know only the second movement. This [movement] is a genuine whole in itself, and the experience of each tone [in it] will be decisively influenced by the whole movement. But normally the experience [of those tones and of the movement itself] will be different if people get to know the whole sonata. The movements are subordinate wholes, *subordinate gestalts* as part of musical reality. [And] within the movement there may be sets of tones forming contrasting wholes. We have therefore a complex realm of gestalts, a vast hierarchy. We can then [in this situation] speak of [sub- and superordinate] gestalts. This terminology is more useful than speaking about wholes and holism, because it induces people to think more strenuously about the relations between wholes and parts. It facilitates the emancipation from strong atomistic or mechanistic trends in analytical thought.

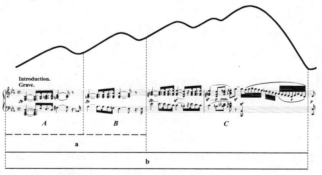

Fig. 9   Arne Næss's graph of the gestalt structure of the opening bars of Beethoven's Sonate Pathétique, *Op. 13. The initial motif, A, is followed by its rhythmic and pitch-contour echo, B. Together, they make up* a. *In C,* a *is echoed in compressed form in the first bar. A, B, and C together make up* b, *which is a yet higher order gestalt. Næss says, "In a similar way the various sections of the entire* Sonate Pathétique *can be understood only with full awareness of their participation in successive orders of gestalts."*

Music

Entering a room, there may be a spontaneous experience of it as a whole, even ... a strong, definite negative or positive colour. Within the room, the experience of a subordinate whole — an arrangement of chairs around a fireplace [for instance] — may change the experience of the room decisively, from a [definitely] negative to a [definitely] positive gestalt. So, within the hierarchy of gestalts, influences may go in any direction. Up or down the hierarchy, or horizontally within one level.

[Additionally,] the gestalt of a complex piece of music is subordinate to the experience of that piece in a particular situation. The piece may be played in the open or in a beautiful or an ugly building. If we have a particular companion, our relation to the companion in that situation influences the experience of the music. No part of the experience stands entirely alone.

*

Gestures occur in a context. Their meaning is a function of this context. The clarity of their resonance determines the coherence of their context. A multiply complex coherent context of gesture is a culture.

LUDWIG WITTGENSTEIN: A Bruckner symphony can be said to have two beginnings: the beginning of the first and the beginning of the second idea. These two ideas stand to each other not as blood relations, but as man and wife.

Bruckner's Ninth is a sort of *protest* against Beethoven's and this makes it bearable in a way it would not be if it were a sort of imitation. It is related to Beethoven's Ninth very much as Lenau's Faust is to Goethe's, that is to say as the Catholic to the Enlightenment Faust, etc., etc.

*

Garry Hagberg observes that in this passage, Wittgenstein has produced "a blizzard of context-linked associations." These associations, he urges, are particular; they resist "overarching generalization." And they are, further, the "embodied, manifest minute parts that constitute a composition's aesthetic content (rather than disembodied compositional ratiocination), parts that ... emerge as salient through comparative or relational juxtaposition, and that — to say it too succinctly — determine the meaning of the work."

Why too succinctly? Because it is not the mere conglomeration of parts — construed as separate entities — that is meaningful. The work's meaning springs from resonant relations among these parts, the dynamic interdetermination of the parts and the whole of which they are parts.

VII

> *"And yet, Socrates," said Parmenides, "the forms inevitably involve these objections and a host of others besides.... As a result, whoever hears about them is doubtful and objects that they do not exist, and that, even if they do they must by strict necessity be unknowable to human nature; and in saying this he seems to have a point; and, as we said, he is extraordinarily hard to win over.... On the other hand, if someone, having an eye on all the difficulties we have just brought up and others of the same sort, won't allow that there are forms for things and won't mark off a form for each one, he won't have anywhere to turn his thought, since he doesn't allow that for each thing there is a character that is always the same. In this way he will destroy the power of discourse entirely."*
>
> — Plato

Wittgenstein's later work is notorious for the view that Platonism is wrong, that there are no unified referents of philosophically charged nouns and adjectives, but only context-bound usages that bear family resemblances to one another.

> LUDWIG WITTGENSTEIN: If I say A has beautiful eyes someone may ask me: what do you find beautiful about his eyes, and perhaps I shall reply: the almond shape, long eye-lashes, delicate lids. What do these have in common with a gothic church that I find beautiful too?

Music   131

Should I say they make a similar impression on me? What if I were to say that in both cases my hand feels tempted to draw them? That at any rate would be a *narrow definition* of the beautiful.

It will often be possible to say: seek your reasons for calling something good or beautiful and then the peculiar grammar of the word 'good' in this instance will be evident.

What is insufficient about this account is that it does not recognize how remarkable it is that we pick up on family resemblances.

*

Wittgenstein argued elsewhere that it was not the business of philosophy to resolve contradictions or advance theses. "The work of the philosopher consists in assembling reminders for a particular purpose." The purpose is to provide a "clear view" of a state of affairs that troubles us. But how do we learn to do this? Which reminders? How assembled? Not all data that a machine could provide would be relevant. What determines salience?

*

Consider: How is it possible to look up in the dictionary a word you don't know how to spell? Or why do mnemonic techniques work? Why, for example, is it possible to remember names by associating the named person with another thing? (Ms White with the image of flour.) Or to remember a series of ideas by 'placing' each in one of the rooms of a familiar house? If it's possible to remember the image attached to the person or to recover the idea once you 'revisit' the 'room,' why isn't it possible to remember the name or the ideas directly?

*

"My, you look like your mother!" we exclaim, though we can't say just why. Or we can add, "You have her carriage," without being able to draw that carriage or give a credible description of it.

*

132   The Experience of Meaning

It's true there's nothing almond-shaped about the cathedral nor anything vaulting about the eyes in the case that Wittgenstein brings to our attention. But what makes us reach for the word 'beautiful' in both instances is the fact of a complex of not-easily-articulable internal structural relations that are deeply resonant. Not the *same* complex in the two cases; but in each case a complex of sufficient integrity that we are drawn or startled.

The experience of the integrity of the complex is strong enough that the thing as a whole arrests our attention.

It is the fact of startling integrity, in each case, that gives rise to the word 'beautiful.'

*

When a simple thing strikes us as beautiful, it is that thing's integrity we have noticed. (It is frequently easier to notice the integrity of simple things than of complex things.)

*

We readily distinguish cases in which someone has been taught to *call* something good or fine and cases in which they have genuinely *recognized* that something is good or fine. The difference shows up most strongly when people are asked to give reasons for their judgments. Where it is merely a matter of socialization, people are often blithe, confused, or defensive. In cases of genuine recognition, they are rarely any of these things: they are often inarticulate, and frustrated by their inability to be more articulate; they often understand why they are being asked to justify their judgment; and though they may end up apologizing for their inability to say much, they remain undefensive, confident they have judged correctly. (Unless, of course, the demand for reasons is unrelentingly hostile.)

*

What Wittgenstein's observations reveal is that there is no paradigmatic case we can point to when asked the meaning of 'beautiful,' as there is in the case of 'blue' or 'tall.' (Though ostensive definitions of 'blue' and 'tall' are also context-dependent, and therefore require gestalt comprehension if we are to understand them as paradigms.) In the case of 'beautiful,' there is nothing we can easily articulate, as in the case of 'fattening' or 'arduous'; nothing we are happy to shrug over, as in the case of 'delicious' (*chacun à son goût*).

Beauty is a phenomenon that has an extraordinary number of manifestations, not all of which will be perceivable by all persons. (A string player can, in most circumstances, tell the difference between a viola playing middle C and a violin playing the same note, but many non-musicians can't.)

Beauty's gestalt character — profound and attracting integrity — makes discernment of it impossible to articulate without engendering the feeling that we have missed the mark. We sense that any attempt to use words in a way that circumscribes resonance is going to lead us astray.

*

There are cultures that have no word for art. Their wise and intelligent members are not typically puzzled by the phenomenon of beauty nor by the fact that music is meaningful.

Our puzzlement is cultural. It is a product of making explicit, analyzable structure the paradigm of meaning. We thereby sculpt intelligence according to a technocratic ideal.

VIII

> *Soulful expression in music. It is not to be described in terms of degrees of loudness and tempo. Any more than a soulful facial expression is to be described in terms of the distribution of matter in space. Indeed, it is not even to be explained by means of a paradigm, since the same piece could be played with genuine expression in innumerable ways.*
>
> — Ludwig Wittgenstein

The attempt to articulate all the aspects of a musical composition that a person has registered and to present the composition's effect as the sum of these piecemeal articulations is an attempt to stuff gestalt comprehension into a calculative straitjacket.

*

I use 'calculative' in the sense of *ratiō*, the Latin etymological root of 'rationality.' *Ratiō* signifies reckoning or calculation, a process that can be represented accurately as a series of explicit steps that require nouns, noun-clauses, or numerals, along with verbs for their accurate formulation. The principles governing this process of reckoning or calculation can also be made explicit.

Analysis is the process that organizes material for the application of calculative reason.

*

Ratiō does not have a Greek root. The word ancient Greeks used for the concept of relative proportion was *logos*.

*

Gestalt comprehension cannot be accurately reconstructed as a 'chain of reasoning' — as a form of calculative thought — because it is not a chain of reasoning.

We can, often enough, construct a chain of reasoning whose conclusion states what gestalt comprehension sees: "His eyes are beautiful." But such a chain of reasoning will not be satisfying; it will be experienced as misleading by someone who has grasped the gestalt, because it misrepresents what has occurred. It misrepresents what has occurred in this way: it represents it as assent to the result of logical operations on premises that articulate ontologically separate facts about the beautiful object. A chain of reasoning does not, cannot, represent what has occurred as the discernment of resonantly attuned aspects.

*

Why should the *way* understanding is represented matter? Why isn't mimicking the result good enough? —— Why isn't mimicking love, or sincerity, or justice good enough?

*

The experience of meaning is the experience of resonant relationship. The deeper and more complex the resonance, the more powerful the experience of meaning. When a mode of representation curtails resonance, it curtails the experience of meaning.

Meaning is *what matters*.

To mimic what matters is to offend against reality and the possibility of genuine engagement with it.

*

When we generate calculative reconstructions of the results of gestalt comprehension, when we attempt to analyze an instance of such comprehension and then put the pieces back together, we enter a different and distinct epistemological mode from gestalt comprehension.

*

What calculative reconstructions cannot do is represent the gestalt character of gestalt insight.

*

What matters is not a mere series of tones or a mere collection of coloured brush marks; what matters is the meaningful gesture.

*

Calculative reconstruction is based on the premiss that there is nothing to meaningful gesture apart from 'experiential atoms' that an analysis can specify. This premiss is false. What matters is the integrity of aspects, their dynamic interrelationship with the whole that determines them as parts.

*

Calculative intelligence represents understanding as a kind of machine.

*

There is no question that gestalt comprehension can be mistaken, and when it is, it is often stubbornly so. There is also no question that calculative intelligence can call attention to such errors. But so can encouraging a person to go back to the misconceived situation and notice other aspects of it.

*

136   The Experience of Meaning

Why are many humans enamoured of machine intelligence? Perhaps we imagine the machine will eliminate error. This, of course, is something it cannot do. The machine will simply alter the nature of the error that can be made.

*

Fascination with machines is one expression of a biological interest in power and control — an interest not limited to the human species, but amplified by its opposable thumb.

*

The perception of feeling in others, the reading of gesture or tone, requires comprehension of wholes through perception of minute, often numerous, details. This perception happens for the most part in a flash. We do sometimes try to figure out what a series of gestures meant ("Did you see Alice catch Deirdre's eye? What do you suppose that was about?") — but frequently what we are attempting to do is to enlarge our gestalt. And sometimes, when we're trying to solve a mystery, we attempt to calculate what a series of gestures could 'add up to.' But this is not the usual case.

IX

So much we have to trust to be able to live our daily day without sinking through the earth!
Trust the masses of snow that cling to the mountainsides above the village.
Trust promises to keep silent and the understanding smile, trust that the telegram about the accident doesn't refer to us and the sudden axe blow from within doesn't come.
Trust the axles that carry us on the highway in the middle of the three hundred times enlarged steel bee swarm.
But none of that is really worth our confidence.
The quintet says that we can trust something else. What else?
Something else, and it follows us a little of the way there.
Like when the light goes out on the stairs and the hand follows — with confidence — the blind banister that finds its way in the darkness.
— Tomas Tranströmer, translated by Samuel Charters

Music   137

The second-most profound experiences of meaning in my life have occurred when I have suddenly grasped a large or complex gestalt — many apparently distinct things, some very distant from each other, suddenly falling into place, dovetailing, beginning to dance with one another.

*

The most profound experiences of meaning I've had have occurred when I've sensed my self dissolving, awareness widening into a world intricate, complex and integrated beyond imagining.

My experience playing chamber music has sometimes fallen between these two: I have, on occasion, felt that I am being played by the music, rather than playing it — that I have become a dynamic aspect of a much larger whole whose unfolding both determines and carries my actions. It is as though my hands and heart, my breath and understanding, are the music's, not my own.

I believe this experience is not uncommon among musicians. Classical musicians have no name for it. Musicians whose practice is improvisatory call it *being in the groove.*

*

In what kinds of cases is it possible to try to say something about how much music has meant in one's life, and hope to be understood?

Over the years, I've talked with several musicians easily and deeply about music. On two separate occasions, different musicians have confessed to me that their experience of listening to a particular piece of music was so intense they thought they would die. They were not exaggerating. They were uttering a simple truth and I understood how it could be so. It seems that what is crucial to attempts to communicate the power of musical meaning is a significant level of trust complemented by a shared context of experience and expertise — a background against which particular remarks and gestures (when the remarks give out) can be understood. A shared vocabulary is developed through long involvement in a common tradition; and intimacy allows expression of feeling.

But a shared vocabulary is defining of all linguistic communities. In other words, a good deal of what makes it possible to try to say something about music's meaning is what is essential for any successful language-use: fluency in a way of life.

*

The way of life that involves Western European classical music is uncommon. It was less uncommon in the circles in which Wittgenstein moved than it is now, but no one writing in mid-twentieth-century Europe could assume deep and universal familiarity with the Viennese tradition, even among intellectuals. Equally problematic for a mid-twentieth-century attempt to talk about the meaning of music was the inhibition around direct expression of feeling in British intellectual culture. And in the particular period in which Wittgenstein was writing, the bias against analogical thought of any sort was on the rise — a situation to which his own early writings had contributed.

These factors would have combined to make it difficult for anyone to say, in a book of philosophy, how much the Viennese tradition had meant to him.

With different emphases (less inhibition about speaking of feeling, increased unfamiliarity with the Western European musical tradition, unabated animus against analogical thought) these factors still combine to make it difficult to write compellingly about music for an educated audience.

*

Are these factors the source of the widespread perception of music's ineffability?

No.

The experience of music's meaning is ineffable because gestalt insight is not structured according to the constraints of calculative, stepwise, analytically organized intelligence. Thought must be capable of discerning resonance if it is to be adequate to gestalt understanding; and it must be capable of embodying resonance if it is to communicate such understanding. Language is frequently resonant in the minds of poets, in the mouths of politicians, and also in the scripts of advertisers; but even when it is informed by resonance, its syntactic rules will, to some degree, restrict the movement of gestalt intelligence.

The aspects of language that can be formalized, that *are* formalized in systems of logic and computation, are what make language a medium that is, to some extent, *foreign* to meaning. We experience the strain whenever we try to describe the experience of gestalt comprehension in words.

Because those formalizable aspects are not all there is to language — because language is also capable of setting images side by side in enactively resonant ways — it is also a medium in which we can nonetheless, at least at times, convey something of the experience of gestalt comprehension.

*

"Aren't *things* — named by nouns — gestalts? How then can you claim that language is foreign to gestalt comprehension? Gestalt comprehension appears to be of its essence!"

Nouns are not language. Nor is naming a calculative, analyzable activity.

> AUGUSTINE: When they (my elders) named some object, and accordingly moved towards something, I saw this and I grasped that the thing was called by the sound they uttered when they meant to point it out. Their intention was shown by their bodily movements, as it were the natural language of all peoples: the expression of the face, the play of the eyes, the movement of other parts of the body, and the tone of voice which expresses our state of mind in seeking, having, rejecting, or avoiding something. Thus, as I heard words repeatedly used in their proper places in various sentences, I gradually learnt to understand what objects they signified; and after I had trained my mouth to form these signs, I used them to express my own desires.

> LUDWIG WITTGENSTEIN, COMMENTING ON THIS PASSAGE: Augustine, we might say, does describe a system of communication; only not everything that we call language is this system.

*

We do not form chains of reasoning that establish things; things are what we think *about*. Chains of reasoning establish *that* things are *thus-and-so*.

Another way to put this: The conclusion of a chain of reasoning is always a sentence, never simply a noun.

*

Language is a medium of calculative thought; it is designed for holding things still while we track or forge linkages, causal or logical, between them and other things.

*

The medium of resonant thought is anything capable of resonance, either literally or metaphorically: music, images, gestures, the sounds of words.

The focus of resonant thought is non-causal, non-logical relationships among things' internal relations — that is, its focus is the internal relations of yet larger things.

> LUDWIG WITTGENSTEIN: I am not a religious man but I cannot help seeing every problem from a religious point of view.

*

The relation between calculative thought and gestalt insight are complex. While calculative thought rarely precipitates gestalt insight directly, it can lead us to look in the right direction, or to look with unusually sustained attention. Or to expect the unexpected.

*

One reason contemporary intellectuals dismiss Romanticism is that, like the cult of rationality against which it reacted, it became a cult itself. Another is that the cult of rationality was, and still is, allied with wealth, exploitation, and power. Calculation, analysis, mechanism, capital: these are the fundamental ideological commitments of technocracy. Their combined effects include not only the imminent death of a good deal of the existing biosphere but nihilism about meaning. If one wishes to remain allied with power, one must ignore or deny these effects.

*

Music so overwhelmingly requires gestalt comprehension that the experience of its meaning is left untouched by attempts to analyze it.

This is why music in the Western European tradition has mattered so much to so many Western European intellectuals. And because they are Western European intellectuals, the power of the music they love baffles them.

*

It is possible that the calculative conundrum that rhythmically and harmonically complex music presents is not confined to Western Europe and its colonial franchises. Technocracy has spread globally and (except in its contacts with some paleolithic cultures) not always at the point of a gun. The inability of consumers — the citizens of technocracy — to act effectively on five decades of *scientific* alarm about climate change is deeply impressive.

It is possible that something not altogether admirable about the neo-lithic human mind achieved its apotheosis in Europe in the sixteenth century and that the dissociation of sensibility to which T.S. Eliot pointed is both widespread and real. It is possible that the flowering of Western European diatonic composition in the seventeenth and eight-eenth centuries is, like the Romantic movement in the nineteenth, a rearguard action against the rise of the technologized intellect; and that the advent of serialism does not mark the exhaustion of tonality's possi-bilities but rather an extension of technocratic control. It is possible that gestalt comprehension depends on widespread neural 'cross-talk' among different areas of the brain and that calculative intelligence requires the inhibition of this cross-talk. It is possible that further human speciation is occurring, driven by environmental factors that include the advent of technocracy.

*

What if the technocratic ideal — the vision of the good life as mech-anized control of the natural world — has been not just an ecological disaster but an epistemological mistake? What if, in technocracy, the domination of the idea of reason by calculative intelligence has broadly undermined human capacities to know the world, even while expanding a narrow subset of those capacities connected with exploitation?

"But how can you suggest that there's an error here? Much of the success of calculative intelligence results from the empirical fact that the book of nature is written in the language of mathematics. The world was waiting for calculative intelligence to come along and reveal its workings."

It is arguable that the world was waiting for geometry; but less clear that it was waiting for algebra.

*

Algebra requires 'arithmetized' mathematics — an idea of mathematics as the manipulation of numbers: lines have numerically specified lengths, areas are products of the lengths of their constituent lines, volumes are further products, ratios of quantities are the quotients of the two numbers that represent them. If this seems too obvious to bear stating, it is a reflection of how profoundly arithmetization has come to dominate our conception of mathematics.

But there is powerful evidence that Greek mathematics, for example, was not arithmetic — that it was conceived instead as an art of rhythm and proportion.

> CLAIRE F. MICHAELS AND CLAUDIA CARELLO: One invariant for a melody happens to be a set of ratios of times and fundamental frequencies....

*

There can be no question that the Pythagoreans, who developed the Greek mathematics of ratio and proportion, understood the natural world to speak the language of mathematics. But they did not view the arithmetized descriptions we rely on to be revealing of its nature.

> MAX WERTHEIMER: To us it seems a great advantage to be able to abstract from the natural relationships of things. It is this facility of thought which we must thank for many technical achievements in our civilization. But there are others [in paleolithic societies] whose thinking may be described thus: Wherever there is no natural relationship, no vividly concrete and relevant

connection amongst things themselves, there is also no logical connection, nor is any logical manipulation of these things possible. In contrast to this stands our kind of thinking whose logic tends in this direction: "Everything can be counted," and "All things can be combined in and-summation."

*

What is emotion good for? Among other things, it is good for perceiving "vividly concrete and relevant connections," that is, real relationships among real things.

X

> *I've listened to music all my life, but the first time I truly heard it I must have been twenty years old, walking across campus to my dormitory. It was autumn, Vermont. Here and there a brilliant red or yellow leaf came see-sawing down, and someone was improvising on piano: the small music building acted as a resonating chamber for sounds that rolled out round and clear and amplified. I stood for some time on the sloping lawn, then sat, and after a while it came to me: the* quality of the sound had changed. *The ornamented, riverine surface of the music had become, abruptly,* articulation — *whose meaning, unfolding, was perfectly obvious — and perfectly untransposable into words.*
>
> — Roo Borson

Acknowledgment of music's meaning is the beginning of a just epistemology.

*

Within the philosophical profession, especially in North America, aesthetics is regarded as a backwater. Centuries of effort have produced nothing definitive. And who cares, when there are reputations to be made with problems that do yield to calculative reconstruction? If one's aim is to become a professional success, aesthetics is not a subdiscipline in which to waste one's time.

*

The key here is that the problems don't yield to calculative reconstruction. Analyses that purport to make everything that matters explicit are deeply implausible. They misrepresent the experience that intrigues us, the experience for which we have a deep need. What should we make of this fact?

What we *have* made of it is this: aesthetic problems are unimportant.

But the phenomenon could equally well be understood in this way: aesthetic problems are the Himalayas of philosophical endeavour. They show that the technocratic paradigm of good thinking is either wrong or incomplete.

*

It is clear that the technocratic paradigm of good thinking is not wholly wrong: witness the stellar achievements of calculative reasoning in technological applications.

I suggest, therefore, that what perennial interest in aesthetics reveals is that the technological paradigm is incomplete.

*

Every question in philosophy is bound up with epistemology: not just aesthetics, but ethics, ontology, metaphysics, the natures of logic and language. The nature of justice and injustice, of truth, of reality, of human happiness, understanding what matters and why — questions about these issues are perhaps most often made explicit in obscure corners of university campuses; but the ways they are answered form the unconscious warp and weft of human societies.

Does intellectual practice reflect cultural ideals or generate them? Both.

*

Let us take music seriously. Let us allow the near-universal testimonies to focus our attention: music is supremely meaningful and yet it resists satisfactory linguistic articulation.

Let us allow this fact to challenge the bewitchment that the image of calculative reason exercises over the intellectual imagination.

Music   145

ROO BORSON: On that long-ago walk back to the dormitory ... — at that moment the music was *spoken*, or I *knew* it, knew what it *was*, or what *I* was, eerily. And where: in an exacting realm where beauty is no longer discretionary, but raw communication.

*

What is gestalt intelligence good for?

Knowing being as resonance.

Recognizing that the world does not aspire to, but actually embodies, the condition of music.

❧ The Inscape of Being

In many cultures, it's taken for granted that there are important connections among poetry, philosophy, and what might be called spiritual insight. Examples would include the *Bhagavad Gita*, *Paradise Lost*, *Raven Travelling* from the west coast of precolonial North America, the *saabis* of West Africa, and the poem of Parmenides. Yet in one very powerful culture, the now-globalized descendant of the European Enlightenment, poetry and philosophy are frequently taken to be mutually exclusive endeavours. That culture is also a culture in which skepticism about anything that might be termed 'spiritual insight' runs high. I believe that these two facts are connected. A common epistemological error — a mistaken picture of *what thinking is* — underlies both. When this neglect is remedied — when we acknowledge the reality and efficacy of gestalt comprehension — we see not only that poetry and philosophy overlap in crucial ways, but that their area of intersection involves a particular kind of ontological awareness. That kind of awareness is, I believe, what is often meant by 'spiritual insight' — what W.T. Stace describes as extrovertive mysticism, for example, or what Aldous Huxley calls "the Perennial Philosophy." The structure of such awareness does not happily accommodate the structure of analytic linguistic thought, but this by no means disqualifies it from being true. Gestalt comprehension allows us to identify tone and gesture correctly, to recognize melodies, faces, distant birds, and landscape contours in a flash. Its products in mathematics and the sciences can be demonstrated to be accurate to even the most crotchety of analytic intellects. Most importantly, it is the foundation of the experience of meaning. The broader and more intense an experience of meaning becomes, I will argue, the more it takes on the lineaments of spiritual insight.

જ

But let me start with poetry.

Lyric poetry, as some readers will recall from their high school English classes, is a form of poetry that tends to brevity and, they were probably also taught, is an outpouring of the poet's personal feeling. This is not wholly erroneous, but it doesn't get to the structural heart of the matter. The word 'lyric' is used in a wide range of contexts — to describe Vermeer's use of oil paint and Bill Evans's use of diatonic tonality, for example, as well as to describe the poems of W.B. Yeats. That general use connects 'lyric' much more firmly to the humming lyre than to the human ego. Its characteristic formal properties are resonance and integrity. Lyric thought is highly *coherent*. Every gesture, even the smallest, counts.

Ludwig Wittgenstein remarked in one of his notebooks, "A poet's words can pierce us." Elsewhere, he wrote, "I believe I summed up my view of philosophy when I said: Really, one should always compress philosophy into poetry." The verb here translated as "compress into poetry" is *dichten*, the root of *Dichtung*, the German word for poetry. *Dichten* conveys the creation of a close-fitting density, a charged compactness of expression, something with such focus that it might indeed pierce. And such density is a hallmark of lyric speech. In a letter to Paul Engelmann, Wittgenstein expanded on the signal virtue of this compression: "And this is how it is: if only you do not try to utter what is unutterable then *nothing* gets lost. But the unutterable will be — unutterably — *contained* in what has been uttered." But how? How does one achieve this meaning-packed density that contains the unutterable without uttering it? It's a deep puzzle. I've encountered apprentice poets who imagine it's done by eliminating articles — 'a' and 'the' — or eliminating punctuation or eliminating the passive voice (sometimes all three). But the problem, as any master poet will tell you, is that there are no universal rules or methods. Each poem must respect its unique subject matter and the unique voice of its human host.

148   The Experience of Meaning

If we are to use language with charged density, one thing we must do is let go of the impulse to explain. When language is used as a vehicle for gestalt thinking, images — or, sometimes, concepts or ideas — may be placed side by side without further explication.

> In a Station of the Metro
>
> The apparition   of these faces   in the crowd :
> Petals   on a wet, black   bough .
> — Ezra Pound

The point is to allow the auditor or reader to perform the gestalt shift on their own. The thinking that the words prompt is wordless, visual.

In this respect, the poem is a linguistic version of the Necker cube:

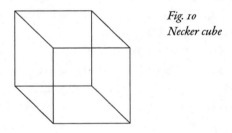

Fig. 10
Necker cube

In the poem, in the cube, distinct gestalts fill the same space; and they do so on the basis of inalienable shared structure.

Inalienable because, without that structure, the thing — the right- or left-pointing box, the apparition of the faces, the petal-laden bough — would not be what it is. The relation between the two gestalts is that of metaphor — which is not, as analytic intelligence would have it, nothing more than a straightforward verbal contradiction with merely phatic content. Or, rather, it *is* a verbal contradiction with phatic content, but the rhetorical emphasis of the analytic view — "nothing more than," "merely" — is wrong. Metaphors make claims that are, strictly speaking, false; but profound metaphors do so in order to point to genuine

The Inscape of Being   149

structural resonance. In metaphoric comprehension, we see x *as* y — see the right-projecting box as the left-projecting box; see the faces as petals. Such seeing-as is not whimsical; in a profound metaphor, it is no more 'impressionistic' than Gauss's recognition that a linear string of integers can be seen as a set of same-summing pairs. It proceeds on the basis of real, though not necessarily describable, shared structure. That structure is crucial to what each thing is; and it is, at the same time, the foundation of the possibility of true, accurate resonance with other gestalts. Haecceity and metaphor have the same ontological root.

ॐ

In order to use language with charged density we must also approach it as a physical medium, as sound.

When we use language as a musical medium, we become alert to sound connections among words — full rhymes, part rhymes, assonance, and alliteration — as well as to connections between the way words sound and what they mean. Lyric language encourages us to attend to silence, too: silence has physical presence in lyric contexts; it shimmers. And we attend to rhythmic patterns. It is frequently at the level of rhythm that lyric language becomes most dense — there are no wasted syllables, there is no meaningless silence. (This does not mean that there is no rhythmic variation: the subtlety and flexibility of free verse lies not in its resemblance to prose, with its absence of a noticeable pulse, but in the non-systematic alternation and mixing of various prosodic feet within the line.) Rhythmic intensity, along with assonance, alliteration, and onomatopoeia, allow lyric thought to *enact* its meaning.

Here's an example:

(1) It was really quiet, but she was starting to enjoy herself, although she was also somewhat creeped out.
(2) The silence slid beneath her skin.

The second sentence has a clear iambic pulse: the *sil*ence *slid* be*neath* her *skin*. The first has none. Noticeable stresses fall on *qui*et, en*joy*, *al*so and *creeped out*, and less noticeable stresses fall elsewhere, but the sentence possesses no obvious rhythmic pattern. The sentence is informative in a

150   The Experience of Meaning

chatty way, but it doesn't *evoke* silence; nor does it convey physical and emotional coolness, as the second does. Now compare the second sentence with a very similar one:

(3) The silence slid under her skin.

It's not as effective. It doesn't convey the sense of slipperiness, the slight eeriness, of the second sentence. Why not? Notice that the last syllable of 'beneath,' *-eath*, sounds like a knife being pulled from its sheath. Neither syllable of 'under' has this kind of enactive sonority. In addition, if you say the two sentences slowly out loud, observing the position of your mouth, you'll find that you say "The silence slid beneath her skin" at the front of your mouth, with your mouth positioned as a rictus. You can't say 'under,' unless you drop your jaw and move your tongue a little way back in your mouth — the sliding sibilance is interrupted. And then there's the rhythm: '*un*der' is a trochee not an iamb. Its presence destroys the smoothness that reinforces the sense of subtle, insinuating movement. (In an attempt to render the third sentence rhythmic, one might read it this way: the *sil*ence slid *un*der her *skin*. But the effect then is not slightly eerie, but slightly comic — at odds with the meaning of the sentence, or at least at odds with the meaning of "the silence slid beneath her skin.")

Let me give an example from a real poem now. These are the opening lines of "Digging" by Seamus Heaney:

Between my finger and my thumb
The squat pen rests; snug as a gun.

Consider the last four words: "snug as a gun." What kind of gun? The monosyllables and the *g* and *u* sounds all by themselves tell us it is a handgun, short and stubby. Would "stubby as a gun" work as well? No. The vowel hasn't changed, the *b* is a dark consonant akin to *g*; but there's that extra syllable, *bee* (spelled '-by'), with its forward, tense vowel, which changes the shape of your mouth as you say it. You can't say "stubby as a gun" without moving your mouth, however fleetingly, into the position of a smile or grimace. "Snug as a gun" accommodates, it invites, the practised impassivity of a hunter. Or a thug.

The Inscape of Being   151

Is the image violent? Not directly in its voicing. The violence is curled within the image, motionless. And consider the *n* sounds, the slant rhyme between *gun* and *thumb*. Compare "snug as a gun" with "snug as a pistol." It's not just the word 'snug' but the physical construction of the lines, the absence of sharp consonants, that suggests a kind of comfortableness, a settledness; 'snug' and 'gun' are experiential as well as alphabetic palindromes.

Well, then, if *n* sounds and the lax, back vowels are part of the power of the line, why not *The round pen rests; snug as a gun*? The pen *is* round, after all; and 'round' is a single syllable like 'squat,' so we wouldn't be changing the rhythm; the *r* alliterates with *rest* and the *oun* extends the *thumb/gun* musical axis. Yet we sense immediately that this substitution would undercut the image rather than strengthen it. Why? It's precisely because the *oun* extends the *thumb/gun* musical axis — it spools out of the *n/ng/m* cluster of the first line in a kind of sing-song. 'Snug' is no longer snug in the line; it becomes the odd syllable out. And now we notice *snug*'s connection with *squat*: a faint but discernible slant rhyme; and how squa*t* and res*ts* are related. Finally, we notice the rhythm. Both lines *can* be scanned as perfect iambic tetrameters; but it's only the first that genuinely exhibits that prosody. Listen to the second line:

The **squat pen rests** [*silence*] snug as a gun.

The strong emphases on each word in 'squat pen rests' — these shut down the iambic movement of the previous line and force a silence before the image of the gun. Notice, too, the pitch. Following the silence, it drops (the shift from the light ě vowel in *pen* and *rests* to the short ŭ in *snug* and *gun*). The entire effect is of ease, understated authority, and deliberate, controlled violence. It is deeply sinister.

Is this the stance an Irish writer in the mid-twentieth century must assume? The poem goes on to meditate on the image of peat-cutters: Heaney's father and grandfather, using their spades. The last three lines of the poem are:

Between my finger and my thumb
The squat pen rests.
I'll dig with it.

152   The Experience of Meaning

This is why the poem is regarded as a masterpiece. Heaney's passionate commitment to Irishness and his equally passionate refusal to take up partisan politics are delineated without a single overt reference to the Troubles. The poem's meaning unfolds viscerally, through the integrity of its music and images. Heaney shows, he doesn't tell.

Here's another example — this time, a whole poem — by Robert Bringhurst:

Poem About Crystal

Look at it, stare
into the crystal because
it will tell you, not
the future, no, but
the quality of crystal,
clarity's nature,
teach you the stricture
of uncut, utterly
uncluttered light.

Figures 11 and 12, on the next page, are attempts to map some of the poem's linguistic music.

The poem enacts the experience of sudden enlightenment: intuition sifting but unfocused, intent gathering, the consonants right, the vowel wrong but finally the mouth finding the right position for the first part of the crucial diphthong, the pressure finally bursting — both unexpectedly and with absolute assurance — into the silence following the arrival of the word "light."

The poem also offers us an image of meditative discipline: those who seek enlightenment must become crystals themselves. To do this, to be emptied of everything except "uncut, utterly uncluttered light," is to undergo severe formation: stricture. Crystals of great size and clarity grow very slowly, in the dark. Thus the moral lesson of the poem is patience: the adept must abandon concern with the future — with crystal *balls* — and inhabit the now. And in a further buried juxtaposition, crystals — enlightened minds — unlike crystal balls — *appear* to be cut; they are cut, as it were, from within. Notice the exact enactive

The Inscape of Being   153

Poem about Crystal

Look at it, <u>stare</u>
into the crystal because
it will tell you, not
the fu<u>ture</u>, no, but
the *q*uality of *c*rystal,
<u>clarity's</u> na<u>ture</u>,
*t*each you the s*t*ric*t*ure
of <mark>uncut, u*tt*erly</mark>
<mark>unclu*tt*ered</mark> light.

L   at *it*
into   ystal
it wi*ll* *t*ell   <mark>not</mark>
<mark>future no but</mark>
*l*ity   ystal [c̄r̄ystal]
[c̄la̅r̄ity's]   <mark>nature</mark>
                    ture
uncut, u*tt*erly
unclu*tt*ered   light
                ah-ee

Fig. 11 (left)   Letters in bold italic are examples of alliterative consonants. Straight and dotted underlines identify two distinct sets of rhyming combinations of vowels and consonants. The gray highlighting identifies a third set.

Fig. 12 (right)   Note the preponderance of lax i vowels (as in 'it') in the first six lines. The poem is also saturated with close configurations of t's and l's (set in bold italic). These are the consonants that frame the final word, 'light,' and both also appear in the key words 'crystal' and 'clarity.' Although 'crystal' and 'clarity' don't rhyme, they do alliterate; indeed, they share all but one of their consonants, as well as the lax i vowel. (The s in 'crystal' is pronounced s; in 'clarity's' it is pronounced z.) Gray highlighting identifies the sound clusters that characterize the poem's fundamental semantic axis. Dotted underlines identify other crucial rhymes.

The vowel in 'light' is a diphthong, the only one in the poem. The first element in the diphthong is very close to the first vowel in 'utterly' and to the first and second vowels in 'uncut' and 'uncluttered.' The second element of that diphthong, 'ee,' rhymes with the final vowel in 'clarity,' 'quality,' and 'utterly' but appears nowhere else in the poem.

multiplicity of the phrase "uncut, utterly / uncluttered": the crystal is not cut, but it looks cut; the words state that it is uncut, but their sound is cutting.

Just as "In a Station of the Metro" presents its two images simultaneously, Bringhurst's poem presents its several meditative strands at once:

it's an extended metaphor. Its lyric meaning resides not only in the individual images themselves, not only in their musical enactment, but in their simultaneity, their multiplicity in unity. It too, then, is a linguistic version of the Necker cube.

Is the Necker cube ambiguous? Yes. But it is not vague; there is nothing indeterminate or fuzzy about it. Its polyvalence is crystal clear. This is true also of well-sculpted lyric thought: multiple, often strictly incompatible, meanings fill the same space, but they do so in utterly distinct and exact ways. This is, in some sense, the core of what analytic thinking can't comprehend about lyric thought. In analytic thought, distinctness requires separability. William Empson famously said, "The machinations of ambiguity are among the very roots of poetry." But Charles Simic put the point more clearly and with the right ontological emphasis: "Ambiguity is the world's condition.... As a 'picture of reality' it is truer than any other. Ambiguity is. This doesn't mean you're supposed to write poems no one understands." "Metaphor," he has also written, "is the supreme way of searching for truth."

æ

How did we come to have two so apparently opposed ways of thinking about the world? The neuropsychiatrist Iain McGilchrist believes they reflect divergent capacities of the left and right hemispheres of the brain.

In *The Master and His Emissary*, McGilchrist draws on an extraordinary range of lesion studies as well as evidence from various kinds of imaging techniques to establish the different tendencies of the two hemispheres. But the first question he asks is why there are two hemispheres in the first place. All brains, throughout the animal kingdom, both vertebrate and invertebrate, have two hemispheres. All these brains display anatomical asymmetries, as well as asymmetries of function, including asymmetries of function that echo those found in humans. This does not mean, McGilchrist is quick to point out, that these functions are completely or simplistically lateralized. What his research shows is that, while both hemispheres are involved in most functions, they are involved in fundamentally different ways. Each hemisphere attends to the world in a distinctive manner. McGilchrist argues that these distinctive

The Inscape of Being   155

forms of awareness are products of evolutionary selection; both modes, he believes, helped us, and helped other animals, to survive.

The smaller of the two hemispheres (usually the left, which controls the right side of the human body) "[pays] narrowly focussed, sharply defined attention" to details of its environment in order to manipulate them — to grab them, to eat them, to thrust them out of the way. "Its aim," McGilchrist says, "is to close down to a certainty and it deals poorly with ambiguity.... [E]lements are decontextualized, seen as more or less interchangeable category members rather than as individuals.... There is an excess of confidence and a lack of insight...." In other words, the left hemisphere doesn't know that there is anything that it doesn't know. Its temporal range is short-term; it analyzes its local environment for immediate use. The left hemisphere's world is the world "of 'me' ... me and my needs, [me] as an individual competing with other individuals, my ability to peck that seed, pursue that rabbit, or grab that fruit." The left hemisphere has no sense of, and thus no interest in, the larger picture in which its focal preoccupations are embedded.

By contrast, the larger of the two hemispheres (usually the right, which controls the left side of the human body) attends to relationships, to patterns of interconnection, to context. Its world is the world at large, the world in which I experience myself "in relation to others, whether they be friend or foe." The awareness of the larger hemisphere is broad, receptive, vigilant and alert for predators, which show up as anomalies against stable or coherent backdrops; at the same time, it is concerned with patterns of association in which we ourselves are closely involved. "Here," McGilchrist suggests, "I may feel myself to be part of something much bigger than myself, and even existing in and through that 'something' ... the flight or flock with which I scavenge, breed and roam, the pack with which I hunt, the mate and offspring that I also feed...."

Or the earth or the sky or the waters of the place I live. In contemporary North America, our relations with others are most often relations with other human beings or their contrivances; and this might tempt us to imagine that the right hemisphere's world was evolutionarily centred on maintaining social relations with others of our kind. Perhaps it was. However, the stories and practices of sustainable cultures show that human relations with nonhuman beings and forces are tremendously significant if one is living close to the land. Relationships with non-human kin may have shaped the right hemisphere's capacities as much as or more than relationships with humans.

"[T]he link between the right hemisphere and holistic or *Gestalt* perception is one of the most reliable and durable of the generalisations about hemispheric differences," McGilchrist notes (citing numerous studies). "The right hemisphere sees the whole, before whatever it is gets broken up into parts in our attempt to 'know' it.... The right hemisphere, with its greater integrative power, is constantly searching for patterns in things.... [I]ts understanding is based on complex pattern recognition."

Emotion, too, is generally the province of the right hemisphere. The right hemisphere is more intimately connected with the evolutionarily ancient limbic system, and it regulates the cortical structures that allow us to be internally aware of our body's condition. The right hemisphere is faster and more accurate than the left at identifying facial expressions, tones of voice, and the import of gestures. It is also crucial to accurate expression of emotion through the same channels. "The one exception to the right hemisphere's superiority for the expression of emotion," writes McGilchrist, "is anger. Anger is robustly connected with left frontal activation." Despite the left hemisphere's generally narrower outlook and involvement with the self, it is the right hemisphere that is responsible for control of emotional arousal, through its regulation of autonomic functions like heart rate and endocrine expression.

How is non-angry, non-self-focused emotion connected to gestalt comprehension? Henri Poincaré argued that the feeling for mathematical beauty, for "harmony of numbers and forms," for "geometric elegance," was emotional; he argued further that it is the foundation of mathematical creativity. Aesthetic emotion, he maintained, sustains and guides the mind in the perception of significant mathematical results, because the most useful results are also often the most beautiful. He described these results as entities that "the mind without effort can embrace [in] their totality while realizing the details." Aimé Césaire, in an echo of this view, says that, in a "climate of emotion and imagination," the poet surrenders language to "the will of the universe"; and the sign that the resulting poem has tracked reality accurately is its beauty. Musical harmonies and melodies — powerful aural gestalts — are also notoriously charged with emotion; indeed, they can feel like descriptions of emotions, or expressions of them that are at least as direct and accurate as physical gestures. Does emotional comprehension underlie all gestalt comprehension? Does every gestalt have an emotional tone? Is gestalt intelligence a species of emotional intelligence? We do not know. What we know is that gestalt comprehension and emotional comprehension are strongly associated in a number of ways, and that they are both strongly right hemisphere dependent.

I suspect that emotions connected with the appreciation of harmony — with fellow-feeling, with the establishment and maintenance of consensual relationship and the coordination of physical activity — do lead and support gestalt comprehension, just as traditional logic leads and supports analysis. (This is not to say that either emotion or logic is always discernible in thinking; the involvement may be faint.) Gestalt thinking *expresses* emotion — when it does — in an attempt to create a field of resonance; it *picks up on* emotion in an effort to co-respond with other minds. 'Positive' emotion, emotion that coordinates individuals with their world, is, I suspect, the right hemisphere's version of language, how it communicates: it evokes and appreciates co-resonance in other beings. (Thus, for example, the way in which music and enthusiastic pleasurable conversation entrain emotional response.) The multiple ways of opening both hand and heart may be to the right hemisphere what analysis is to the left: its way of trying to understand.

Poincaré's observation about the way beautiful mathematical entities allow the mind to embrace totalities and details at the same time leads me to the final characteristic of right-hemispheric intelligence that I wish to discuss. For it is also the right hemisphere that is alive to the uniqueness of individuals. They spring into vivid focus for it; it resists seeing things in terms of categories or generic objects. How is this connected to its other proclivities? McGilchrist says: "[I]t is precisely its capacity for holistic processing that enables the right hemisphere to recognise individuals. Individuals are, after all, *Gestalt* wholes: that face, that voice, that gait, that sheer 'quiddity' of the person or thing, defying analysis into parts."

This claim is remarkable for a number of reasons. It echoes the Gestalt theorists' claim that many kinds of perceptual awareness *start* with wholes, and that parts are abstracted from these wholes — 'sense data'

158   The Experience of Meaning

are not the building blocks of right-hemispheric perception. Second, it sheds important light on two distinct conceptions of wholeness. Abstraction understands wholes as impenetrable lumps, as atoms: the indistinguishable 'uncuttables' of existence. Gestalt thought, by contrast, understands wholes as harmonies, as highly various open-textured individuals. Sometimes what gestalt thought understands is horrific — it correctly senses impending disaster in the trend of events, or it perceives the moral monster beneath a cloak of righteousness. Often, though, the wholes that gestalt thought perceives are experienced as attractive precisely because of their harmonious character. These wholes, or individuals, are also often experienced as fragile: as individuals, they are mortal; their internal harmony can be disregarded; the net of resonant relations in which they exist may be unperceived. Lyric insight may be defined as that species of gestalt comprehension most alert to, most emotionally affected by, the tension between the world experienced as a resonant whole and the world experienced as a colloquy of distinct, mortal beings.

Another neurophysician, Sigmund Freud, also thought that there were two distinct modes of mental functioning. He called them primary and secondary process. Although his understanding of these processes came to be coloured by his purely psychological investigations, it was grounded in his early study of the neurophysiology of eels. His characterizations share significant features with those McGilchrist documents. Primary process thought, as Freud describes it, is highly associative and imagistic; it plays down standard causal connections and emphasizes metaphorical ones; it tolerates paradox and contradiction in the service of metaphor, and it displays little awareness of time. Secondary process thought, according to Freud, inhibits primary process — that's its job, and why it's called secondary process. It is aimed at manipulating the world to ensure satisfaction of desire: its hallmark is syntactically unexceptional language-use; it does not tolerate paradox or apparent contradiction.

Significantly, primary process thought also lacks a sense of self; and this, Freud hypothesized, was the key to the differences between the two systems. (Recall that McGilchrist characterizes left-hemispheric thought as 'me'-thought.) Freud argued that there was a locus of neurophysiological activity at the core of secondary process: he hypothesized that it operated on a hydraulic model of energy transfer to shut down

The Inscape of Being   159

the associative, nonlinear connections of primary process. He called this neurophysiological structure the ego. How or why we experience this neuronal organization as the self is not explained by Freud; but there is now a growing body of evidence that he got the basic idea right. Imaging studies have revealed a neuronal organization that has earned an unwieldy moniker — the default mode network. It appears to act to inhibit freely associative activity in the brain. When its activity is curtailed, subjects report a loss of sense of self. They also report that their experiences are ineffable. The default mode network is not lateralized in the way that, say, Broca's area is lateralized, but preliminary research indicates that "leftward functional connectivity" is greater in fundamental nodes of the network.

Why all this fuss about neurophysiology and neuropsychology? Science, synapses, lab reports, and fMRI data are things analytic, left-hemispheric, secondary process thought feels comfortable with. It's suspicious of psychoanalysis, but it will listen to tales about the dissection of eels. One of my aims is to establish the *reality* of lyric, gestalt-based comprehension for an intellectual culture that has sidelined it for centuries: to establish not only that it is itself a real phenomenon, but that it perceives and understands the real world. We do not stand a chance of producing a viable epistemology, or a viable metaphysics, ontology, or ethics, until we open a genuine dialogue between the two ways of knowing. And the problem is urgent. In the absence of that dialogue, I believe we are fated to continue to ignore the facts of ecological cataclysm and to imagine they'll be fixable by piecemeal measures. They won't be. The fate of the species depends on the left hemisphere coming to the table.

෨

In the context of a discussion about simplicity, I quoted Robert Hass on the minimalist imagism of haiku. His words are relevant to the present discussion, too, and bear repeating:

> Often enough, when a thing is seen clearly, there is a sense of absence about it ... as if, the more palpable it is, the more some immense subterranean displacement seems to be working in it; as if at the point of truest observation the visible and invisible exerted enormous counterpressure.

160   The Experience of Meaning

This is a gnomic observation; one can tell that Hass is trying to get at something that he's finding difficult to put into words. I believe that what he's pointing to is *synoptic* gestalt experience: the seeing of a particular for the unique gestalt that it is and, at the same time, sensing that it is an aspect of a much larger gestalt. In other words, it's an illustration of McGilchrist's claim that the capacity for seeing integrated wholes is a version of the capacity for recognizing unique individuals. Or, to reverse the polarity: the capacity for perceiving particulars as the particulars they are is a function of the capacity for perceiving large, integrated, non-analytically-structured gestalts. Poincaré's description of what's involved in the perception of beautiful mathematical entities — the simultaneous embrace of totalities and details — relies on the same kind of awareness. The capacity for synoptic gestalt experience is, I believe, key to understanding the relationships among lyric poetry, lyric philosophy, and spiritual insight — their differences as well as their similarities. Before attempting to summarize those relationships, though, I'd like to offer some more descriptions of the experience.

Jane Hirshfield calls it "concentration":

> By concentration, I mean a particular state of awareness: penetrating, unified, and focused, yet also permeable and open.... Aldous Huxley described it as the moment the doors of perception open; James Joyce called it epiphany. The experience of concentration may be quietly physical — a simple, unexpected sense of deep accord between yourself and everything. It may come as the harvest of long looking and leave us, as it did Wordsworth, amid thought "too deep for tears."... Concentration can also be placed into things — it radiates undimmed from Vermeer's paintings, from the small marble figure of a lyre-player from prehistoric Greece, from a Chinese three-footed bowl....
>
> ... [T]here may be some strong emotion present — a feeling of joy, or even grief — but as often, in deep concentration, the self disappears. We seem to fall utterly into the object of our attention, or else vanish into attentiveness itself.

Hirshfield has trained for many years in the Buddhist tradition. Tim Lilburn trained in a different tradition, that of Ignatius, but he, too, sees fundamental connections between poetry and what he calls contemplation. He also sees fundamental connections between "ecstatic appetite" and desire to fully perceive "individuality":

> More than any other speech, poetry is tolerant of a nostalgia for Paradise.... Its vector and velocity is desire leaning into the [unlanguageable] individuality of things; poetry is the artifact of this desire. Around everything is an epidermis of narrative, a layer of hypotheses, orders, causal grids by which the world is rendered intelligible. Poetry's fundamental appetite is ecstatic; its curiosity yearns beyond this barrier of intelligibility to know the withinness of things.

Elsewhere, Lilburn characterizes the substance of contemplative life as "a light, mobile transfixity" and says:

> My hunch ... is that contemplation and poetry do not share an identical telos, but that what both want strikes each as the same — as quintessentially compelling and as unutterable.... [T]he deeper into the practice you travel, the emptier you become.... Contemplation and poetry are forms of knowing where the knower and her powers are first shaved by the world then are swallowed by the world.

The mind of concentration placed into things, ecstatic vision leagued with the perception of utter individuality: a similar kind of synoptic gestalt experience is the foundation of a great deal of Rainer Maria Rilke's poetry. Recall the conclusion of "Archaic Torso of Apollo":

> Otherwise this stone would stand defaced, cut off
> under the shoulders' diaphanous plunge,
> and wouldn't shimmer like the pelt of some wild beast;
>
> and wouldn't burst from all its boundaries
> like a star: for there is no place
> that does not see you. You must change your life.

The poem is about seeing a particular so clearly that we see *through* it to the immense resonance of the world as a whole. Rilke called this kind

162   The Experience of Meaning

of seeing *einsehen* — 'seeing-into.' We experience vision that is eyeless, itself a form of light, light in which we ourselves are seen, that is, embraced, and to which we must respond — with which we co-respond. The radiance is a resonance that sets everything ringing. In experiencing it, we *realize* it: we, just like the headless torso, become an embodiment of the world's resonance.

In lyric awareness, we don't know at arm's length, we know *as* part of a larger whole. The 'I' is, and yet it isn't, too; it has undergone immense subterranean displacement. Both it and the particular to which it attends have become the dimensionless meeting points of their respective relata — like the nodes of an immense, flexing geodesic sphere.

In conversation with Mark Doty, an unnamed interlocutor remarks on the connection between the last line of Rilke's poem and the penultimate line of the poem "The Fish" by Elizabeth Bishop. "You get there [to the awareness Bishop describes]," the interlocutor says, "by acutely paying attention to the thing.... that same vivid attention ... all of a sudden blossoms into this bigger sensation."

In the poem, Bishop has just caught a "tremendous" fish and is holding it half out of the water beside the boat. Her description is a string of extraordinary similes and metaphors evoking an ancient scarred beauty: full-blown roses stained with age, rags of green weed; she imagines the flesh packed in like feathers, looks into the yellow eyes, their irises backed with tarnished tinfoil:

> They shifted a little, but not
> to return my stare.
> – It was more like the tipping
> of an object toward the light.

Then she sees, hanging from the fish's great lip, five old pieces of fishline, the hooks all grown firmly into its mouth. The poem concludes:

> Like medals with their ribbons
> frayed and wavering,
> a five-haired beard of wisdom
> trailing from his aching jaw.
> I stared and stared
> and victory filled up

the little rented boat,
from the pool of bilge
where oil had spread a rainbow
around the rusted engine
to the bailer rusted orange,
the sun-cracked thwarts,
the oarlocks on their strings,
the gunnels — until everything
was rainbow, rainbow, rainbow!
And I let the fish go.

What is the victory here? It isn't letting the fish go, much less catching it. It is the vision of everything — old, cracked, rusted, like the fish — illuminated from within, it is being itself restored to vision through seeing what the fish is. It is the recognition that beauty and its promise of renewal are quick now, here, now, always.

Anyone familiar with the work of Mary Pratt will recognize the same kind of ontological attention at work in her paintings. Particulars leap off the canvases, shaking with the enormity of their existence.

(above) Mary Pratt: *Salmon on Saran;* *(opposite, above)* Mary Pratt: *Eggs in Egg Crate;* *(opposite, below)* Mary Pratt: *Roast Beef*

It is no accident, I think, that the things that arrest Pratt's attention are dead, eviscerated, used up, a kind of invisible domestic matériel; that Bishop's fish is near dead, scarred and damaged; that Rilke's Apollonian torso is ancient, broken and apparently inert: these, even these, if we attend in the right way, are saturated — we reach for the word, the paradox almost silencing us — saturated *with life*.

Like Rilke, Bishop is changed by her seeing: she feels victory in having landed the unlandable fish, but the vision of the fish's reality is even more powerful — she lets it go. In all such cases, this change *in us* is the litmus of truth. We see this in Tolstoy's portrait of Pierre Bezukhov, whose moment of spiritual insight on the frozen march from Moscow altered the course of his life. Skepticism is the philosopher's worry that maybe reality is all just in our heads, a projection of cultural bias, or, in the fully consistent case, a single brain hallucinating in a vat. On its own grounds — the contextless, arm's length discourse of rational analysis — skepticism is indefeasible. But gestalt experience shows those grounds to be incomplete. This — this *this*ness, this haecceity — is real; that it is real is the most obvious thing about it. That's why we have to change our lives.

ᴆ

Pratt's ecstatic vision, Bishop's ecstatic vision, Rilke's *einsehen*, Lilburn's erotic attention to the "withinness of things," Hirshfield's "concentration," Hass's "point of truest observation" — all, I believe, are versions of what Gerard Manley Hopkins called the perception of inscape.

Inscape is the shape a thing takes on because of what Hopkins called its *instress*, its vibrant interior structure. The best example I can think of comes from hockey. Hockey is a very fast-moving game; to the uninitiated it can appear chaotic. Wayne Gretzky, the highest scorer the National Hockey League has ever known, was renowned for his ability to sense the order inside the chaos. He could pick up on a game's instress and, as a result, was able to skate off to the place the puck *was going to be* five seconds later. Hopkins claimed that really to know what a thing is is to sense its inner order, its developing pattern of interior relations.

What must be underlined here is this: when we see into a thing, we perceive the inalienable structure that makes the thing what it is — its

166   The Experience of Meaning

"sheer quiddity," in McGilchrist's phrase — *which structure is also* the foundation of the thing's genuinely resonant relations with other things. Seeing-into has the same ontological root as seeing-as. In seeing-as we sense how the instress of one thing resembles the instress of another. When we see into a thing, we press more and more deeply into its in-scape, we sense more and more the complexity of its instress.

But the more sheer the quiddity, the greater the pressure from the other side, as Hass would say. Dennis Lee writes:

> How did I
> miss it? that
> haltingly, silently,
> stubbornly, home,
> each mortal being announces the pitch of itself
> in a piecemeal world. And
> here! it was always here, the living coherence.
> Not abstract harmonies but, rather, that
> each thing gropes to be itself in time and what is lovely
> is how, once brought to a pitch, it holds & presides
> in the fragile hum of its own galvanic being.
> And more: as it persists it tunes to
> every thing that is, neither in outright
> concord nor yammer but half alive on
> all those jumbled wave-lengths,
> inciting a field of near-coherence
> in the spacey surround.
>
> One luminous deed, amid the daily
> gumbo of motives; a well-made
> journey, or tree, or
> law; a much-loved parent, the fullness of grief —
> whatever: let that
> flourish in its completeness,
> and every nearby thing begins to
> quicken, tingle, dispose itself in relation,
> till smack in the clobber & flux,
> coherence is born ...

The Inscape of Being

To perceive inscape is, I suggest, to experience the resonance of being — all motions arising from its inner relations — *in* a particular thing.

And the inscape of being itself? We might say it is a Very Large Gestalt. The gestalt of gestalts, the coherence of coherences.

"In all ten directions of the universe," as Ryōkan says,

> there is only one truth.
> When we see clearly, the great teachings are the same....
> Look: this ball in my pocket:
> can you see how priceless it is?

ès

Earlier, I mentioned the crucial role of crystal-clear ambiguity in gestalt thought. Here's another example:

道可道非常道

名可名非常名

dào kě dào fēi cháng dào
míng kě míng fēi cháng míng

Dào that can be dàoed is not Dào.
Name that can be named is not name.

These are lines of poetry, but they are also the opening sentences of one of the seminal texts of lyric philosophy, the *Dào Dé Jīng*. Philosophy, generally, may be defined as 'thinking in love with clarity.' Lyric philosophy is philosophy that is also driven by profound intuitions of coherence. Lyric thought understands clarity as resonance and is willing to override at least some of the protocols of logico-linguistic syntax in order to achieve it. The opening lines of the *Dào Dé Jīng* exhibit extreme compression, both musically and in the form of apparently incompatible gestalts that arise simultaneously: the gesture consists of language used to undo language. Not, as Eliot would have it, the articulate raid-

168   The Experience of Meaning

ing the inarticulate, but the other way around: wordless thought using words for its own ends.

Here's another example from a canonical text of lyric philosophy, this time one of the closing propositions of Wittgenstein's *Tractatus Logico-Philosophicus*, §6.522. The sentences are not as musically charged as the very last proposition — "Wovon man nicht sprechen kann, darüber muß man schweigen" — but their verbal gestures are nonetheless overtly lyric.

Es gibt	*There are*
allerdings	*indeed*
Unaussprechliches. Dies	*unspeakables. This*
zeigt sich, es ist	shows *itself, it is*
das Mystiche.	*the mystical.*

I've laid the passage out as free verse to point some of the emphases and to give a sense of its tone. Note the preponderance of one-syllable words (in a language famous for its polysyllabic constructions): the claim announces itself as one that stands forth plainly. The striking exception to the short one-syllable words is *Unaussprechliches* — which is a part rhyme with *Mystiche*. *Es gibt* is a part rhyme with *es ist*, and an echo of *es ist* occurs palindromically in *Mystische*. The vowels and consonants of the second sentence are, with the exceptions of *zeigt*, closely related: *Dies/das*; *ies/sich/es/ist/ys/tich/e*. It is not, I believe, an accident — or if it is, it is an unaccountably happy one — that *zeigt* shares its vowel with *schweigen* ("be silent"), the final word of Wittgenstein's book, which arrives three propositions later. (To say that it is not an accident is not to claim that Wittgenstein himself deliberately contrived the echo.)

And here is a third example from the lyric philosophical canon — Herakleitos' Fr. 1 — which uses both linguistic music and etched ambiguity to carry its gestalt:

τοῦ δὲ λόγου τοῦδ' ἐόντος αἰεὶ ἀξύνετοι γίνονται ἄνθρωποι....

tou de logou toud' eontos aiei axunetoi ginontai anthrōpoi....

[of the logos which is forever unaware are born humans....]

*The Logos is eternal
but men have not heard it
and men have heard it and not understood.* (Guy
  Davenport)

*Although this account holds forever, men ever fail to
  comprehend....* (Charles Kahn)

What is the relation between lyric poetry and lyric philosophy? In many cases, I think they're indistinguishable. This becomes especially apparent if we draw a distinction between poetry and what we might call versifying. Versifying involves laying language out in strict patterns of metre and rhyme; Hallmark greetings are good examples, but so are many fine pre-twentieth-century poems in numerous European languages. Versified language, too, can be lyric when it enacts lyric comprehension. But when the patterns are forced, where language has been squeezed into a prosodic corset, it rarely dances with life. The versification turns out to be merely an aid to memorization or, sometimes, an end in itself. There are many instances of linguistically musical utterance that are not versified, whose images-cum-concepts trace and evoke ontological resonance. These might be laid out like free verse, or even rhymed verse; or they might be laid out like prose — as Wittgenstein laid out his aphorisms, and as editors have laid out the fragments of Herakleitos that have come down to us. Even when they're laid out to look like prose, though, the sentences of Wittgenstein and Herakleitos don't strike us as standard prose. Their voicing is powerfully enactive, and their structure is often aphoristic. Like lyric poems, they set things side by side without much explication, compelling readers actively to discern the intended gestalt.

Still, the intuition persists that there is *some* difference between lyric poetry and lyric philosophy. I think it comes to this: At one end of the spectrum — where we find a high concentration of lyric poetry, and also lyric visual art — there is gestalt thinking that focuses on the perception of being's resonance *in* particulars. It concerns itself with *seeing into* the inscapes of individuals. At the other end of the spectrum — where we find a high concentration of lyric philosophy — there is gestalt thinking that concerns itself with *seeing through* individuals to a Very Large

Gestalt, to the inscape of being-as-a-whole. In both cases, the thinking points to the same phenomenon — the interdetermination of haecceity and the world. It's just that the emphasis is different. In the middle of the spectrum, lyric poetry and lyric philosophy overlap: the work speaks both to the inscapes of particulars and to the immense inscape of which particulars are aspects.

And spiritual insight? It is rooted in exactly the same phenomenon. Its distinguishing characteristic — to the extent that it has one — is its deep focus, its simultaneous concentration both on individuals and on being-as-a-whole. It gazes from the inscape of being-as-a-whole into the particular, while gazing through the particular into the inscape of being. Arne Næss spoke of a process he called "precisation" — the discrimination and refinement of parts within a gestalt — which can be followed by re-integration of the precised parts in a new comprehensive gestalt. The result is deepening awareness of the gestalts of the parts as well as the gestalt of their whole. Another way to speak about spiritual insight is to say that it perceives, with ever-increasing clarity, an enormous range of these sub- and super-ordinate gestalts.

Just as lyric poetry and lyric philosophy overlap, so both overlap with spiritual insight. Because of its scope, spiritual insight is especially hard to wrangle into words. In the Western European tradition, it has often been more comfortable using music as its medium of communication; but it frequently resorts to poetry or lyric prose. Or it simply keeps its mouth shut and becomes manifest in a form of life. There are also works that appear to possess the deep ontological focus I've described, but which are not lyric in form — the theological writings of the Franciscan friar Richard Rohr, for example.

Asking for hard and fast criteria that will allow us to distinguish whether, in any given case, we're dealing with lyric poetry, lyric philosophy, or spiritual insight is like asking for criteria that will allow us to distinguish every instance of prose from every instance of free verse. Such criteria can't be had. I'm told they can't always be had in biology, either; or linguistics. I suspect that most classificatory schemes are, in at least some respects, approximations. It is the demand for exceptionless criteria that appears to be the problem. What is the origin of this demand? Its root is the same as the root of skepticism about the existence of a mind-independent world: the need never to be mistaken.

The Inscape of Being   171

What we can say about lyric poetry, lyric philosophy, and spiritual insight is that they are distinguishable — when and if they are distinguishable — by characteristic emphases of attention. More important, however, is that a single kind of intelligence is active in all three. The ontological structures that kind of intelligence evolved to comprehend are real and, as its presence in science and mathematics demonstrates, it informs thought even in the inner precincts of technocracy.

This may seem to be an attempt to secularize spiritual insight, to sever its connections with organized religion. I don't wish to refuse connections with organized religion, but I propose, in keeping with a version of Perennialism, that religions are the iconographic clothes in which a culture traditionally dresses spiritual insight. They are neither the body of such insight nor its ground. Its ground is the kind of awareness we find in Edward Thomas's portrait of Morgan Rhys:

> He went seldom to a chapel, and when he went, did something more than escape boredom, by the marvelous gift of inattention which enabled him to continue his own chain of thought or fancy from beginning to end of the service. He was quite unhindered by hymn, prayer, or sermon, and accepted what he heard, as elderly persons accept fairies, without even curiosity....
>
> When a child of five he had been left alone for half a day in a remote chamber of a great house, and at nightfall was found sitting at a window that commanded an orchard and a lawn, and when he did not rise to greet his friends, and was questioned, merely said "Look!" Nobody could see anything, or rather, they saw everything as usual; nor could he explain.... [H]e admitted that he was intoxicated by the mere trees and the green lawn. In the same way he was often found listening to silence....
>
> ... [H]e valued poetry not so much because it was full of music for ear and spirit, though that he loved;... [but] because it revealed to him the possibility of a state of mind and spirit in which alone all things could be fully known at their highest power....
>
> One evening he came into the farmhouse in deep excitement because (as he said) he had been part of the music of the spheres. He had walked through village after village, over the mountains and along the rivers, under great motionless white clouds. The air

had been so clear that every straw of the thatch gleamed separately. He had passed through the lonely places with a sense of passing through a crowd because the rich spring air had been so much a presence.... He had looked at the sky, the flushed mountain sheep, the little stony lanes that led steeply up to farmyard and farm, the jackdaw making suitable music high up in the cold bright air, the buzzard swirling amidst the young bracken, and he had approved, and had been approved, in ecstasy.... Thus he spoke in ejaculations, to our great joy.... [And when] he became silent ... for a time the whole world shimmered and darkened as if it had been some tapestry which Rhys had made. The most pious member of the party, a Christian if ever there was one, remarked that he "wished he had felt like that sometimes." To which Rhys replied that he could not possibly wish that, as he would then be damned like himself: and the other agreed.

Let me stress again that there is nothing fantastical or inexplicable about spiritual insight. The capacity for such insight is continuous with the capacity for gestalt understanding of any sort. What *is* remarkable is the aggressive neglect of this capacity by technocratic culture. This neglect reveals itself not only as deafness to poetry and blindness to environmental crisis; it has penetrated deeply into many aspects of our intellectual, moral, and political lives and become part of our self-understanding. It reveals itself further in the fact that technocratic culture regards all claims to spiritual insight as delusional.

Such claims are not universally delusional. The ontological insight that underlies many of them is quite real. Such insight evades routine description; but so, it turns out, do gestalt insights of almost any level of complexity. The reasons for taking the pan-cultural core of broad, intense ontological insight seriously are as good as the reasons for trusting computer programs to accurately calculate load, or lift, or sheer: gestalt intelligence evolved, just as analytic intelligence did, as a successful way of negotiating reality.

It would be pointless to hope for universal enlightenment; we need to remember that even the saints could not sustain it. We're human — we have our talkative, self-preoccupied, analytically oriented other halves. What we can do is respect lyric intelligence, strengthen and cultivate it as an instrument of discernment; we can use it to sense shapes emerging in the swirl of cultural change and disintegration, and to honour the individuals and landscapes that are dying; and we *must* use it to remind ourselves that, however dark the times, there is always cause for celebration and joy. *This* being, *this* one — and this, and this, and this! The extraordinary music of existence, which, as long as there is something rather than nothing, sounds through each of us.

❧ Appendix
A Few Outstanding Questions

In what is now his best-known essay, "Untersuchungen zur Lehre von Gestalt," Max Wertheimer formulated a number of 'factors' or 'principles' that cause arrays of distinct objects to be perceived as single things or wholes. He mentions the following:

- proximity (proximate objects will be seen as a single 'thing');
- similarity (similar objects will be seen as a single 'thing');
- common fate (objects moving together will be perceived as a group or thing, as in marching bands or flocks of starlings);
- *Einstellung* or set (consider a set of variations on a pattern; it turns out that the order of presentation of the variations can influence whether or not the pattern is perceived in certain of the variations);
- good continuation or direction (regular, continuous patterns without sharp interruptions, both visual and auditory, are perceived even when proximity or similarity would suggest a different grouping);
- 'good curve' (this appears to be a subspecies of the more general factor of good continuation);
- symmetry and 'inner equilibrium' (also mentioned in connection with good continuation; Wertheimer specifies that symmetry is "by no means simply an 'equality' of components");
- closure (discontinuous contours are often perceived as 'whole' shapes);
- habit or past experience (we see what we've been conditioned to see).

Wertheimer also mentions, midstream between common fate and *Einstellung*, a factor he calls *Prägnanz* — a word that means, roughly, *fullness of meaning*. (Sometimes it is translated as 'pithiness.' Michael Wertheimer and K.W. Watkins offer 'salience.' Willis D. Ellis leaves the word in the original German.) The idea is this: Given an array, a 'good' gestalt of it, Wertheimer argued, will be one that is as simple, orderly, coherent, unified, *et cetera*, as possible. Some Gestalt theorists, like Wolfgang Metzger and Friedrich Wulf, regarded *Prägnanz* as the overarching principle to which other factors contribute. In addition to the factors mentioned or described by Wertheimer, Metzger discusses several others, including simplicity, enclosedness, and having a common centre.

Wertheimer offers numerous examples to illustrate the various factors. Although these examples are compelling, Wertheimer's discussion reveals an issue that his own work was unable to resolve. In situations where more than one factor is in play — most real-world situations — it is extremely difficult to determine in advance which factors will dominate. Wertheimer discusses examples that involve both proximity and similarity, and also an example in which 'good curve' pre-empts closure, but he draws no principled conclusions that can be applied to all situations. The 'laws' of his title turn out to be tendencies in, rather than determinants of, gestalt perception. This raises the question of whether *specifiable* necessary and sufficient conditions exist — or if real-world cases are simply too complex. Can we predict without knowledge of context which tendencies will dominate? Even with detailed knowledge of context, can we predict with certainty? What, exactly, is the relation between the factors, such as they are, and the principle of *Prägnanz*? And how, for example, do the factors illuminate the notion of a simple proof in mathematics? Are we to consider a flock of starlings 'orderly'? Lab work done by Wertheimer and Metzger in the 1920s and '30s focused almost exclusively on simple visual stimuli; some auditory correlates of visual phenomena have been established, but little work has been done since on other sense modalities or on coordinated sense modalities, let alone on complex thought.

Wertheimer did not pretend all the problems with Gestalt theory's fundamental re-formulation of epistemology had been solved: "My terms should not give the impression that the problems are settled; they themselves are loaded with — I think — [the very kinds of] problems

176   Appendix

[I am trying to draw to your attention]." He repeatedly called for further rigorous investigation. But Gestalt theory did not capture the postwar North American intellectual imagination. Wertheimer's inability to produce a major book may have been an exacerbating factor; but it is not the main reason. His colleague Wolfgang Köhler was a fluent writer and an articulate lecturer who published a number of well-regarded books. Kurt Koffka's work at Smith College had a significant influence on the development of James J. Gibson's views. The problem was not an absence of credible exponents. The problem was, and still is, the phenomena themselves. Laboratory investigation may help us to describe gestalt perception and comprehension in more detail, but it will never successfully *reduce* them to forms of analytic comprehension. What makes an analysis an analysis is that the parts it identifies are not interdefined.

Over the last three decades, laboratory research in the US has focused on ways in which language-use appears to interfere with gestalt perception and comprehension. In 1990, Jonathan Schooler and Tonya Engstler-Schooler published the initial paper on a phenomenon they called 'verbal overshadowing.' They described experiments in which subjects had been asked to describe the individual features of faces they had seen or to use an Identi-Kit to reconstruct those faces. These subjects proved less successful at recognizing the faces in subsequent trials than controls who had not been asked to describe or otherwise analyze the faces. Schooler's and Engstler-Schooler's results substantiated some earlier studies that had shown similar effects, particularly a study by Roy Malpass that had sought to establish effective ways of improving face recognition, only to find that training subjects to characterize aspects of faces verbally actually reduced their capacity to remember them.

Schooler and his associates have gone on to investigate the possible interference of verbalization on other phenomena, including (but not exhausted by) colour recognition, bi-stable configurations like the Necker cube, memory of visual images, grasp of analogies, and subsequent satisfaction with aesthetic judgments. A 1995 study that Schooler co-authored with Joseph Melcher, "The Ineffability of Insight," is especially interesting. It explores the difference between analytic problem solving — where solutions depend on "a stepwise set of logical arguments" — and insight, which Schooler and Melcher define as "the sudden solution to a problem that one has been working on without

A Few Outstanding Questions   177

any sense of progress." Among other things, Schooler and Melcher attempted to determine if 'non-reportable' processes were involved in insight by asking subjects to think aloud while they tried to solve various problems. They found that if the problems involved analysis, thinking aloud had no effect on success, whereas if the problems involved the restructuring of gestalts, chances of success were diminished. Subjects working on insight problems were much more likely than subjects working on analytic problems to say that they just weren't able to keep talking about their thought processes. They were also much more likely to report that they had reached an impasse. How the impasses were overcome was not clear — to anyone. In another series of experiments which attempted to correlate the capacity for insight with ten other 'cognitive measures,' the single best predictor of insight performance turned out to be the ability to recognize out-of-focus pictures.

For a period, Schooler was at the centre of a controversy over the repeatability of his results. But in 2014, a very large, multi-site replication study was released, confirming unequivocally that verbal overshadowing exists. Since then, Schooler has been attempting to draw attention to the so-called 'decline effect' — the fact that often, surprisingly often, initial findings are not confirmed by subsequent attempts to replicate them. It is important to note that it's not just Schooler's results, nor even just results in psychology, that show the decline effect. The problem appears to afflict many branches of science. Schooler is to be commended for his insistence that the problem requires attention from all scientists. It is far from clear what underlies it.

There remains the vexed issue of the metaphysical status of gestalts, a problem that Max Wertheimer recommended we avoid. Is the world that we perceive mind-independent, or isn't it? We shouldn't be trying to address of this question, Wertheimer claimed, when what we need are *facts* about how perception works. But what are facts? Are they real things 'out there' in the world, or are they mental entities 'here inside' our heads? Lab research isn't going to solve this problem, and ignoring it isn't going to make it go away. All serious philosophical inquiry, in all traditions, in ethical, aesthetic, and religious matters, as well as in epistemology and metaphysics, involves, somewhere along the line, an attempt to address the question *What is a gestalt?* Versions of this question include: *Are facts distinct from values? What is the nature of reality? What is truth? How can I be certain?*

The last version is the one that has dominated Anglo-American epistemology since the Enlightenment. Instead of asking whether certainty is possible or needed, this tradition assumes that certainty is available and inquires only how to get it. It has proposed two answers: skepticism about the existence of an 'external world' which, when pursued rigorously, leads to solipsism; and reductionism, the idea that if we analyze a situation into its component parts, and then analyze those parts into their components, and then analyze those components into their micro-components, and so on, and on, we will eventually arrive at a point where analysis must stop. "There! *That's* brute reality!" The problem is that all attempts to find separate, indivisible particles of brute reality have so far failed, both in physics and in psychology. Are there ultimate uncuttables? Who knows. It's time to ask ourselves why we *need* them to be there.

I've suggested that we and other living beings negotiate the world by reading it. I do not mean by this that the world consists of, or is wholly conditioned by human language. Nor do I mean that all perception is perception of an unfolding sequence, such as a sentence or a melody. What I mean is that it's not just in ambiguous figures like the duck-rabbit and the Rubin vase that the concepts of perception and conception cross. They are indisseverably present — perhaps indistinguishable — in everything we intuitively count as perception.

Another way to put this is to say that perception is not generally the two-stage process that reductionist epistemology claims it is. What we intuitively count as perception doesn't consist of registering 'raw' data and then transforming that data into something meaningful. When the process *is* two-stage, it's because perception isn't working. When we are initially confused or uncertain, when we have to struggle to make sense of a situation, we are *aware* of two stages. When our attempts to discern a gestalt are unsuccessful, when we're forced to register impressions that strike us as meaningless, we feel uncomfortable. We say things like "I can't see what's going on!" That is: we claim that our ability to perceive is being thwarted. When our ability to perceive is not being thwarted,

A Few Outstanding Questions   179

we have no sense of a stage in which we lack a gestalt. Not even for a split second.

What about gestalts like sentences or stories that 'take time' to perceive? Aren't stages involved in those cases? In the beginning, and then, and then...? This is a challenging question. For melodies, those archetypal gestalts, are also sequenced. No one disputes that melodies are apprehended as wholes; they are not experienced as distinct notes with plus signs between them. It is possible to play a series of individual notes and experience it as just that: a series of individual notes. Nonetheless, the order of the notes in a melody surely matters. If we mix them up, we get a different melody — or a series of individual notes. How, then, do we comprehend orders as wholes? I don't know; but there's reason to think that such comprehension may not have anything to do with time. Order also matters in the Gauss problem: the numbers must form a sequence. (The sequence doesn't have to be 1, 2, 3, ... 100; it can be 3, 6, 9, ... 60 or −2, −4, −6, ... −248; but it can't be 1, 73, 12, 50, 13.) Yet the Gauss problem, famously, has an apparently instantaneous solution.

One striking thing about sequenced gestalts whose comprehension appears to require time is that their basic form is aural, not visual. Both stories and melodies now have written instantiations in many cultures, but they can happily dispense with their visual clothing and continue to exist. Do aural gestalts depend on time in a distinctive way? Humming a melody 'takes time'; so does listening to one. But this is time registered by the clock. We look up from our engagement with music or a story — whether we're reading or playing or singing, or listening, or watching and listening, as at a play, or dancing — and are astonished to find that time 'has flown.' Melodies and narratives have shapes; it is those shapes we've grasped when we're confident we can sing or retell them. Sometimes, independently of the gestalt's sequenced or unsequenced structure, we perceive complex, multiple resonances altogether, in a flash; and sometimes understanding, like the dawn, comes slowly. Is it ontologically, metaphysically, or epistemologically significant that some gestalts take us more clock-measured time to absorb than others? I suspect not, but that's only a guess. (*What then is time? If no one asks me, I know; if I want to explain it to a questioner, I do not know.*)

Although in saying that all perception is a form of reading I'm construing reading in a broad sense, I wish nonetheless to focus briefly on what is involved in reading written language. It's useful to consider this

180   Appendix

narrow case because a reductionist account of what's going on can seem especially plausible. The lessons it can teach us have wide application.

Take Pound's poem "In a Station of the Metro." The reductionist will urge that the images of faces and petals are *interpretations*: 'interior,' 'subjective,' 'mental constructs' provoked by what's 'really out there,' namely, a bunch of squiggles — the glyphs of which the written text is composed. These glyphs are, in and of themselves, meaningless, the reductionist maintains, and must be *transformed* into meaningful images by the alchemy of 'consciousness'; once they have been transformed by the alchemy of consciousness, the black squiggles have a different metaphysical status. They've become mind-dependent; and they are therefore, according to the reductionist, less real.

It's true that the squiggles are really out there. But so are the images of the faces and the petals. What the reductionist account misses is that to perceive the glyphs *as glyphs* is also to perceive gestalts. A person who can read does not see meaningless black squiggles *at any point* in her encounter with a text. (More on this in a moment.) It is also true that something is not perceived until it is perceived. But this doesn't mean that if it isn't perceived, it doesn't exist (the crime that was covered up for decades — or is still covered up); nor does it mean that when it *is* perceived, it's just 'all in our head' (the crime again). (Does the tree falling out of any being's earshot in the woods make a sound? If you define sound as 'the sensation produced through the ear,' as the *Concise Oxford Dictionary* does, then of course not; if you define sound as 'vibrations causing sensation that can be detected by the ear,' which the *Concise Oxford* offers immediately after the first definition, then of course it does.) To insist that the squiggles are 'more real' than the images because they are in some sense less 'mental' is to assume reductionism is true rather than to demonstrate that it is. "But anyone can see the squiggles! Not everyone can read them!" Reading is indeed an acquired skill. Anyone can see that the sun moves across the sky. Does it follow that that's what's 'really out there' — a bright hot disc arcing over motionless earth?

Reading — of any sort: written language, spoken language, tones of voice in a conversation that's too distant for us to make out the words, ocean currents, the weather, the health of a patch of shortgrass prairie — involves the perception of gestalts. When we are acquiring skill in reading, we do first have to learn some basics. In the case of learning to read written language, we learn to recognize (not to interpret, to recognize)

A Few Outstanding Questions   181

the gestalts of characters (alphabetic letters, in many scripts; syllabic letters in some; what are called 'logograms' — *zi* — in Han Chinese). After that, we learn to recognize the gestalts of words, usually by sounding them out if the script is alphabetic or syllabic, or by rote memorization if the script is logographic. And finally we learn to recognize the larger gestures made by concatenations of words. (See J.L. Austin's *How to Do Things with Words*, as well as Wittgenstein's *Philosophical Investigations*.) But once we are proficient at reading we cannot, without considerable effort, recapture what it's like to see a page in a language we can read the way someone who cannot read sees the same page. As Simone Weil says, a fluent reader experiences meaning "reaching immediately into her mind ... without her participation, as sensations seize us."

Weil also notes that when one is proofreading, "it is necessary to force oneself to read a different meaning, not that of words or sentences, but that of letters of the alphabet, without completely forgetting the first [namely, words and sentences]." This is another way to put the key point. Arne Næss would couch it in yet other terms: the gestalts of glyphs, characters, words, sentences, images, gestures are sub- and superordinate with respect to one another. Whether one is reading letters of the alphabet or sentences, one is grasping gestalts. Grasping them directly, not decoding them, or deducing them, or figuring them out.

If fluent reading of texts were a kind of reverse analysis — a remarkably speedy version of first recognizing characters, then recognizing words, then interpreting the concatenations of words — proofreading would not be the challenge that it is. Word-processing programs, whose crucial sub-routines can be fully analyzed into discrete steps, are flawless proofreaders — up to a point. Humans, on the other hand, hve no truoble readinq stait thorough eggegrius ty:pos. Humans can also spot solecisms, infelicities of style, that no program has yet been able to detect.

The images of the faces and the petals in Pound's "In a Station of the Metro" do not behave like 'mere interpretations.' There is no effort, no puzzling over what could be meant, no sense the evidence is insufficient. Nor are there clear candidates for other readings. (Compare "Her hesitancy might be interpreted as disinterest, but it's possible she was just nervous" and "The first line of Pound's poem might be interpreted as an evocation of an image of faces in a crowd, but it's possible that what he hoped we'd see is a bunch of table napkins.") If we're forced to ana-

182   Appendix

lyze the images, to articulate their shared features, we will — if the lab reports are anything to go by — become less good at recognizing them and less responsive to the resonance between them. Those abstracted features are the 'mere interpretation'; *they* are the invention, the projection of analytic intelligence.

If a piece of writing is inept, either in its physical execution or in its command of language, we often do have to guess at its meaning. We have to interpret it. Where the meaning is complex (because the images are deliberately ambiguous, say, or because the story involves multiple perspectives or episodes), we may need to re-read several times, to live with the piece of writing, to savour it or converse with others about it, before its full richness becomes present to us. This can happen with brilliantly dense haiku as well as thousand-page novels. But such re-reading and savouring is not the same as puzzling over execrable handwriting or bad grammar; nor does it involve the projection of a meaning that 'isn't really there.' Some pieces of writing have no meaning; in some the meaning is confused, or poorly realized, or undercut by an unacknowledged agenda. These, too, are real features of real texts, and being able to read allows us to discern them. I don't wish to deny that human beings do, frequently enough, project; they incorrectly attribute meanings (or attribute incorrect meanings) to gestures, to sentences, to works of art, to passing remarks on the street. That is: human beings are capable of misreading. What we must notice is that in at least some situations we can tell that we have (or someone else has) misread. We can distinguish projection from accurate perception.

The test of an experience of meaning — its force, its intensity — is the way in which we ourselves are changed by what we perceive. (When we're projecting, that's often what we're trying to avoid: being changed.) Touching meaning, being touched by it, shakes us up. In the case of the Necker cube, there is that slight startle, a moment of astonishment, as the gestalts shift for the first time. A similar sensation of astonishment does not occur when we force ourselves to view the figure as a meaningless array of lines; the effort brings no reward, no sense of recognition.

This is true also of the *phi* phenomenon. There, the perception of a single moving light affords no surprise; nothing about it draws our attention, nothing fixes the experience indelibly in memory. What surprises us, what is memorable, is the demonstration that the experimental apparatus contains no moving light, but only two lights that flash on

A Few Outstanding Questions   183

and off in sequence. This demonstration, however, does not register as an "Aha!"; it registers as a "Huh?" or a "Whoa!" And this reaction shows not that we've perceived something 'more basic' than our original gestalt, but that we've encountered a gestalt that we can't coordinate with the rest of our experience. We then have to figure out what to let go of: the new evidence, the old evidence, or the whole shebang.

When we can dismiss the hypothesis that the experimenters are quickly switching out the apparatus to confound us; when we move back and forth between the apparatus and the precisely positioned chair, observing that when we're just a bit to one side of it or behind it, there appear to be two flashing lights — we are then in a position to conclude that our perceptual experience from the vantage point of the chair is not reliable. But notice that we don't then say that the two flashing lights are 'more basic'; we say that our perception of a single moving light is flat-out *wrong*. Where gestalt perception is wrong — from the *phi* phenomenon to the terracentric universe — we don't cease using it in order to perceive the truth (or truths). We shift to a larger gestalt that coordinates both the earlier mistaken gestalt and other, equally powerful gestalts that contradict it. When we can't find such a gestalt, we experience puzzlement, frustration, bewilderment, or worse.

Is the world that we perceive mind-independent, or isn't it? Are the gestalts that we perceive really 'out there,' or not? Our answer will depend on the depth of our need for certainty and the degree to which we feel required to affirm the existence of things other than ourselves. Reductionism has been unable to demonstrate the existence of brute, 'ungestalted' atoms of perceptual experience. If we also reject the skeptical position — which assures us of certainty, since nothing exists but our own momentary experience — we are left with something like the following: Since we and other beings demonstrate the capacity for accurate gestalt perception in a wide variety of situations, evolutionary theory suggests that such a capacity must be adaptive; if the capacity is adaptive, what it registers is real; ergo, gestalts must be mind-independent. At least, they are as mind-independent as it gets. *How* mind-independent is mind-independent reality? No physicist or philosopher has been able to propose a fully satisfactory answer to this question. Like Wertheimer, I propose to leave it open.

NOTES

"WHAT IS GESTALT THINKING?"

page 3

Frege 1956: 289, 290, 291, 292. (In Strawson: 17, 19, 20.)

Quine 1970: xi.

Haack 1978: 3.

page 4

The word Gestalt ... *came to prominence in German philosophy ... with the work of Christian von Ehrenfels*: Edmund Husserl, Alexius Meinong, and Carl Stumpf also made significant early contributions to the early development of Gestalt theory. See "Gestalt Theory: An Essay in Philosophy," the first chapter of Smith 1988, for an overview.

page 5

Mitchell Ash speculates: See Ash 1995: 405–12.

"There are contexts ...": Wertheimer 1925a: 43.

"parts do not become parts ...": Wertheimer, Michael 1980: 213, my emphasis.

page 6

as Aristotle might say: Aristotle: *Physics* II.7 198b2–4.

the details of [Aristotle's] views are notoriously difficult to pin down: For a clear overview of the issues, see Ainsworth 2016.

"Piecewise" methods ... have obscured what any intelligent unschooled *child can see*: Wertheimer, Max 1959, "The Area of the Parallelogram": 13–78, esp. 17, and "The Famous Story of Young Gauss": 108–42, esp. 117. For 'piecewise' see Ellis's abridged translation of Wertheimer 1925a, 2.

we have so profoundly committed ourselves to an erroneous view of what the facts must be: For a provocative diagnosis of what might underlie this cultural commitment, based on contemporary neurophysiological research, see McGilchrist 2009, especially Part I.

the socio-political wing of Wertheimer's project: For Wertheimer's writings on social and political issues, see Part 1 of Henle 1961. For his critique of educational theory and practice, see Wertheimer, Max 1959; the introduction gives an overview of his critique, and he there lists the chapters of the book that pursue it in more detail.

page 7

"concrete scientific work": Wertheimer 1925a: 43. Similar sentiments appear in the introduction to Wertheimer, Max 1959.

quip attributed to Oscar Wilde: For an exhaustive discussion of the attribution, with detailed bibliographic references, see https://quoteinvestigator.com/2015/10/25/comma/.

page 9

structure is real: See previous reference to Aristotle on page 6.

page 10

The Gestalt school rejected ...: For a summary of the views that the Gestalt school rejected, see the introduction to Metzger 1936 (English translation: xv–xxv). Metzger's Idealist conclusions (xxv) were not advocated by other major Gestalt theorists, most notably Köhler.

page 11

what Max Wertheimer called the phi *phenomenon*: Wertheimer, Max 1912b: 186 (English translation: 23). D. Brett King and Michael Wertheimer state that he called the phenomenon "by the Greek letter phi, φ, for 'phenomenon'" [King and Wertheimer 2005: 100]. 'The phenomenon phenomenon' doesn't make much conceptual sense, however, especially given that 'phenomenon' (or *Phänomen* in German) is here being used to mean 'object of study.' I speculate that Wertheimer used the letter φ to recall the Greek word φαίνομαι (*phainomai*), which was a verb meaning 'appears.' In other words, Wertheimer was attempting to create a shorthand for the phenomenon of *apparent motion*.

page 12

"so-called genius": Shahn 1957: 21.

What single-digit integer is contained in this figure?

The figure appears in Köhler [1929] 1930: 155.
Necker cube: See Necker 1832.

page 13

    Rubin vase: After Rubin 1921: Fig. 3 [p. 249].

page 14

    Proof of the Pythagorean Theorem: The Pythagorean theorem states that for any right triangle, the square on the hypotenuse equals the sum of the squares on the other two sides. The visual proof offered here depends on seeing that the two large squares are both identical in area: both have sides of length $a + b$. Then we notice that within each large square are four identical triangles with sides a, b, and c. If we subtract these triangles from the first large square, we have a single square, with sides of length c, built on the hypotenuse of the triangle with sides a, b, and c. If we subtract the four identical triangles from the second square, we are left with two squares, one built on the shortest side of the right triangle, a, the other built on the second-shortest side, b. The area of these two squares added together must equal the area of the single square in the first triangle, because the large squares are equal in area and the same areas — those of the four identical triangles — have been subtracted from each.

    "[m]any of our concepts *cross*": Wittgenstein [1958] 1972, II.xi: 211; see also 197 and 199.

    Recent neuropsychological research confirms: Spillman 2001: 138.

    the traditional distinction between sense perception and thought: The distinction has been active in Western European philosophy since Parmenides. It has been questioned in various ways since Kant, who proposed that there is no such thing as naïve perception — the mind actively structures all experience. Many thinkers in the phenomenological tradition start from this premise and some, like Husserl and Merleau-Ponty, have been actively interested in Gestalt theory. Phenomenology, however, rejects the view that we are aware of a robustly mind-independent world; and because I am morally and politically committed to that view, I have not pursued phenomenological versions of Gestalt precepts.

page 15

    Sartorius says: Sartorius 1856: 12. (English translation: 4.)

page 16

    50 times 101 is 5,050: Wertheimer notes that there are alternate non-piecemeal solutions and recounts one offered to him by a twelve-year-old. Wertheimer, Max 1959, "The Famous Story of Young Gauss": 112.

    Poincaré's famous description: Poincaré 1929: 387.

    Newton's equally famous account: See Stuckeley 1752: 15 recto.

Kepler's vision of the relations of the planetary orbits: Kepler [1596/1621] 1981. The appearance of the polyhedral hypothesis has many of the classic features of a gestalt shift: Kepler had been puzzling over the problem for some time, but the idea came to him "by a certain mere accident" [*leui quadam occasione propius*] during the course of a lecture in July of 1595. (65/64) "What delight I have found in this discovery I shall never be able to express in words." [*Et quidem quantam ex inuentione voluptatem perceperim, nuquam verbis expressero.*] (69/68) As E.J. Aiton writes, "Almost all the astronomical books written by Kepler (notably the *Astronomia nova* and the *Harmonice mundi*) are concerned with the further development and completion of themes that were introduced in the *Mysterium cosmographicum*. The ideas of this work did not constitute just a passing fancy of youth but rather the seeds from which Kepler's mature astronomy grew. When a new edition was called for, he decided against changing the text itself, for a complete revision would have required the inclusion of all the main ideas of his other books." (29) (Aiton refers his readers to Kepler 1937: 8, 10.)

page 17

"I stand at the window and see a house ...": Wertheimer, Max 1923: 301. Translation by Willis D. Ellis in Ellis 1938: 71.

gestalts, once comprehended, are hard to undermine: On the incorrigibility of gestalts see Lorenz 1959: 153–4. (In English translation: 312–13.)

page 18

it is just the answer Aristotle gave: Aristotle: *Nichomachean Ethics*, Book, §§1–4.

Wertheimer had a series of conversations with Albert Einstein: "Einstein: The Thinking That Led to the Theory of Relativity" in Wertheimer, Max 1959: 213–33.

"*These thoughts,*" *Einstein said*: Wertheimer, Max 1959: 228, n7. A letter from Einstein, printed as an appendix to Jacques Hadamard's 1949 essay *The Psychology of Invention in the Mathematical Field*, repeats the claim that Einstein made to Wertheimer that he very rarely thought in words [Hadamard 1949: 142–3]. In the letter, Einstein adds: "The ... elements [of thought] are, in my case, of visual and some of muscular type. Conventional words or other signs have to be sought for laboriously only in a secondary stage." [143]. In the main text, in a section entitled "Words and Wordless Thought," Hadamard includes testimonials from Francis Galton to the same effect. [66–71, esp. 68–71.] He also notes the tendency among philosophers to assume that all logical thought must be in words. [95–96]

page 19

Konrad Lorenz claimed: Lorenz 1959: 154. (For this and subsequent references in English translation: 313–15. Translations in text by Zwicky.)

"sensitivity to self-observation": Lorenz 1959: 154.

"Rationally controlled attention ...": Lorenz 1959: 154.

Lorenz quotes Goethe: Lorenz 1959: 155. *Faust: Teil II*, Dritter Akt, Vor dem Palaste des Menelas, lines 8691–2.

"the innumerable, multi-directional relationships" and "linear, temporal sequence of spoken language": Lorenz 1959: 155.

a failure of memory: Lorenz 1959: 155.

Jonathan Schooler ... contends: See Appendix for references and more detailed discussion.

the thinking *that produces the poem does not occur ... in words*: See, for example, Bringhurst 2009a, "Everywhere Being is Dancing, Knowing is Known": 15–16; Domanski 2006: 15; Lee 1998, "Poetry and Unknowing": 180; McKay 2001, "Baler Twine": 26; Page 2007, "Traveller, Conjuror, Journeyman": 47.

page 20

"Wertheimer's [manner of speaking] ...": Aldrich 1946: 1471. I am indebted to D. Brett King and Michael Wertheimer, in King and Wertheimer 2005, for drawing my attention to this review, and for suggesting that Wertheimer had anticipated and replied to Aldrich's complaint. (See Appendix, pages 176–7.)

POETRY AND MEANINGLESSNESS

page 22

Epigraph: ALL CARDS, REMOVE YOURSELF: This poem originally appeared in Murdoch 2011. Murdoch, it should be noted, is not a defender of flarf. This poem is an experiment, an attempt to come to grips with the genre. Murdoch put it together by collating phrases that were turned up by a Google search of "the maps are wrong." He says, "[I] tried hard to make it [the piece of flarf] mean something, to be personal, lyrical even, but it won't be going in the big red folder."

page 25

"a little pop in [the] mind": Sharon Mesmer, quoted in Fischer 2009.

Flarf got started: This account is taken from Fischer 2009.

Notes to pages 18–25   189

page 30

Fresh is always fresh: Roo Borson, personal communication.

page 31

P.K. Page insisted on drawing a distinction: Page drew this distinction during a poetry reading in Victoria, BC, sometime in the early 2000s. It echoes the distinction T.S. Eliot draws between verse and poetry in his essay "Rudyard Kipling" (Eliot 1957: 240). But although Eliot draws the distinction in order to credit Kipling with achievements beyond mere verse, he does not attempt to define the two terms.

"I am far from sure ...": Page 2007: 3.

you can walk the path: Robert Bringhurst, personal communication.

page 32

Epigraph: "Sometimes we go into a man's study ...": Ludwig Wittgenstein, quoted in Janik and Toulmin 1973: 207. (From Toulmin's notes for the academic year 1946–47.)

page 36

"memorable speech": Auden and Garrett 1938: v.

page 39

"In sense perception ...": Weil [1947] 1988: "L'attention et la volonté," 197.

Epigraph: "We must not insist on knowing ...": Hopkins 1959: 267.

page 40

Frye ... it is better to expand literary taste than to restrict it: "On the ethical level we can see that every increase in appreciation has been right, and every decrease wrong: that criticism has no business to react against things, but should show a steady advance toward undiscriminating catholicity." Frye 1957: 25.

page 42

T.S. Eliot refused to draw the distinction ... in prosodic terms: Eliot 1930: 8–9.

page 43

what Dennis Lee has called 'pointing': Lee 1998, "Body Music": §§ 26 –31.

page 49

Epigraph: "At the burial of an epoch ...": Akhmatova [1973] 1997: first stanza of "In 1940."

τὸ γὰρ αὐτὸ νοεῖν ἐστίν τε καὶ εἶναι [*to gar auto noein estin te kai einai*], *said Father Parmenides*: Coxon Fr. 4; Diels-Kranz, Fr. 3.

page 52

As I argued earlier: See *There is no one thing a poem means!*, pages 32–5.

page 53

Knowledge ... is always a function of the interpenetration of facts and character: See Heiti 2018 for a detailed discussion.

page 54

Hopkins called character inscape: Hopkins 1959: from 1868 on *passim*.

Hopkins describes: Hopkins 1959: "melodious," 11 July 1868: 172; "slow tune," 14 March 1871: 205.

page 55

"that unified complex of characteristics ...": W.H. Gardener, quoting W.A.M. Peters, S.J., in Hopkins [1953] 1981: xx. Gardener cites W.A.M. Peters, S.J., *Gerard Manley Hopkins: A Critical Essay towards the Understanding of His Poetry*, OUP, 1948, without giving a page number.

"But *instress* is not only the unifying force *in* the object ...": W.H. Gardener in Hopkins [1953] 1981: xxi.

page 56

"Walked down to the Rhone glacier....": Hopkins 1959, 20 July 1868: 178.

Hopkins says it's better to be alone: Hopkins 1959, 25 July 1868: 182.

"with a companion ...": Hopkins 1959, 12 December 1872: 228.

page 58

"The ashtree ...": Hopkins 1959, 8 April 1873: 230.

SIMPLICITY AND THE EXPERIENCE OF MEANING

page 59

Simplicity is frequently touted as an ideal in art, mathematics, and the sciences: Examples will be offered as the discussion proceeds. See also the note to page 71 below.

page 60

Wittgenstein called it Sehen als: "seeing-as": Wittgenstein [1958] 1972, Part II Section xi.

Gerard Manley Hopkins called it the sensation of inscape: Hopkins 1959, 1868–1875 passim. See, for example: 19 July 1868; June (later), 1871; 19 July 1872. See also W.H. Gardner's introduction to Hopkins 1953: xx–xxi.

Plato described it as κατ᾽ εἶδος λεγόμενον [*kat' eidos legomenon*]: "understanding according to a form that collects particulars into a unity": *Phaidros* 249b.

the old Taoists called it awareness of zìrán (自然): "self-evidencing": See Ames 1986: 341. "[Things that are 'self-evidencing'] are self-disclosing within the conditions of their unique contexts, and cannot be explained fully by appeal to principles independent of them. Significantly, given the intrinsic relatedness and interdependence of particulars, the 'self-evidencing' of any one particular requires the 'self-evidencing' of its environing conditions."

page 61

"[F]orm is not just the intention of content ...": Shahn 1957: 70.

It served Mies van der Rohe as a motto: See, for example, http://ca.phaidon.com/agenda/architecture/articles/2014/april/02/what-did-mies-van-der-rohe-mean-by-less-is-more/. Or Mertins 2014.

Browning 1855: line 78.

as old as Hesiod: *Works and Days*, line 40: νήπιοι, οὐδὲ ἴσασιν ὅσῳ πλέον ἥμισυ παντὸς [*nēpioi, oude isasin hosoi pleon hēmisu pantos*]: "Simpletons, they have no idea how much more the half is than the whole."

"The enormous, endless bivouac ...": Tolstoy [1869] 2007: 1020.

page 62

"In captivity, in the shed ...": Tolstoy [1869] 2007: 1060.

"almost unchanged in his external ways": Tolstoy [1869] 2007: 1104.

"much simpler": Tolstoy [1869] 2007: 1105.

"Formerly he had been unable to see ...": Tolstoy [1869] 2007: 1104.

page 63

"Often enough, when a thing is seen clearly ...": Hass 1984: 274–5.

Næss points out: Naess 1973, Point 6. This essay has been much anthologized and is readily available on line.

page 64

Wittgenstein claimed: Wittgenstein 1980: 34. (In Wittgenstein's remark, the last lines are rendered "Each minute and unseen part, / For the gods are everywhere.")

"[V]ery nearly the whole of the higher artistic process ...": Cather 1920: 102.

page 65

the effect of presenting the ... visual proof of the Pythagorean theorem on page 14 and saying simply "Behold!": It is reported that Baskārā, in the twelfth century, did just this; the truth, however, is a little less dramatic. See Brahmagupta and Bhāskara 1973 §§146–7.

"January 16 was a holiday ...": Hass 1984: 274.

page 66

"Paul Erdős, the great twentieth-century mathematician ...": Wikler Senechal 2008: xiii.

"Since I had become acquainted with Euclid's proof ...": Koestler 1954: 351–2.

pages 68–9

what Næss called subordinate and superordinate gestalts: Næss 1995: 243.

page 69

To paraphrase the homespun philosopher: For a version of this possibly apocryphal figure, see Hawking 1988: 1.

nobody understands quantum mechanics: Feynman 1994: 122–3.

to understand *something just is to perceive its relevant structural similarity.… The perception of telling similarity is the litmus*: Wertheimer, Michael 1985, esp. 24; Wertheimer, Michael 1980, esp. 210 and 230–1; Wittgenstein [1958] 1972, §151.

page 70

it may have been a concern with cosmological clutter: Copernicus argued that his system was to be preferred to Ptolemy's because it had fewer spheres: Copernicus [1543] 1978: 20, lines 43–8. The problem was, and Copernicus came to see this, that his system actually required more epicycles than Ptolemy's. See Koestler [1959] 1989: Part III, Chapter 2, "The System of Copernicus."

Aristotle said: Aristotle: *Metaphysics* A: 980a21–981a7. The participle usually translated "to know" in Aristotle's famous opening line — "All men naturally desire to know" — is εἰδέναι, a word that connotes seeing that something is so, that is, 'getting it.' This kind of knowing, based in experience, is the foundation of τέχνη, or art, which is described a few sentences later as "a grasp of those similarities in view of which they are a unified whole" (trans. Richard Hope in Aristotle 1975).

the so-called Law of Prägnanz … *the 'factors' remained tendencies*: See Wertheimer, Max 1923. The Appendix provides a summary of Wertheimer's discussion as well as references to discussions by other Gestalt theorists.

it isn't, as Poincaré notes, any odd or bizarre combination: Poincaré 1929: 386.

page 71

Great physicists and philosophers have argued that the big cosmological picture has to be simple: Or, in some cases, as simple as possible. See, for example:
Aristotle: *On the Heavens* I.4 271a33–4 ("God and nature create nothing that is pointless," trans. J.L. Stocks in Aristotle 1984); *Posterior Analytics* I.25 86a34–5 ("Let that demonstration be better which, other things being equal, depends on fewer postulates or suppositions or propositions," trans. Jonathan Barnes in Aristotle 1984);
Ptolemy *Almagest* III.1 ("We consider it appropriate to explain the phenomena by the simplest hypotheses possible, in so far as there is nothing in the observations to provide a significant objection to such a procedure," trans. Gerald Toomer);

medieval axioms cited by scholars from Odo Rigaldus through Duns Scotus and Ockham (for example: "A plurality is not to be posited without necessity" and "It is useless to do with more what can be done with fewer"; see Maurer 1984 for an overview);

Thomas Aquinas, *Summa Theologica*, Part I, Q 2, Third Article, Objection 2 ("it is superfluous to suppose that what can be accounted for by a few principles has been produced by many," trans. Fathers of the English Dominican Province);

Nicolaus Copernicus, as mentioned above in the note to page 70;

Isaac Newton, Rule 1 at the opening of Book III of *Principia Mathematica* ("We are to admit no more causes of natural things than such as are both true and sufficient to explain their appearances. To this purpose the philosophers say that Nature does nothing in vain, and more is in vain when less will serve; for Nature is pleased with simplicity, and affects not the pomp of superfluous causes," trans. Andrew Motte in Newton 1803: Vol. II, 160);

Albert Einstein in Einstein 1959 ("conceptual systems ... aim at greatest possible sparsity of their logically independent elements (basic concepts and axioms)," trans. Paul Arthur Schilpp, 13);

Richard Feynman in Feynman 1994 ("It always bothers me that, according to the laws as we understand them today, it takes a computing machine an infinite number of logical operations to figure out what goes on in ... a [tiny] region of space.... So I have often made the hypothesis that ultimately physics will not require a mathematical statement ... and the laws will turn out to be simple." 51–2).

page 72

Jonathan Schooler's work in experimental psychology: See Appendix for references to Schooler's own work and to research by his associates.

Schooler cites mid-twentieth-century studies ... whose results were subsequently overlooked: Belbin 1950 and Kay and Skemp 1956.

uses up time that might otherwise be devoted to 'visual encoding': Bahrick and Boucher 1968 and Nelson and Brooks 1973.

caused them to focus on schematic aspects of pictures: Pezdek et al. 1988.

the negative effects observed were anomalous: Woodhead, Baddeley, and Simmonds 1979.

training may need to be more intensive: Ellis, Hadyn 1984. Ellis is clear, however, that face-recognition involves gestalt perception (13, 35), and that it is extremely difficult both to maintain the image of a face in memory and to 'decompose' it in order to extract information from it (35).

"verbal processing has been assumed to be the 'deepest' ...": Schooler and Engstler-Schooler 1990: 67.

PLATO AND GESTALT OR WHY THERE IS NO THEORY OF FORMS

page 75

"There is not, nor will there be ...": Plato *Letter VII*, 341c–d.

page 76

Some, like Wolfgang Köhler: The view, in its most succinct form, is stated in Köhler 1969, "Gestalt Psychology and Natural Science," esp. 65–6. Elsewhere, Köhler says, "I share the opinion of those who contend that all [psychological] phenomena without any exception are the correlates of somatic processes in the nervous system." (Köhler [1938] 1959: 70) For a more detailed discussion see Köhler 1920; an English translation of a portion of the introduction to this book may be found in Arnheim 1998.

Others, like Wolfgang Metzger: Metzger 1936, "Einleitung: Überblick über die Geschichte der Lehre vom Sehen": vii–xvi, esp. §3. (Spillman [2006] 2009, "Introduction: Overview of the History of Visual Theory: xv–xxv.)

He explicitly divided the problem into two parts: See, for example, Wertheimer, Max 1959, "The Famous Story of Young Gauss" §III: 120–1.

"freely, open-mindedly" *and* "inner relation": Wertheimer, Max 1959, "The Famous Story of Young Gauss": 121.

page 77

"illuminating and making transparent essential structural features ...": Wertheimer, Max 1959, "The Famous Story of Young Gauss": 121.

"Solve the problem without counting.": Wertheimer, Max 1959, "The Famous Story of Young Gauss": 110 and 112.

he then offered cases for comparison: Wertheimer, Max 1959, "The Famous Story of Young Gauss": 121.

or he asked leading questions: Wertheimer, Max 1959: 40, n10.

Often, Wertheimer noted, young children who had not been thoroughly schooled: Wertheimer, Max 1959, "The Famous Story of Young Gauss": 117. See also Wertheimer, Max 1959, "The Area of the Parallelogram": 17.

Köhler in "What Is Thinking?": Köhler 1969, 133–64.

The first stage he called elenkhos,... *The second,...* dialektikē: References to both occur throughout Plato's corpus. See, for example, *Sophist* 230b–d and 253d–e, where the *elenkhos* is described as "the greatest and most efficacious of purifications" and dialectic is described as the method of collection and division. In *Meno*, following the *elenkhos*, at 80d–81e and in *Protagoras*, at 348c–d, Socrates is made to emphasize the conversational, truth-seeking nature of philosophic enterprise, although the word 'dialectic' does not occur in either passage. A similar emphasis occurs at *Republic* 539a–d. See also *Letter VII*, 344b–c.

Plato defined the method of collection and division: *Phaidros* 265d–e.

page 78

Plato does provide some examples: See fourth note for this page.

Konrad Lorenz, however, is more vocal: Lorenz 1959. Lorenz's suggestion that inductive hypotheses are not random evokes Plato's own 'method of hypothesis,' referred to in both *Meno* and *Republic*. Plato, however, gives so few details that there is no consensus either on what the method was or on its relationship to the method of collection and division.

"Of myself …": Lorenz 1971: xxii–xxiii.

Plato shows the method of collection and division in action: angling: *Sophist* 218e–221c; sophistry: *Sophist* 221c–223b, 222c–226a, and finally 264e–268d; statecraft: *Politikos*: a summary of the lengthy initial discussion is given at 267a–c; madness: *Phaidros* 244a–245c and 249d–e.

an abstract summary of the method that includes brief examples: *Philebos* 16d–17e.

indications that the hierarchies can be remade: *Sophist* 223c–226a, for example.

biologists actively involved … say: Dr Curtis Björk, University of British Columbia, Beaty Biodiversity Museum, personal communication.

page 79

his characters complain explicitly: See *Sudden Insight After Much Hard Work*, below, pages 84–6.

teaching employs analogies and leading questions: The use of analogies combined with the absence of procedural rules is especially striking. Cf. Wittgenstein [1958] 1972, §127: "The work of the philosopher consists in assembling reminders for a particular purpose" (trans. Anscombe). Cf. Weil 1970: 270: "There is a pitfall here for the human mind, which constitutes the *essential* difficulty (and which Descartes failed to see).… If there is a remedy, it consists in substituting *series* in place of *generalizations*."

page 80

Early in Politikos, *there is a methodological digression*: 263a–c.

it is never mentioned again: Though Socrates does complain about people who go about the matter improperly at *Politikos* 285a–c, and reiterates his lack of interest in talking further about how to go about things correctly.

196   Notes to pages 77–80

page 81

"the paper is frequently referred to ...": Michael Wertheimer in Wertheimer, Max 1959: 260, note to title.

In a paper ... published in 1912: Wertheimer, Max 1912a. The quotation that follows is drawn from pages 346–7; in Ellis 1938: 270–1. I rely here on Ellis's perspicacious rendering of Wertheimer's prose, but have, in places, silently added punctuation in an attempt to make the thought clearer.

page 82

Again, in a paper published in 1923: Wertheimer, Max 1923. A summary of his discussion is provided in the Appendix.

Wertheimer's ... 1912 ... research into apparent motion: Wertheimer, Max 1912b.

page 83

Wertheimer's discussion mentions: Wertheimer, Max 1923: *von Ehrenfels*, 165 (English translation 4); *what's going on in the eyes*, 246 (English translation, 75); *speculation regarding wholistic processes*, 251 (English translation, 78).

Kepler's sudden vision: See previous note to page 16.

Lorenz also mentions the "fundamental incorrigibility" of Gestalt perception: Lorenz 1959: 153. (In Lorenz 1971: 312.) Lorenz's citation for the incident reported by Alexander Bavelas appears in Lorenz 1959 on page 165. It reads:

> Bavelas, A., "Group Size, Interaction, and Structural Environment." Group Processes, Transactions of the Fourth Conference, 1957, The Josiah Macy Jr Foundation, New York.

The citation is, however, incorrect. Bavelas did lead a seminar with this title at the 1957 Josiah Macy Jr Foundation conference on group processes, and the issue of randomness was broached; but there was no discussion of experiments or their aftermaths. None of the other four volumes of proceedings contains a description of the incident, though in Volume 11, the proceedings for the 1955 conference (published in 1956), Bavelas evinces an interest in the subject of randomness during both H. Blauvelt's and William J.L. Sladen's seminars. I conjecture that Bavelas reported the incident that Lorenz describes, and did so at the conference, as Lorenz indicates; but that the discussion occurred when the tape recorder was not running. I have not found a report of the experiment in the papers by Bavelas that I have been able to locate, but I am not confident that I have been able to locate everything he published. I would appreciate hearing from anyone who knows more.

page 84

"immortal discourse": *Phaidros* 277a.

ἐπιστήμη (epistēmē) — *a term Plato often uses for comprehension of forms*: See, for example, *Meno* 85c or *Republic* 534a. But Plato himself says that the vocabulary should not be regarded as technical (*Republic* 533e). And at *Republic* 511d–e, for instance, the term he uses for comprehending forms appears to be νόησις (*noēsis*); this usage is echoed in *Timaios* (see fourth note for this page). In *Politikos*, at 258e, ἐπιστήμη is the term used for all knowledge, which is then divided into two parts, practical knowledge and "solely" intellectual knowledge, for which the term μόνη γνῶσις (*monē gnōsis*) is used. At *Phaidros* 247d–e, ἐπιστήμη also appears to signify all knowledge, and knowledge of forms is described as ἐπιστήμη ἀκήρια (*epistēmē akēria*) — knowledge that is pure in the sense of being untouched or undefiled.

ἐπιστήμη *is defined as "conception of the soul ...*": *Definitions*, trans. D.S. Hutchinson, in Cooper 1997: 1683, col. 1 (414b–c).

"immovable by persuasion": *Timaios* 51e.

"the starting point of knowledge": *Definitions*, trans. D.S. Hutchinson, in Cooper 1997: 1682, col. 2 (414a).

Plato's Lecture on the Good: Aristoxenos, *Elements of Harmony* II.30–1 in Findlay 1974, Appendix I: 413.

not what is likely, *but what is conceptually* necessary: See, for example, *Symposium* 200a–b.

page 85

"Only the *result* of the organizing process is usually experienced": Köhler 1969, "What Is Thinking?": 163–4.

"Only with much hard toil ...": *Letter VII*, 344b–c.

The need for hard work: *Parmenides* 133b and 135a–c, as well as 137c ff; *Symposium* 210a–e; *Sophist* 217e–218a; *Politikos* 257c–d. See also *Republic* 494d, 503e–504e.

"[The young boy] asked ...": Wertheimer, Max 1959, "The Famous Story of Young Gauss": 112.

page 86

"I certainly don't know how to do *that*": Wertheimer, Max 1959, "The Area of the Parallelogram": 47–8. Ivana Marková provides a summary of historical and contemporary discussion of the suddenness of insight in Marková 2005, §2.1.1: 40–8.

"When someone has reached this point ...": *Symposium* 210e.

there is scholarly debate about whether it is genuine: See, most notably, Tarrant 1983.

page 87

ῥέω *occurs there twice*: *Theaitētos* 205d–e.

Fowler: Plato 1921.

Levett and Burnyeat: Cooper 1997.

Cornford: Cornford [1935] 1960.

Morrow: Cooper 1997: 1659.

Bury: Plato 1929: 531.

the claim that knowledge of the forms is strictly ineffable ... is not supported: Cf. Findlay 1974: 301.

page 88

as Arne Næss would say: Næss 1995: 243. See also pages 68–9.

the special offices of the Like and the Unlike: *Sophist* 254d–257a. In biology, it is bacteria that effect the sharing of genetic material between species that are not related to one another according to the clad structure of the midscale macro-evolutionary tree.

We have independent confirmation of his interest in eros *and erotics from Xenophon*: *Memoirs* 2.6.28; 3.11.16; 4.1.2. *Symposium* 8 *passim*. Charles Kahn notes that the "theme of Socratic *eros* ... is the topic most fully represented" in the material that survives from other writers of Socratic dialogues. (Kahn 1996: 4).

page 89

ground of philosophical insight: I use 'ground' here rather than 'object' because I am sympathetic to Francisco Gonzalez's suggestion that the forms are in fact the conditions of possibility of intelligible discourse [Gonzalez 2002]; and for that reason, like 'logical form' in Wittgenstein's *Tractatus*, inarticulable.

What we love when we're embodied: *Phaidros* 246a–253c.

we find excited puppyish play: *Republic* 539b, echoed at *Philebos* 15e.

'*directedness*': "Gruppe einer Richtung" in Wertheimer, Max 1923: 322.

"*a place toward which the attention is attracted*": Wertheimer, Max 1912b, in Wertheimer, Max 2012: 76.

a fundamental feature in Einstein's thinking: Wertheimer, Max 1959, "Einstein": 228, n7; also 231.

it constitutes the moral foundation of all scientific activity: Wertheimer, Max 1934 in Henle 1961: 28.

"Just as a task, a problem situation …": Wertheimer, Max 1959; "The Famous Story of Young Gauss": 141–2.

page 90

"Why do such revolutions …": Köhler 1969, "What Is Thinking?": 164.

truth connotes wholeness: The English word 'whole' is etymologically related to 'health.' In Arabic, the words for truth and health have the same root.

"that relationship to the things themselves …": Wertheimer, Max 1934 in Henle 1961: 28.

page 91

Plato is usually credited with a 'two realms' doctrine: See *Phaidros* 246d–247e or *Timaios* 51d–52b, for example. Some commentators, however, have questioned whether Plato really believes there is a 'place' in which forms exist. See Gonzalez 2002: 31–83, esp. 36–9 and n45.

Aristotle escaped: See page 6 and notes thereto.

page 92

a grumpy essay from 1929: Lund 1929.

"The Gestalt … is assumed to be of non-empirical origin …": Lund 1929: 320.

page 93

I take the objections as read: One significant objection should be that there's a passage in *Theaitētos* that appears to articulate the central claim of Gestalt theory — that wholes are distinct from the sums of their parts — only to deny its validity: 204a–205a. I would reply that I trust Cornford's reading of this passage. He argues that it's not actually about the central claim of Gestalt theory. Theaitētos' *intuition* is roughly that claim, but the view that's actually on trial is a strictly aggregative one. Socrates is arguing that the *aggregative* view *defines* things as sums of parts and therefore has no room for Theaitētos' intuition. See Cornford [1935] 1960: 149.

Another objection concerns the roles that ἐπιστήμη (*epistēmē*) and νόησις (*noēsis*) play in Plato's discussion of forms. Does he use them in a technical sense? The Divided Line passage (509d–511e) in *Republic* suggests that νοῦς (*nous* – a form of νόησις) may indeed be a technical term. But I've argued earlier that we should take Plato at his word: he did not intend to develop technical vocabulary. (See the note regarding ἐπιστήμη (*epistēmē*) on page 84.) This doesn't mean that there isn't *preferred* vocabulary; it means only that we can't conclude from the way a term is used or defined in one dialogue, or even one passage, that it is being used in *exactly* the same sense in all other contexts – or that a technical distinction proposed in one context is operating in all contexts.

The Divided Line passage, with its suggestion of technical vocabulary, also seems to drive a wedge between the apprehension of necessary truths in mathematics (διάνοια – *dianoia*) and the apprehension of forms (νοῦς). This suggests another objection: that Plato can't have anything like gestalts in mind when he's thinking about forms, since paradigm cases of gestalts involve the apprehension of necessary truths in mathematics. My suggestion is that the vagueness of the passage allows us to speculate that Plato distinguishes two genera of gestalts: one whose species are moral and ontological (and include beauty, which it would be wrong to call an 'aesthetic' species in this context precisely because it doesn't have to do with sense perception), and another whose species are mathematical. Both are characterized by the experience of epistemic necessity.

The passage at the end of Book VI in *Republic* also raises a question about how the so-called method of hypothesis, which is also mentioned in *Meno*, is related to the method of collection and division. I don't know. It is possible that the method of hypothesis involves what Lorenz calls intuition — we make a good guess and then show what follows on our guess; if what follows coheres with other things we know or intuit, we're justified in thinking we're on the right track. But this is different from feeling certain that our intuitions are correct. Confirming intuitions involves long practice with collection and division.

There are many other objections of this sort.

the figure 4 in the two-shape line drawing: See page 12.

page 94

"innumerable, multi-directional": Lorenz 1959: 155. See page 19.

'human being is the measure of all things': A claim attributed to Protagoras, a fellow citizen of Socrates and a sophist. (Sextus Empiricus, *Against the Mathematicians* 7.60, in Diels-Kranz [1951] 1996: 80B1.) Many have seen in Plato's corpus an attempt to show that Socrates was condemned to death because he was falsely thought to be a sophist.

"SHOW, DON'T TELL"

page 96

"Beauty is truth, truth beauty ...": John Keats, "Ode on a Grecian Urn," lines 49–50.

page 98

As Carlo Ginzburg has pointed out: Ginzburg 1980.

"in contemplative mood": Stuckeley 1752: 15 recto.

page 99

> *the factors of closure and good continuation*: Wertheimer, Max 1923: 324–6 (in English translation, Wertheimer 2012: 154–5, or Ellis 1938: 83); and Metzger 2009: 10 and 21. For brief summaries, see the Appendix.
>
> *branch with a sprout*: I owe the idea of this illustration to Wertheimer, Max 1923: 324.
>
> *rectangle occluding the intersection point of a pair of crossed lines*: I owe this illustration to Metzger 2009: 134.

page 102

> "The Dry Salvages," opening lines: Eliot 1943.

page 103

> Tranströmer, "Elegy," trans. Bly: In Tranströmer 1986: 119.

page 105

> *The gestalt factor operating in local and extended metaphors is … similarity*: Wertheimer, Max 1923: 308–15 (in English translation, Wertheimer 2012: 135–43, or Ellis 1938: 74–7); and Metzger 2009: 32–5 (for example). For a brief summary, see the Appendix.

pages 105–6

> *Einstein … Lorenz … Schooler*: See pages 18–19 and 72, and pages 177–8 in the Appendix.

page 106

> *There is also recent evidence that Freud … was right*: See Carhart-Harris et al. 2008, Carhart-Harris and Friston 2010, and Tagliazucchi 2016. See also Griffiths et al. 2006 for evidence that suspension of the ego is correlated with ineffable states of mind.
>
> *each [hemisphere] has a fundamentally different style*: See McGilchrist 2009, Part I. McGilchrist's work is discussed in more detail in "The Inscape of Being," pages 155–60.
>
> *I suspect that we share both styles of thought with other species*: See Andics et al. 2016 and Corballis 2014. Corballis, unlike Andics, persists in the view that "language itself is uniquely human." McGilchrist also maintains that the two styles of thought are present in all animals with bihemispheric brains.

page 107

> "irritable reaching after fact and reason" and "uncertainties, Mysteries, doubts": See Keats's letter to George and Thomas Keats, 21 (27?) December 1817, in Keats 1952.

page 108

> "a friend to man": "Ode on a Grecian Urn," line 48.

MUSIC

page 109

§I epigraph: Ludwig Wittgenstein, reported in conversation with M.O'C. Drury, "Some Notes on Conversations with Wittgenstein." In Rhees 1984: 76–96 at 79.

Langer [1942] 1951: 197 and 206–7.

Jankélévitch 1961: 94.

Scruton 1997: 360–4.

Einstein 2011: 237–8 passim.

Hugo 1864: 120.

page 110

Michaels and Carello 1981: 25.

page 111

§II epigraph: Goethe 1984, 23 March 1829: 246.

pages 112–14

The view that music fundamentally concerns tonal organization is elaborated in Hanslick 1854, Zuckerkandl 1956, and Scruton 1997. I shall have more to say about Scruton's views presently.

page 113

Rhythm is perceived aurally, kinaesthetically, and proprioceptively: See Todd and Lee 2015.

page 114

§III epigraph: Epstein 1987: 30.

pages 115–17

Johansson 1973: 202–4.

page 117

If … humans possess so-called mirror neurons: The existence of mirror neurons in humans is disputed. The Wikipedia entry on mirror neurons contains references to several up-to-date discussions. For a speculative proposal that connects comprehension of music to mirror neurons, see Molnar-Szakacs and Overy 2006.

page 118

§IV epigraph: Richard Rorty, "Relations, Internal and External" in *The Encyclopedia of Philosophy*, 1967: VII.126.

Scruton 1997: 39, 88, and 91.

page 119

Eliot 1957, "What Is Minor Poetry?" [1944]: 49–50.

page 120

"The rain is Art Blakey …": Heiti 2011, from "Rain Sutra."

page 122

§v epigraph: Issa, ["Blossoms at night"], trans. Robert Hass, in Hass 1994: 163.

page 124

Blake 1982, "[A Vision of the Last Judgement]" [1810]: 565–6.

page 125

§vi epigraph: Ludwig Wittgenstein, reported in conversation with M.O'C. Drury, in "Conversations with Wittgenstein." In Rhees 1984: 97–171 at 157.

page 126

Darwin 1871, in Part iii, "Voice and Musical Powers": 572.

Jordania 2006, in Part 3, "Few Preliminary Questions and Answers": 298.

Mithen 2005, and Cross 1999. Mithen argues that an evolutionary precursor to both music and language, which he calls Hmmmmm, was important to social bonding among early hominids. In addition to arguing that music promoted social bonding among early humans, Cross argues that "proto-musical" behaviours played a crucial role in expanding hominin cognitive development by integrating activity across various neurophysiological domains.

page 128

Imberty 2000: 459.

Davenport 1982: 218.

pages 129–30

Næss [1989] 1990: 58–9. Minor alterations have been made to the translation to increase its readability in English.

page 130

Wittgenstein [1980] 1984: 34e [1938], with minor alterations to Peter Winch's translation.

Hagberg 2017: 74–5.

page 131

§vii epigraph: Plato, *Parmenides*, 134e–135c, trans. Mary Louise Gill and Paul Ryan with minor alterations, in Cooper 1997.

pages 131–2

Wittgenstein [1980] 1984: 24e [1933].

page 132

"The work of the philosopher ...": Wittgenstein [1958] 1972: §127.

"clear view": Wittgenstein [1958] 1972: §125.

page 134

§VIII epigraph: Wittgenstein [1980] 1984: 82 [1949], trans. Zwicky.

page 137

§IX epigraph: Tomas Tranströmer, excerpt from "Schubertiana," trans. Samuel Charters, in Tranströmer 1986.

page 140

Augustine, *Confessiones* I.8 (trans. G.E.M. Anscombe?) in Wittgenstein [1958] 1972: §1.

Wittgenstein [1958] 1972: §3.

page 141

Wittgenstein, reported in conversation with M.O'C. Drury, in "Some Notes on Conversations with Wittgenstein." In Rhees 1984: 76–96 at 79.

page 142

the dissociation of sensibility to which Eliot pointed: "The Metaphysical Poets" [1921], in Eliot 1951: 281–91.

It is possible that gestalt comprehension depends on widespread neural 'crosstalk': See Carhart-Harris et al. 2008, Carhart-Harris and Friston 2010, and Tagliazucchi 2016.

page 143

Greek mathematics: See Fowler 1987. Regarding contemporary mathematical thought, and how attempts to model it with a series of algorithms is proving difficult, see Gromov 2017: 109–10 and 114–15.

Michaels and Carello: see Note to page 110.

Wertheimer, Max 1912a, in Ellis 1938: 267.

page 144

§X epigraph: Borson 1995: 123–4.

page 146

Borson 1995: 131.

THE INSCAPE OF BEING

page 147

what is often meant by 'spiritual insight': Stace 1960: 15–17; Huxley 1945: vii. (Huxley claims that the phrase *philosophia perennis* was coined by Leibniz. Agostino Steuco was, in fact, its originator. See Schmitt 1966.) See also James 1963, Lectures XVI and XVIII: 379–82; and compare Underhill 1945: 81.

page 148

"A poet's words can pierce us": Wittgenstein 1967: §155.

"I believe I summed up my view ...": Wittgenstein [1980] 1984: 24 [1933–1934], trans. Zwicky.

"And this is how it is ...": Wittgenstein in Englemann 1968: 7.

page 150

Gauss's recognition: See page 15.

page 155

Empson 1946: 3.

Simic 1990: 67 and 88.

page 156

"[pays] narrowly focussed, sharply defined attention": McGilchrist 2016: 11.1.

"Its aim ... is to close down to a certainty ...": McGilchrist 2016: 11.3.

the world "of 'me'": McGilchrist 2009: 25.

"in relation to others ...": McGilchrist 2009: 25.

"Here I may feel myself to be part of something much bigger than myself ...": McGilchrist 2009: 25.

page 157

"[T]he link between the right hemisphere and holistic or Gestalt perception ...": McGilchrist 2009: 46–7.

Emotion ... is generally the province of the right hemisphere: McGilchrist 2009: 58–60.

"The one exception ... is anger": McGilchrist 2009: 61.

the right hemisphere ... is responsible for control of emotional arousal: McGilchrist 2009: 59.

Poincaré 1929: 37.

Césaire 1990: xliii, l, and lv (Sixth Proposition).

page 158

the right hemisphere ... resists seeing things in terms of categories or generic objects: McGilchrist 2009: 51.

"[I]t is precisely its capacity for holistic processing ...": McGilchrist 2009: 51.

page 159

Freud's conceptions of primary and secondary process: These notions lie at the foundation of Freud's thought from first to last. Most of the characteristics of primary process are described in Freud [1915] 1957: 187. See also Freud [1911] 1958. In Freud 1960: 316–18, Freud also remarks that primary processes "[exert] on somatic processes an influence of intense plastic power which the conscious act can never do." Nowhere in Freud's corpus is there a neat summary of the characteristics of secondary process, however. Relevant passages include Freud [1915] 1957, §VII: 196–204 and 209–15; Freud [1923] 1961, §II: 19–27; Freud [1920] 1955, §IV, and the opening of §V; Freud [1900] 1958, Ch. VII §§E and F, esp. 598–611; and especially Freud [1895] 1966, Pt I §§1 and 14–18 and Pt III. I have elsewhere argued that Freud was mistaken in attributing consciousness only to secondary process. (See "What Is Ineffable?" in *Alkibiades' Love*, McGill-Queen's University Press, 2015.)

primary process thought also lacks a sense of self: This claim and the correlative claim that secondary process thought represents the inhibitory activity of a neuronal complex corresponding to the ego is the burden of Freud [1895] 1966.

page 160

    the default mode network: See, for example, Goldberg et al. 2006, Griffiths et al. 2006, and especially Carhart-Harris et al. 2008, Carhart-Harris and Friston 2010, and Tagliazucchi et al. 2016. Some of this material is summarized in Pollan 2015.

    "leftward functional connectivity" *is greater*: See Saenger et al. 2012.

    "Often enough, when a thing is seen clearly ...": Hass 1984: 274–5. See page 63.

page 161

    Hirshfield 1997: 3–4.

page 162

    "More than any other speech ...": Lilburn 1995: 163. After consultation with Lilburn, I have modified the original text, which spoke of the "unknowable individuality of things." By 'knowledge,' Lilburn understands cognition characterized by identification, analysis, and classification [Lilburn 2017: 168] — in other words, McGilchrist's left-hemispheric way of knowing. Lilburn agrees that both poetry and contemplation perceive and comprehend important truths, but that their insight is fundamentally nonlinguistic.

    "a light, mobile transfixity": Lilburn 2017: 164.

    "My hunch ...": Lilburn 2017: 169.

    Recall the conclusion of "Archaic Torso of Apollo": See page 59.

page 163

    nodes of an immense, flexing geodesic sphere: See page 63.

    In conversation with Mark Doty: See https://www.poets.org/poetsorg/text/archaic-torso-apollo?page=1.

page 166

> *Pierre Bezukhov's moment of spiritual insight*: See pages 61–2, including references.

> *what ... Hopkins called the perception of inscape*: See pages 54–6, including references.

page 167

> Lee 2017: 265–6.

page 168

> Ryōkan: "In all ten directions of the universe ..." translated by Stephen Mitchell in Mitchell 1989.

page 170

> Davenport 1995: 158.

> Kahn 1979: 29.

page 171

> *Arne Næss spoke of a process he called "precisation"*: Næss 1989: 42–3.

> *sub- and super-ordinate gestalts*: Næss 1995: 243. See pages 68–9 in the text.

pages 172–3

> Thomas 1905: 88–93.

APPENDIX

page 175

> "by no means simply an 'equality' of components": Wertheimer, Max 1923: 325 (in English translation, Wertheimer 2012: 1154).

page 176

> Prägnanz: In the context of Gestalt theory, the first published use of the term *Prägnanz* that I have been able to uncover is in Köhler 1920, where it occurs in the title of the fifth section of Part IV, "Die Richtung auf Prägnanz der Struktur," and then again in sub-sections 249 and 264. Parts of this book are reprinted in Ellis 1938; see pages 51 and 54. As far as I can discover, the term *Prägnanzstufen* (roughly, *stages of configural stability*) first occurs in Wertheimer's work in "Untersuchungen zur Lehre von Gestalt," published in 1923. However, D. Brett King and Michael Wertheimer offer evidence that the "law of the *Prägnanz* of the Gestalt" had occurred to Max Wertheimer as early as 1914. Chapter 7 of King and Wertheimer 2005 tracks the historical development of the notion.

> *Michael Wertheimer and K.W. Watkins offer 'salience'*: Wertheimer, Max 2012: 144–7.

> Metzger 1936: Ch. 2 §3. (English translation: 19–21.)

> Wulf 1922: 372. (English translation: 148.)

Metzger discusses several others: Metzger 1936 *passim*. He uses *Gesetz* (law) where Wertheimer uses *Faktor* or *Prinzip*. Nothing, as far as I can tell, hangs on the terminology.

"My terms should not give the impression ...": Wertheimer, Max 1959: 4.

page 177

laboratory research in the US: The studies are legion. Here, in chronological order, are a few of the most notable. Those with asterisks contain useful summaries of earlier research: Schooler and Engstler-Schooler 1990; Schooler, Ohlsson, and Brooks 1993; Brandimonte and Gerbino 1993; Schooler and Melcher 1995; *Schooler, Fiore, and Brandimonte 1997; Sieck, Quinn, and Schooler 1999; Lane and Schooler 2004; *Chin and Schooler 2008.

Schooler's and Engstler-Schooler's results substantiated some earlier studies: In addition to Malpass 1981, see Belbin 1950 (which focuses on recall of a street safety poster), Kay and Skemp 1956 (which focuses on recall of a picture of holiday park scene), and Matthews 1985 (which focuses on childrens' ability to recall and draw, trace, or describe their routes to school). Other experiments have shown that, in the case of face-identification, focusing on 'holistic' impressions (personality or presumed occupation) improves subsequent recognition over focusing on isolated features of faces. The role of language, if any, in the latter is not understood. See Wells and Hryciw 1984.

Schooler and his associates have gone on to investigate: *colour recognition*, Schooler and Engstler-Schooler 1990; *bistable configurations*, Brandimonte and Gerbino 1993 (the figure used in this study was a version of Jastrow's duck-rabbit, familiar to those who know the work of Ludwig Wittgenstein; Jastrow, in Jastrow 1900 reports that the drawing in his own text is "from *Harper's Weekly*, originally in *Fliegende Blätter*" [295]); *memory of visual images*, Brandimonte, Hitch, and Bishop 1992; *grasp of analogies*, Sieck, Quinn, and Schooler 1999; Lane and Schooler 2004; *subsequent satisfaction with aesthetic judgements*, Wilson, Lisle, Schooler, et al. 1993. There are also studies published before Schooler began his investigations that confirm similar results. See Belbin 1950, Kay and Skemp 1956, Malpass 1981, and Ellis, Hadyn 1984. See also notes to page 72.

"a stepwise set of logical arguments": Schooler and Melcher 1995: 98.

"the sudden solution ...": Schooler and Melcher 1995: 98.

page 178

the single best predictor: Schooler and Melcher 1995: 123; Schooler, Fallshore, and Fiore 1995: 577.

Schooler was at the centre of a controversy: See Lehrer 2010.

a very large, multi-site replication study: See Alogna 2014.

Schooler [insists] ... that the problem requires attention: Schooler 2014.

page 179

figures like the duck-rabbit and the Rubin vase: See note to page 177 (*bistable configurations*) for the first and page 13 for the second.

page 180

the Gauss problem: See page 15.

What then is time? Augustine [written 397] 1993: 242. (Many editions are available. See Book XI, ch. 14.)

page 181

Pound's poem "In a Station of the Metro": See page 149.

page 182

we cannot, without considerable effort, recapture what it's like: Can a fluent reader recapture the experience of a non-reader by picking up a text in a language she doesn't know? If the text uses a script with which she's familiar, then the characters are still recognizable, although their combinations may not be comprehensible. Even in a case where the script as well as the language is unfamiliar, a reader will know she is confronting meaningful text of some sort — consider Linear A. Olmec may provide an even better example. Archaeologists are not certain that the characters incised on the Cascajal Block belong to a script. Nonetheless, a reader — of any language — who views the block will immediately look for repeated glyphs and try to discern patterns or relationships among them. Do humans who cannot read look at the Cascajal Block in a similar way? I do not know.

"reaching immediately into her mind ...": Weil 1946: 14. See Heiti 2018 for an extended and insightful discussion of this passage. We are, here, in the metaphysical territory Wertheimer resolutely refused to explore.

"it is necessary to force oneself to read a different meaning ...": Weil 1946: 14; and Heiti 2018: 272.

Arne Næss would couch it in yet other terms: Næss 1995: 243. Previous discussion on pages 68–9.

page 183

there is that slight startle, a moment of astonishment: Cf. Wittgenstein 1982: §565.

the phi phenomenon: See page 11.

REFERENCES

Ainsworth, Thomas. 2016. "Form vs. Matter." *The Stanford Encyclopedia of Philosophy*. Spring 2016 Edition. Ed. Edward N. Zalta. <https://plato.stanford.edu/archives/spr2016/entries/form-matter/>

Akhmatova, Anna. [1973] 1997. *Poems of Akhmatova*. Ed. and trans. Stanley Kunitz with Max Hayward. Boston: Houghton Mifflin.

Aldrich, Virgil C. 1946. "Learning by Insights: Productive Thinking by Max Wertheimer." *Christian Century* 63.49 (4 December): 1471.

Alogna, V.K. et al. 2014. "Registered replication report: Schooler and Engstler-Schooler (1990)." *Perspectives on Psychological Science* 9.5: 556–78.

Ames, Roger T. 1986. "Taoism and the Nature of Nature." *Environmental Ethics* 8: 317–49.

Andics, Attila, et al. 2016. "Neural mechanisms for lexical processing in dogs." *Science* 353.6303: 1030–2.

Aristotle. 1975. *Metaphysics*. Trans. Richard Hope. Ann Arbor: University of Michigan Press.

—— 1984. *The Complete Works of Aristotle*. Rev. Oxford Translation. Ed. Jonathan Barnes. Princeton: Princeton University Press.

Aristoxenos. See Findlay 1974.

Arnheim, Rudolf. 1998. "Wolfgang Köhler and Gestalt Theory: An English Translation of Köhler's Introduction to *Die physischen Gestalten* for Philosophers and Biologists." *History of Psychology* 1.1.: 21–6.

Ash, Mitchell G. 1995. *Gestalt Psychology in German Culture, 1890–1967: Holism and the Quest for Objectivity*. Cambridge: Cambridge University Press.

Auden, W.H. and John Garrett, eds. 1938. *The Poet's Tongue*. London: G. Bell and Sons.

Augustine. *Confessions*. [written 397–8] 1993. Trans. F.J. Sheed. Indianapolis: Hackett.

Austin, J.L. 1962. *How to Do Things with Words*. Ed. J.O. Urmson. Cambridge, MA: Harvard University Press.

Bahrick, H.P. and Barbara Boucher. 1968. "Retention of Visual and Verbal Codes of the Same Stimuli." *Journal of Experimental Psychology* 78.3: 417–22.

Belbin, Eunice. 1950. "The Influence of Interpolated Recall upon Recognition." *Quarterly Journal of Experimental Psychology* 2.4: 163–9.

Berkeley, George. [1710] 1965. *The Principles of Human Knowledge*. In *Berkeley's Philosophical Writings*. Ed. David M. Armstrong. London: Collier-Macmillan.

Bishop, Elizabeth. [1946] 1983. "The Fish." In *Elizabeth Bishop: The Complete Poems 1927–1979*. New York: Farrar, Straus and Giroux. The poem was originally published in *North & South*, Boston: Houghton Mifflin.

Blake, William. 1982. *The Complete Poetry and Prose of William Blake*. Newly rev. ed. Ed. Daniel V. Erdman. Berkeley: University of California Press.

Borson, Roo. 1995. "Poetry as Knowing." In *Poetry and Knowing*. Ed. Tim Lilburn. Kingston: Quarry Press, 123–31.

Brahmagupta and Bhāskara. [1817] 1973. *Algebra, with Arithmetic and Mensuration, from the Sanscrit of Brahmagupta and Bháscara*. Trans. Henry Thomas Colebrooke. London: John Murray.

Brandimonte, M.A. and W. Gerbino. 1993. "Mental Image Reversal and Verbal Recoding: When Ducks Become Rabbits." *Memory & Cognition* 21.1: 23–33.

Brandimonte, M.A., G.J. Hitch, and D.V.M. Bishop. 1992. "Influence of short-term memory codes on visual image processing: Evidence from image transformation tasks." *Journal of Experimental Psychology: Learning, Memory, and Cognition* 18.1: 157–65.

Bringhurst, Robert. 1975. "Poem About Crystal." In *Bergschrund*. Delta, BC: Sono Nis. The poem has been reprinted in a number of Bringhurst's collections since 1975.

— 2009a. *Everywhere Being Is Dancing: Twenty Pieces of Thinking*. Berkeley: Counterpoint.

— 2009b. Foreword. In Lunde 2009.

Browning, Robert. 1855. "Andrea del Sarto." In *Men and Women*. London: Chapman and Hall.

Burtynsky, Edward. *Feng Jie #4, Three Gorges Dam Project, Yangtze River, 2002*. See, for example, http://www.mascontext.com/tag/three-gorges-dam/.

Carhart-Harris, R.L., Helen S. Mayberg, Andra L. Malizia, and David Nutt. 2008. "Mourning and melancholia revisited: correspondences between principles of Freudian metapsychology and empirical findings in neuropsychiatry." *Annals of General Psychiatry* 7.9 (24 July 2008): https://doi.org/10.1186/1744-859X-7-9.

— and K.J. Friston. 2010. "The default-mode, ego-functions and free-energy: A neurobiological account of Freudian ideas." *Brain* 133.4: 1265–83.

— See also Tagliazucchi 2016.

Cather, Willa. [1920] 1953. "On the Art of Fiction." In *On Writing: Critical studies on writing as an art.* New York: A.A. Knopf, 99–104. Originally published in *The Borzoi 1920: Being a sort of record of five years' publishing.* New York: Alfred A. Knopf, 1920, 7–8.

Césaire, Aimé. 1990. "Poetry and Knowledge." In *Lyric and Dramatic Poetry 1946–82.* Trans. Clayton Eshleman and Annette Smith. Charlottesville: University Press of Virginia: xlii–lvi.

Chin, Jason M. and Jonathan W. Schooler. 2008. "Why Do Words Hurt? Content, Process, and Criterion Shift Accounts of Verbal Overshadowing." *European Journal of Cognitive Psychology* 20.3: 396–413.

Cooper, John M., ed. 1997. *Plato: Complete Works.* Indianapolis and Cambridge: Hackett.

Copernicus, Nicolaus. [1543] 1978. *On the Revolutions.* Ed. Jerzy Dobrzycki. Trans. Edward Rosen. Baltimore: Johns Hopkins University Press.

Corballis, Michael. 2014. "Left Brain, Right Brain: Facts and Fantasies." *PLOS Biology* 12.1: 1–6.

Cornford, F.M. [1935] 1960. *Plato's Theory of Knowledge.* London: Routledge & Kegan Paul.

Coxon, A.H. 1986. *The Fragments of Parmenides.* Assen/Maastricht and Wolfeboro, NH: Van Gorcum.

Croce, Benedetto. 1902. *Estetica come scienza dell'esspressione e linguistica generale.* Milan: R. Sandron. Available in English as *Aesthetic as Science of Expression and General Linguistic*, trans. Douglas Ainslie, New York: Noonday Press, [1909] 1953.

Cross, Ian. 1999. "Is Music the Most Important Thing We Ever Did? Music, Development and Evolution." In *Music, Mind, and Science.* Ed. Suk Won Yi, Seoul: Seoul National University Press, 10–39.

Dalley, Stephanie. 2013. *The Mystery of the Hanging Garden of Babylon: An Elusive World Wonder Traced.* Oxford: University of Oxford Press.

Darwin, Charles. 1871. *The Descent of Man, and Selection in Relation to Sex.* London: John Murray.

Davenport, Guy. 1982. *Tatlin!* Baltimore: Johns Hopkins University Press.

— 1995. *7 Greeks.* New York: New Directions.

Diels, Hermann, rev. Walther Kranz. [1951] 1996. *Die Fragmente des Vorsokratiker.* 6th ed. Zürich: Weidmann.

Domanski, Don. 2006. *Poetry and the Sacred.* Nanaimo, BC: Institute for Coastal Research.

von Ehrenfels, Christian. 1890. "Über 'Gestaltqualitäten.'" *Vierteljahrsschrift für wissenschaftliche Philosophie* 14: 249–92. Available in English translation in Smith 1988.

Einstein, Albert. 1959. "Autobiographical Notes." In *Albert Einstein: Philosopher-Scientist*. Ed. Paul Arthur Schilpp. New York: Harper Torchbooks.

— 2011. *The Ultimate Quotable Einstein*. Ed. Alice Calaprice. Princeton: Princeton University Press.

Eliot, T.S. 1930. Preface to St.-J. Perse, Anabasis. Trans. T.S. Eliot. London: Faber & Faber.

— 1943. *Four Quartets*. New York: Harcourt, Brace & World.

— 1951. *Selected Essays*. London: Faber & Faber.

— 1957. *On Poetry and Poets*. London: Faber & Faber.

Ellis, Hadyn D. 1984. "Practical Aspects of Face Memory." In G.L. Wells and E.F. Loftus, eds., *Eyewitness Testimony: Psychological Perspectives*. Cambridge: Cambridge University Press, 12–37.

Ellis, Willis D. 1938. *A Source Book of Gestalt Psychology*. London: Routledge & Kegan Paul.

Empson, William. [1930] 1946. *Seven Types of Ambiguity*. New York: New Directions.

The Encyclopedia of Philosophy. 1967. Ed. Paul Edwards. New York: Macmillan.

Englemann, Paul. 1968. *Letters from Ludwig Wittgenstein with a Memoir*. New York: Horizon Press. [First published by Basil Blackwell, 1967.]

Epstein, Helen. 1987. *Music Talks: Conversations with Musicians*. New York: McGraw-Hill.

Exner, Sigmund. 1875. "Über das Sehen von Bewegungen und die Theorie des zusammengesetzten Auges." *Sitzungsberichte der Kaiserlichen Akademie der Wissenschaften. Mathematisch-Naturwisssenschaftliche Classe. Abt. 2, Mathematik, Physik, Chemie, Physiologie, Meteorologie, physische Geographie und Astronomie*. 72.3: 156–90.

Feynman, Richard. 1994. *The Character of Physical Law*. New York: The Modern Library.

Findlay, J.N. 1974. *Plato: The Written and Unwritten Doctrines*. London: Routledge & Kegan Paul.

Fischer, Shell. 2009. "Can Flarf Ever Be Taken Seriously?" http://www.pw.org/content/can_flarf_ever_be_taken_seriously (July/August 2009; posted 1 August 2009)

Fowler, D.H. 1987. *The Mathematics of Plato's Academy: A New Reconstruction*. Oxford: Clarendon Press.

Frege, Gottlob. 1956. "The Thought: A Logical Inquiry." Trans. A.M. and Marcelle Quinton. *Mind* 65.259: 289–311. Reprinted in Strawson, P.F., ed., *Philosophical Logic*. Oxford University Press, 1967.

Freud, Sigmund. [1895] 1966. "Project for a Scientific Psychology." In *The Standard Edition of the Complete Psychological Works of Sigmund Freud* Vol. 1. Ed. and trans. James Strachey, 281–397. London: Hogarth.

— [1900] 1958. *The Interpretation of Dreams*, Chapter VII, §§E and F. In *The Standard Edition of the Complete Psychological Works of Sigmund Freud*. Edited and translated by James Strachey. Vol. 5: 588–621. London: Hogarth.

— [1911] 1958. "Formulations on the Two Principles of Mental Functioning." In *The Standard Edition of the Complete Psychological Works of Sigmund Freud*. Edited and translated by James Strachey. Vol. 12: 213–26. London: Hogarth.

— [1915] 1957. *The Unconscious*. In *The Standard Edition of the Complete Psychological Works of Sigmund Freud*. Edited and translated by James Strachey. Vol. 14: 159–215. London: Hogarth.

— [1920] 1955. *Beyond the Pleasure Principle*. In *The Standard Edition of the Complete Psychological Works of Sigmund Freud*. Edited and translated by James Strachey. Vol. 18: 1–64. London: Hogarth.

— [1923] 1961. *The Ego and the Id*, Chapter 2. In *The Standard Edition of the Complete Psychological Works of Sigmund Freud*. Edited and translated by James Strachey. Vol. 19: 1–66. London: Hogarth.

— [1960] 1975. *Letters 1873–1939*. Ed. E.L. Freud. Trans. T. and J. Stern. New York: Basic Books.

Frye, Northrop. 1957. *Anatomy of Criticism: Four Essays*. Princeton: Princeton University Press.

Gibson, James J. 1979. *The Ecological Approach to Visual Perception*. Boston: Houghton Mifflin.

Ginzburg, Carlo. 1980. "Morelli, Freud, and Sherlock Holmes: Clues and Scientific Method." Trans. Anna Davin. *History Workshop Journal* 9: 5–36.

von Goethe, Johann Wolfgang. 1984. *Conversations with Eckermann*. Trans. John Oxenford. San Francisco: North Point.

Goldberg, Ilan, Michal Harel, and Rafael Malach. 2006. "When the Brain Loses Its Self: Prefrontal Inactivation during Sensorimotor Processing." *Neuron* 50 (20 April 2006): 329–39.

Gonzalez, Francisco J. 2002. "Plato's Dialectic of Forms." *Plato's Forms: Varieties of Interpretation*. Ed. William A. Welton. Lanham, MD: Lexington Books.

Goodman, Nelson. [1969] 1976. *Languages of Art: An Approach to the Theory of Symbols*. Indianapolis: Hackett.

Gray, Robert. 1990. "Under the Summer Leaves." In *Selected Poems*. London: Angus & Robertson.

Griffiths, R.R., W.A. Richards, U. McCann, and R. Jesse. 2006. "Psilocybin can occasion mystical-type experiences having substantial and sustained personal meaning and spiritual significance." *Psychopharmacology* 187: 268–83.

Gromov, Misha. 2017. "Math Currents in the Brain." In *Simplicity: Ideals of Practice in Mathematics and the Arts*. Ed. Roman Kossak and Philip Ording. Springer, 107–18.

Haack, Susan. 1978. *Philosophy of Logics*. Cambridge: Cambridge University Press.

Hadamard, Jacques. 1949. *The Psychology of Invention in the Mathematical Field*. Princeton: Princeton University Press.

Hagberg, Garry. 2017. "Wittgenstein, Music, and the Philosophy of Culture." In *Wittgenstein on Aesthetic Understanding*. Ed. Garry L. Hagberg. Cham, Switzerland: Palgrave Macmillan, 61–95.

Hanslick, Eduard. 1854. *Vom Musikalisch-Schönen*. Leipzig: Rudolf Weigel. There are numerous subsequent editions. Available in two English translations: *The Beautiful in Music*, ed. Morris Weitz, trans. Gustav Cohen, New York: Liberal Arts Press, 1957; and *On the Musically Beautiful*, ed. and trans. Geoffrey Payzant, Indianapolis: Hackett, 1986.

Hass, Robert, ed. and trans. 1994. *The Essential Haiku: Versions of Bashō, Buson and Issa*. New York: Ecco Press.

— 1984. "Images." In *Twentieth Century Pleasures: Prose on Poetry*. New York: Ecco, 269–308.

Hawking, Stephen W. 1988. *A Brief History of Time*. Toronto: Bantam.

Heany, Seamus. 1966. "Digging." In *Death of a Naturalist*. London: Faber & Faber.

Heiti, Warren. 2011. *Hydrologos*. Toronto: Pedlar Press.

— 2018. "Reading and Character: Weil and McDowell on Naïve Realism and Second Nature." *Philosophical Investigations* 41.3 (July): 267–90.

Henle, Mary, ed. 1961. *Documents of Gestalt Psychology*. Berkeley: University of California Press.

Hesiod. [1914] 1936. *Works and Days*. Loeb Classical Library. New and rev. edition. Trans. Hugh G. Evelyn White. Cambridge, MA and London: Harvard University Press.

Hirshfield, Jane. 1997. *Nine Gates: Entering the Mind of Poetry*. New York: HarperCollins.

Hopkins, Gerard Manley. [1953] 1981. *Gerard Manley Hopkins: Poems and Prose*. Ed. W.H. Gardner. Harmondsworth: Penguin Books.

— 1959. *The Journals and Papers of Gerard Manley Hopkins*. 2nd ed. Ed. Humphry House, completed by Graham Storey. London: Oxford University Press.

Howe, Marie. 1998. "The Mother," "From My Father's Side of the Bed," and "The Attic." In *What the Living Do*. New York: W.W. Norton.

Hugo, Victor. 1864. *William Shakespeare*. Paris: A. Lacroix.

Huxley, Aldous. 1945. *The Perennial Philosophy*. New York: Harper & Brothers.

Imberty, Michael. 2000. "The Question of Innate Competencies in Musical Communication." In *The Origins of Music*. Ed. Nils L. Allin, Björn Merker, and Steven Brown. Cambridge, MA: MIT Press, 449–62.

James, William. [1902] 1963. *The Varieties of Religious Experience*. Enlarged edition. New York: University Books.

Janik, Allan and Stephen Toulmin. 1973. *Wittgenstein's Vienna*. New York: Simon & Schuster.

Jankélévitch, Vladimir. 1961. *La musique et l'ineffable*. Paris: Seuil.

Jastrow, Joseph. 1900. *Fact and Fable in Psychology*. Boston and New York: Houghton, Mifflin.

Johansson, Gunnar. 1973. "Visual perception of biological motion and a model for its analysis." *Perception & Psychophysics* 14.2: 201–11.

Jordania, Joseph [I.M. Zhordania]. 2006. *Who Asked the First Question? The Origins of Human Choral Singing, Intelligence, Language and Speech*. Tbilisi: Logos. Available at: http://citeseerx.ist.psu.edu/viewdoc/download?doi=10.1.1.470.3973&rep=rep1&type=pdf

Kahn, Charles. 1979. *The Art and Thought of Heraclitus*. Cambridge: Cambridge University Press.

— 1996. *Plato and the Socratic Dialogue*. Cambridge: Cambridge University Press.

Kay, Harry and Richard Skemp. 1956. "Difference Thresholds for Recognition – Further Experiments on Interpolated Recall and Recognition." *Quarterly Journal of Experimental Psychology* 8.4: 153–62.

Keats, John. 1952. *The Letters of John Keats*. Ed. Maurice B. Foreman. London: Oxford University Press.

— 1973. John Keats: *The Complete Poems*. Ed. John Barnard. Harmondsworth: Penguin.

Kepler, Johannes. 1937–. *Gesammelte Werke*. Bd. I, ed. Walther von Dyck, Max Caspar, Franz Hammer, and Matha List. Munich: 8, 10.

— [1596/1621] 1981. *Mysterium Cosmographicum: The Secret of the Universe*. Trans. A.M. Duncan. Introduction and commentary by E.J. Aiton. New York: Abaris Books.

King, D. Brett and Michael Wertheimer. 2005. *Max Wertheimer and Gestalt Theory*. New Brunswick, NJ: Transaction Publishers.

Kivy, Peter. 1980. *The Corded Shell: Reflections on Musical Expression*. Princeton: Princeton University Press.

Koestler, Arthur. 1954. *The Invisible Writing*. New York: Macmillan.

— [1959] 1989. *The Sleepwalkers*. London: Arkana.

Köhler, Wolfgang. 1920. *Die physischen Gestalten in Ruhe und im stationären Zustand, Eine naturphilosophische Untersuchung*. Braunschweig: Friedrich Vieweg and Sohn. Heavily abridged English translation, under the title "Physical Gestalten," in Ellis 1938, 17–54.

— [1929] 1930. *Gestalt Psychology*. London: G. Bell and Sons.

— [1938] 1959. *The Place of Value in a World of Facts*. New York: Meridian.

— 1969. *The Task of Gestalt Psychology*. Princeton: Princeton University Press.

Lane, Sean M. and Schooler, Jonathan W. 2004. "Skimming the Surface: Verbal Overshadowing of Analogical Retrieval." *Psychological Science* 15.11: 715–19.

Langer, Susanne. [1942] 1951. *Philosophy in a New Key*. New York: Mentor.

Lee, Dennis. 1998. *Body Music*. Toronto: House of Anansi.

— 2017. "Not Abstract Harmonies But." In *Heart Residence: Collected Poems 1967–2017*. Toronto: House of Anansi. The poem was originally published, in a different version, in *The Gods*, Toronto: McClelland & Stewart, 1979.

Lehrer, Jonah. 2010. "The Truth Wears Off." *The New Yorker* 86.40 (13 December): 52–7.

Lerdahl, Fred and Ray Jackendoff. 1983. *A Generative Theory of Tonal Music*. Cambridge, MA: MIT Press.

Lilburn, Tim. 1995. "How to Be Here?" In *Poetry and Knowing*. Ed. Tim Lilburn. Kingston: Quarry Press.

— 2017. "Thinking the *Rule of Benedict* within Modernity." In *The Larger Conversation*. Edmonton: University of Alberta Press.

Lorenz, Konrad. 1959. "Gestaltwahrnehmung als Quelle wissenschaftlicher Erkenntnis." *Zeitschrift für experimentelle und angewandte Psychologie* 6: 118–65. Subsequently published as "Gestalt perception as a source of scientific knowledge." In Lorenz 1971: 281–322.

— 1971. *Studies in Animal and Human Behaviour* Vol. II. Translated by Robert Martin. London: Methuen.

Lund, Frederick H. 1929. "The Phantom of the Gestalt." *Journal of General Psychology* 2.2: 307–21.

Lunde, Ken. 2009. *CJKV Information Processing*. Sebastopol, CA: O'Reilly Media.

Malpass, Roy S. 1981. "Training in face recognition." In *Perceiving and remembering faces*. Ed. G.M. Davies, H.D. Ellis, and J.W. Shepherd. London: Academic Press, 271–85.

Marková, Ivana. 2005. *Insight in Psychiatry*. Cambridge: Cambridge University Press.

Matthews, M.H. 1985. "Young children's representation of the environment: a comparison of techniques." *Journal of Environmental Psychology* 5: 261–78.

Maurer, Armand. 1984. "Ockham's Razor and Chatton's Anti-Razor." *Medieval Studies* 46: 463–75.

McGiffin, Emily. 2014. "The Hanging Gardens," a section of "Nine Meditations on Edward Burtynsky." In *Subduction Zone*. St. John's, NL: Pedlar Press.

McGilchrist, Iain. 2009. *The Master and His Emissary: The Divided Brain and the Making of the Western World*. New Haven: Yale University.

—2016. "'Where shall I go for truth?'" Unpublished text of the three 2016 Laing Lectures, Regent College, Vancouver, BC.

McKay, Don. 2001. *Vis à Vis: Fieldnotes on Poetry and Wilderness*. Kentville, NS: Gaspereau Press.

Mertins, Detlef. 2014. *Mies*. London and New York: Phaidon.

Metzger, Wolfgang. 1936. *Gesetze des Sehens*. Frankfurt am Main: W. Kramer. Translated as *Laws of Seeing* by Lothar Spillman et al. Cambridge, MA: MIT Press, [2006] 2009.

Michaels, Claire F. and Claudia Carello. 1981. *Direct Perception*. Englewood Cliffs: Prentice-Hall.

Mitchell, Stephen, ed. 1989. *The Enlightened Heart: An Anthology of Sacred Poetry*. New York: HarperCollins.

Mithen, Steven. 2005. *The Singing Neanderthals*. London: Weidenfeld & Nicolson.

Molnar-Szakacs, Istvan and Katie Overy. 2006. "Music and mirror neurons: from motion to 'e'-motion." *Social Cognitive and Affective Neuroscience* 1.3 (December): 235–41.

Murdoch, Jim. 2011. "How to Write Flarf." http://jim-murdoch.blogspot.ca/2011/09/how-to-write-flarf.html (7 September 2011).

Næss, Arne. 1973. "The Shallow and the Deep, Long-Range Ecology Movements: A Summary." *Inquiry: An Interdisciplinary Journal of Philosophy* 16: 95–100.

—1989. *Ecology, community and lifestyle*. Ed. and trans. David Rothenberg. Cambridge: Cambridge University Press.

—1995. "Ecosophy and Gestalt Ontology." In *Deep Ecology for the 21st Century*. Ed. George Sessions. Boston: Shambhala, 240–5.

Necker, L.A. 1832. "Observations on some remarkable Optical Phenomena seen in Switzerland; and on an Optical Phenomenon which occurs on viewing a Figure of a Crystal or a Geometrical Solid." *London and Edinburgh Philosophical Magazine and Journal of Science* 1.5 (November): 329–37.

Nehamas, Alexander and Paul Woodruff. 1995. *Plato: Phaedrus*. Indianapolis: Hackett.

Nelson, Douglas L. and David H. Brooks. 1973. "Functional Independence of Pictures and Their Verbal Memory Codes." *Journal of Experimental Psychology* 98.1: 44–8.

Newton, Isaac. 1803. *The Mathematical Principles of Natural Philosophy*. Trans. Andrew Motte, London: H.D. Symonds.

Page, P.K. 2007. *The Filled Pen: Selected Non-fiction*. Toronto: University of Toronto Press.

Parmenides. See Coxon 1986 and Diels-Kranz [1951] 1996.

Pezdek, Kathy et al. 1988. "Picture Memory: Recognizing Added and Deleted Details." *Journal of Experimental Psychology: Learning, Memory and Cognition* 14.3: 468–76.

Plato. *Complete Works*. See Cooper 1997.

— 1921. *Theatetus [Theaitētos]* and *Sophist*. Loeb Classical Library. Trans. H.N. Fowler. Cambridge, MA, and London: Harvard University Press.

— 1929. *Timaeus [Timaios]* and *Epistles [Letters]*. Loeb Classical Library. Trans. R.G. Bury. Cambridge, MA, and London: Harvard University Press.

Poincaré, Henri. 1929. "Mathematical Creation." Ch. III, "Science and Method," in *The Foundations of Science*. Trans. George Bruce Halsted. New York: Science Press.

Pollan, Michael. 2015. "The Trip Treatment." *The New Yorker* 90.47 (9 February 2015): 36–47.

Pound, Ezra. 1913. "In a Station of the Metro." *Poetry* 2.1 (April 1913): 12. The poem was first reprinted in *Lustra, with earlier poems*, New York: Knopf, 1917, and has been reprinted many times since, for example in *Personae: The Collected Poems of Ezra Pound*, New York: New Directions, 1926.

Quine, W.V.O. 1970. *Philosophy of Logic*. Englewood Cliffs, NJ: Prentice-Hall.

Raffman, Diana. 1993. *Language, Music, and Mind*. Cambridge, MA: MIT Press.

Rhees, Rush, ed. 1984. *Recollections of Wittgenstein*. Rev. ed. Oxford: Oxford University Press.

Rilke, Rainer Maria. 1987. "Archaïscher Torso Apollos." In *New Poems [1908]: The Other Part*. A bilingual edition with translations by Edward Snow. North Point: San Francisco.

Rorty, Richard. 1967. "Relations, Internal and External." See Edwards 1967.

Rubin, Edgar John. 1921. *Visuell wahrgenommene Figuren: Studien in psychologischer Analyse*. Gyldendalske: Copenhagen.

Saenger, Victor M., F.A. Barrios, M.L. Martínez-Gudiño, and Sarael Alcauter. 2012. "Hemispheric asymmetries of functional connectivity and grey matter volume in the default mode network." *Neuropsychologia* 50.7 (June): 1308–15.

Sartorius von Waltershausen, Wolfgang. 1856. *Gauss zum Gedächtnis*. Leipzig: S. Hirzel. English translation by Helen Worthington Gauss under the title *Carl Friedrich Gauss: A Memorial*. Leipzig: S. Hirzel, 1966.

Schenker, Heinrich. 1906–1935. *Neue musikalische Theorien und Phantasien*, especially Bd. III, *Der freie Satz* [1935]. Stuttgart: J.G. Cotta. Available in English as *Free Composition*, ed. and trans. Ernst Oster, New York: Longman, 1979. See also Zbikowski 2002, especially pages 127–31.

Schmitt, Charles. 1966. "Perrenial [*sic*] Philosophy: From Agostino Steuco to Leibniz." *Journal of the History of Ideas* 27.1 (Oct.–Dec. 1966): 505–32.

Schooler, Jonathan W. 2014. "Turning the Lens of Science on Itself: Verbal Overshadowing, Replication, and Metascience." *Perspectives on Psychological Science* 9.5: 579–84.

— and Engstler-Schooler, Tonya Y. 1990. "Verbal Overshadowing of Visual Memories: Some Things Are Better Left Unsaid." *Cognitive Psychology* 22: 36–71.

—, Stellan Ohlsson, and Kevin Brooks. 1993. "Thoughts Beyond Words: When Language Overshadows Insight." *Journal of Experimental Psychology: General* 122.2: 166–83.

—, Marte Fallshore, and Stephen M. Fiore. 1995. "Epilogue: Putting Insight into Perspective." In *The Nature of Insight*. Ed. Janet E. Davidson and Robert J. Sternberg. Cambridge, MA: MIT Press, 559–87.

— and Joseph Melcher. 1995. "The Ineffability of Insight." Chapter 5 in *The Creative Cognition Approach*. Ed. Steven M. Smith, Thomas B. Ward, and Ronald A. Finke. Cambridge, MA: MIT Press, 97–133.

—, Stephen M. Fiore, and Maria A. Brandimonte. 1997. "At a Loss from Words: Verbal Overshadowing of Perceptual Memories." *Psychology of Learning and Motivation* 37: 291–340.

Schopenhauer, Arthur. [1819] 1937–1941. *Die Welt als Wille und Vorstellung*. Ed. Arthur Hübscher. Leipzig: F.A. Brockhaus. Available in English as *The World as Will and Representation*, trans. E.F.J. Payne, New York: Dover, 1969.

Scruton, Roger. 1997. *The Aesthetics of Music*. Oxford: Oxford University Press.

Shahn, Ben. 1957. *The Shape of Content*. Cambridge, MA: Harvard University Press.

Sieck, Winston R., Clark N. Quinn, and Jonathan W. Schooler. 1999. "Justification Effects on the Judgement of Analogy." *Memory & Cognition* 27.5: 844–55.

Simic, Charles. 1990. *Wonderful Words, Silent Truth*. Ann Arbor: University of Michigan Press.

Smith, Barry, ed. 1988. *Foundations of Gestalt Theory*. Munich and Vienna: Philosophia Verlag.

Spillman, Lothar. 2001. "Gehirn und Gestalt: 11. Neuronale Mechanismen." *Kognitionswissenschaft* 9: 122–43.

Stace, W.T. 1960. *The Teachings of the Mystics*. New York: The New American Library.

Stuckeley, William. 1752. *Memoirs of Sir Isaac Newton's Life*. Published online by the Royal Society. http://ttp.royalsociety.org/ttp/ttp.html?id=1807da00-909a-4abf-b9c1-0279a08e4bf2&type=book

Tagliazucchi, Enzo, Leor Roseman, Mendel Kaelen, Amanda Fielding, David J. Nutt, R.L. Carhart-Harris, et al. 2016. "Increased Global Functional Connectivity Correlates with LSD-Induced Ego Dissolution." *Current Biology* 26: 1043–50.

Tarrant, Harold. 1983. "Middle Platonism and the Seventh Epistle." *Phronesis* 28: 75–103.

Tolstoy, Leo. [1869] 2007. *War and Peace*. Trans. Richard Pevear and Larissa Volokhonsky. New York: Random House.

Thomas, Edward. 1905. "Morgan Rhys." In *Beautiful Wales*. London: A.C. Black, 88–95. Reprinted in *A Language Not to Be Betrayed: Selected Prose of Edward Thomas*. Ed. Edna Longley. New York: Persea Books, 1981, 257–9.

Todd, Neil and Christopher S. Lee. 2015. "The sensory-motor theory of rhythm and beat induction 20 years on: a new synthesis and future perspectives." *Frontiers in Human Neuroscience* 26 August 2015. https://doi.org/10.3389/fnhum.2015.00444.

Tranströmer, Tomas. 1986. *Selected Poems 1954–1986*. Ed. Robert Hass. New York: Ecco.

Underhill, Evelyn. 1945. *Mysticism: A Study in the Nature and Development of Man's Spiritual Consciousness*. London: Methuen.

Weil, Simone. [1947] 1988. *La pesanteur et la grâce*. Paris: Librairie Plon. English translation by Emma Craufurd available as *Gravity and Grace*, London: Routledge, [1952] 1987.

— 1946. "Essai sur la notion de lecture." *Les Études philosophiques* NS. 1 (January–March): 13–19. Translated by Rebecca Fine Rose and Timothy Tessin as "Esaay on the Notion of Reading." *Philosophical Investigations* 13.4 (October 1990): 297–303.

— 1970. *First and Last Notebooks*. Trans. Richard Rees. London: Oxford University Press.

Wells, Gary I. and Brenda Hryciw. 1984. "Memory for Faces: Encoding and Retrieval Operations." *Memory and Cognition* 12.4: 338–44.

Wertheimer, Max. 1912a. "Über das Denken der Naturvölker: 1. Zahlen und Zahlgebilde." *Zeitshcrift für Psychologie* 60: 321–78. Reprinted in Wertheimer, Max 1925b. Abridged English translation, under the title "Numbers and Numerical Concepts in [Indigenous] Peoples," in Ellis 1938, 265–73.

— 1912b. "Experimentelle Studien über das Sehen von Bewgung." *Zeitschrift für Psychologie* 61.1: 161–265. Available in English as "Experimental Studies on Seeing Motion," in Wertheimer, Max 2012. Trans. Michael Wertheimer and K.W. Watkins, in Wertheimer, Max 2012: 1–91.

— 1923. "Untersuchungen zur Lehre von der Gestalt. II." *Psychologische Forschung* 4: 301–50. Full English translation by Michael Wertheimer and K.W. Watkins, under the title "Investigations on Gestalt Principles," in Wertheimer, Max 2012: 127–82. Abridged English translation, under the title "Laws of Organization in Perceptual Forms," in Ellis 1938: 71–88.

— 1925a. "Über Gestalttheorie." Lecture for the Kant Society, Berlin, 17 December 1924. *Philosophische Zeitschrift für Forschung und Aussprache* 1: 39–60. Also published separately, Erlangen: Philosophische Akademie, 1925: 1–24. Full English translation by Kurt Riezler in *Social Research* 11.1 (1944): 78–99. Abridged translation, under the title "Gestalt Theory," in Ellis 1938, 1–11.

— 1925b. *Drei Abhandlungen zur Gestalttheorie*. Erlangen: Philosophische Akademie.

— 1933. "Zu dem Problem der Unterscheidung von Einzelinhalt und Teil." *Zeitschrift für Psychologie* 129: 353–7. Available in English as "On the Problem of the Distinction Between Arbitrary Component and Necessary Part," trans. Michael Wertheimer in Wertheimer, Max 1959: 260–5.

— 1934. "On Truth." *Social Research* 1.2 (May): 135–46. Reprinted in Henle 1961, 19–28.

— 1959. *Productive Thought*. 2nd Edition. Ed. Michael Wertheimer. New York: Harper & Row.

— 2012. *On Perceived Motion and Figural Organization*. Ed. Lothar Spillmann. Cambridge, MA: MIT Press.

Wertheimer, Michael. 1980. "Gestalt Theory of Learning." In *Theories of Learning: A Comparative Approach*, ed. G.M. Gazda and R.J. Corsini. Itasca, IL: F.E. Peacock, 208–53.

— 1985. "A Gestalt Perspective on Computer Simulations of Cognitive Processes." *Computers in Human Behaviour* 1.1: 19–33.

Wikler Senechal, Marjorie. 2008. "Introduction." In *The Shape of Content: Creative Writing in Mathematics and Science*. Ed. Chandler Davis, Marjorie Senechal, Jan Zwicky. Wellesley, MA: A K Peters.

Wilson, T.D., D.J. Lisle, J.W. Schooler, et al. 1993. "Introspecting about reasons can reduce post-choice satisfaction." *Personality and Social Psychology Bulletin* 19.3: 331–9.

Wittgenstein, Ludwig. [1922] 1972. *Tractatus Logico-Philosophicus*. Trans. D.F. Pears and B.F. Mcguinness. London: Routledge & Kegan Paul.

— [1958] 1972. *Philosophical Investigations*. Trans. G.E.M. Anscombe. Oxford: Basil Blackwell. Third English edition of *Philosophische Untersuchungen*, originally published in 1967.

— 1967. *Zettel*. Ed. G.E.M. Anscombe and G.H. von Wright. Trans. G.E.M. Anscombe. Oxford. Basil Blackwell.

— [1980] 1984. *Culture and Value*. Ed. G.H. von Wright with Heikki Nyman. Trans. Peter Winch. Chicago: University of Chicago Press.

— 1982. *Last Writings on the Philosophy of Psychology*, Vol. 1. Ed. G.H. von Wright and Heikki Nyman. Trans. C.G. Luckhardt and Maximillian A.E. Aue. Chicago: University of Chicago Press.

— See also M.O'C. Drury, "Some Notes on Conversations with Wittgenstein" and "Conversations with Wittgenstein" in Rhees 1984, 76–96, and 97–171 respectively.

— See also Englemann 1968.

Woodhead, M.M., A.D. Baddeley, and C.C.V. Simmonds. 1979. "On Training People to Recognize Faces." *Ergonomics* 22.3: 333–43.

Wulf, Friedrich. 1922. "Über die Veränderung von Vorstellungen (Gedächtnis und Gestalt)." *Psychologische Forschung* 1: 333–73. Abridged English translation in Ellis 1938, 136–48.

Xenophon. 1990. *Conversations of Socrates*. Ed. Robin Waterfield. Trans. Hugh Tredennick, and Robin Waterfield. Harmondsworth: Penguin.

Zbikowski, Lawrence. 2002. *Conceptualizing Music: Cognitive Structure, Theory, and Analysis*. New York: Oxford University Press.

Zuckerkandl, Victor. 1956. *Sound and Symbol: Music and the External World*. Trans. Willard R. Trask. Princeton: Princeton University Press.

ACKNOWLEDGMENTS

My sincere thanks to the individuals, audiences, and editors who read or listened to versions of these essays and responded with generosity and insight. I am especially grateful to Robert Bringhurst, Warren Heiti, and Scott Howard, whose literary and philosophical labours on my behalf have been unstinting. Many thanks, too, to Mark Abley, Laurie Graham, Dennis Lee, and two anonymous referees for the press: their perspicacious and acute readings have helped make this a much better book. Jane McWhinney's spritely, capacious intelligence saved me from numerous infelicities — I hereby, with much gratitude, absolve her of all responsibility for those that we both know remain.

❧

The publisher and author acknowledge, with thanks, permission to reprint the following copyright material:

Elizabeth Bishop, two excerpts from the poem "The Fish," by permission of Penguin Random House UK.

Excerpts from "The Fish" from *Poems* by Elizabeth Bishop. Copyright © 2011 by The Alice H. Methfessel Trust. Reprinted by permission of Farrar, Straus and Giroux. Publisher's Note and compilation copyright © 2011 by Farrar, Straus and Giroux.

Excerpt from "The Dry Salvages" from *Four Quartets* by T.S. Eliot. Copyright © 1941 by T.S. Eliot, renewed 1969 by Esme Valerie Eliot. Reprinted by permission of Houghton Mifflin Harcourt Publishing Company. All rights reserved.

Excerpts from "Digging" from *Death of a Naturalist* by Seamus Heaney by permission of Faber and Faber Limited.

Excerpts from "Digging" from *Opened Ground: Selected Poems 1966–1996* by Seamus Heaney. Copyright © 1998 by Seamus Heaney. Reprinted by permission of Farrar, Straus and Giroux.

Extract from *Invisible Writing* by Arthur Koestler reprinted by permission of Peters Fraser & Dunlop (www.petersfraserdunlop.com) on behalf of the Estate of Arthur Koestler.

"In a Station of the Metro" by Ezra Pound, from *Personae*, copyright © 1926 by Ezra Pound. Reprinted by permission of New Directions Publishing Corp.

Mary Pratt, *Salmon on Saran* (1974). Bruneau Family Collection. Permission granted by the Estate of Mary Pratt.

Mary Pratt, *Eggs in Egg Crate* (1975). The Rooms Provincial Art Gallery, Memorial University of Newfoundland Collection. Permission granted by the Estate of Mary Pratt.

Mary Pratt, *Roast Beef* (1997). Collection of Museum London, London, Ontario. Art Fund, 1977. Permission granted by the Estate of Mary Pratt.

The author and McGill-Queen's University Press apologize for any errors or omissions in the preceding list and would be grateful to be notified of corrections that should be incorporated in any subsequent edition of this volume.

ॐ

The author and publisher also wish to thank the following individuals:

Robert Bly for his permission to reprint four lines of his translation of "Elegy" by Tomas Tranströmer from Tomas Tranströmer's *Selected Poems 1954–1986*, edited by Robert Hass, published by Ecco Press, 1987.

Roo Borson for her permission to reprint material from her essay "Poetry as Knowing" in *Poetry and Knowing*, edited by Tim Lilburn, published by Quarry Press, 1995.

Robert Bringhurst for his permission to reprint "Poem About Crystal" from *Selected Poems*, published by Gaspereau Press, 2009.

Robert Gray for his permission to reprint an excerpt from "Under the Summer Leaves" from *Selected Poems*, published by Collins/Angus & Robertson, 1990.

Dennis Lee, for permission to reprint an excerpt from "Not Abstract Harmonies But" from *Heart Residence: Collected Poems 1967–2017*, published by House of Anansi, 2017.

Emily McGiffin for her permission to reprint "Hanging Gardens" from *Subduction Zone*, published by Pedlar Press, 2014; and Beth Follett, publisher of Pedlar Press, for her additional permission.

Jim Murdoch for permission to reprint "All cards, remove yourself," from his blog *The Truth About Lies* ("How to Write Flarf," Wednesday, 7 September 2011).

ॐ

Dorothea Lange's *Migrant Mother*, also known as *Destitute pea pickers in California. Mother of seven children. Age thirty-two. Nipomo, California*, is reproduced courtesy of the Library of Congress, Prints & Photographs Division, FSA/OWI Collection. Library of Congress LC-DIG-fsa-8b29516.

Diego Velázquez's *Portrait of Juan de Pareja* is reproduced courtesy of the Metropolitan Museum of Art.

ॐ

A version of "Poetry and Meaninglessness" originally appeared in serialized form in *Brick: A Literary Journal*, Nos. 97–100; it was subsequently anthologized in *Best Canadian Essays 2018*, edited by Christopher Doda and Mark Kingwell (Toronto: Tightrope Books, 2018). A version of "Simplicity and the Experience of Meaning" appeared under the title "The Experience of Meaning" in *Simplicity: Ideals of Practice in Mathematics and the Arts*, edited by Roman Kossak and Philip Ording (Springer, 2017).

FIGURES AND ILLUSTRATIONS

Beethoven, opening of Op. 13, 129
branch and sprout, 99
broken circle, 99
buried numeral 4, 12
mirror word, 12
Lange, Dorothea, *Migrant Mother*, 55
Necker cube, 12
π is greater than 3, 102
Pratt, Mary, *Eggs in Egg Crate*, 165
Pratt, Mary, *Roast Beef*, 165
Pratt, Mary, *Salmon on Saran*, 164
Pythagorean theorem, 14
rectangle occluding crossed lines, 99–100
Rubin vase, 13
Velázquez, Diego, *Portrait of Juan de Pareja*, 55

INDEX

abstract, abstraction, 17, 105, 159; 'elements' abstracted from wholes, 5, 158, 183; Wertheimer critical of, 81, 143–4

aesthetics. *See* philosophy

Akhmatova, Anna, 49

Aldrich, Virgil, 20

ambiguity, 155, 168

analogy, 50, 72, 102; analogical thinking, 44, 73, 119, 139; critical to experience of understanding, 69; in Plato, 79

analysis, analyze, 49, 128, 158; connection with left hemisphere, 106, 156; defined, 135; distinctness requires separability, 155; 'elements' a product of, 5, 183; emancipation from analytic thought, 129; language as tool of, 44; and metaphor, 149; and North American philosophy, 73; 'piecewise,' piecemeal, or stepwise approaches, 6, 8, 51, 177; and reductionism, 177–9; undermines gestalt comprehension, 19, 94–5, 134, 145. *See also* intelligence; logic; reductionism; *and* thought, calculative

Aristotle, 9, 94; on character, 54, 124; and desire to understand, 70; on form, formal causation, 6–7, 91; and role of practice, 18; on simplicity, 193

Ash, Mitchell, 5

atoms, 11, 19–20, 69, 136. *See also* analysis; elements; *and* reductionism

Auden, W.H., 36

Augustine, 140; quoted, 180

Bartók, Béla, 43, 114

Bavelas, Alexander, 83

beauty, 58, 132–4, 146, 164; mathematical, 95, 157, 161; moral, 84, 95; natural, 50, 101; and truth (Keats), 96, 107; (Césaire), 157

Beethoven, Ludwig van, 129, 130

being, 73–4, 146, 168, 170–1. *See also* ontology: ontological awareness

Berkeley, George, 94, 100

Big Data, viii

Bishop, Elizabeth, 163–4

Black Mountain poetics, 47

Blake, William, 44, 124

Borson, Roo, 30, 42, 144, 145

Brahe, Tycho, 68, 69

Bringhurst, Robert, 31, 153–4

Browning, Robert, 61

Bruckner, Anton, 130

Burnyeat, Miles, 87

Burroughs, William S., 24

Burtynsky, Edward, 103

Bury, R.G., 87

Buson, 65, 67

calculation, calculative thought. *See* thought, calculative

Carello, Claudia, 110, 143

Cather, Willa, 64–5

causality, cause-and-effect, causal reasoning: in Aristotle, 6–7; in *I Ching*, 50; and language, 51, 141; in narrative, 162; and prose, 42, 48; and right-hemispheric thinking, 159

certainty: demand for, 52, 54, 95, 179

Césaire, Aimé, 157

'chain of reasoning,' 135, 140–1

character: knowledge a function of, 53, 54, 93–4, 124

clutter, 60–1, 64, 66, 68–70

collection and division, method of. *See* Plato

complexity *vs.* complicatedness, 63–4, 66

context-dependence: of distinction between necessary part and arbitrary component, 82, 93; of evaluation of prose texture, 41; of gestalt recognition, 82, 93–4, 130, 176; of gestural meaning, 45, 130; of metaphoric truth, 119; of ostensive definition, 133; of what constitutes a poem, 40; in Wittgenstein, 132

cool, 29

Copernicus, 67, 70, 193, 194

Cornford, Francis, 87

courage, 53

Croce, Benedetto, 111

Cross, Ian, 126

culture, defined, 130; language-use and way of life, 138–9. *See also* technocracy

cut-up technique, 24, 39

Dada, 23–4

Dalley, Stephanie, 104

Dào Dé Jīng, 168–9

Darwin, Charles, 126

Davenport, Guy, 128, 170

decline effect, 178

default mode network. *See* self, sense of

discernment, 17, 32–9, 97; aim of thinking, 95, 139; and gestalt comprehension, 28, 101, 120, 135, 170; and imagistic or lyric thought, 44, 174; no recipe for, 32, 38, 128

Doty, Mark, 163

doubt, logic of, 33, 52–3

ecological crisis, 49, 57–8, 142, 173–4; and lack of respect for gestalt comprehension, 71, 141, 160

ecology, 50, 57, 110. *See also* land *and* nature

ecosystem(s), 5, 63. *See also* ecology *and* land

von Ehrenfels, Christian, 4–5, 83, 94

einsehen (in Rilke), 162–3, 166. *See also* seeing-into

Einstein, Albert, 18, 89, 105–6, 109, 194

elements, 5, 8, 19, 68. *See also* analysis *and* atoms

Eliot, T.S. 23, 60, 102, 119, 168; and dissociation of sensibility, 142; and distinction between prose and poetry, 42–4

Ellis, Willis D., 176

emotion(s), 120, 157; as aspects of gestalts, 124–5; education of, 121, 125–7; emotional tone, 38–9, 103; and gestalt comprehension, 158; and mathematics, 157; and perception, 144; a subclass of feeling(s), 123. *See also* feeling(s)

Empson, William, 155

Engstler-Schooler, Tanya, 177

entrainment, 126

epistēmē. See Plato

epistemology, 145; just, 144
Epstein, Helen, 114
eros. See Plato
Euclid, 66–7
Evans, Bill, 148
Exner, Sigmund, 82

family resemblance(s). *See* gestalt(s)
feeling(s), 122–5; characterized, 123–4; emotion(s) a subclass of, 123; examples, 122; are gestalts, 124; and gesture, 121, 122; how expressed by music, 121, 134. *See also* emotion(s)
Feynman, Richard, 69, 194
flarf, 25
form: according to Ben Shahn, 61
forms, Platonic: characteristics, 75; comparison with gestalts, 75–9; and difficulties with language-use, 86–8; examples of, 78, 89; ontological status, 91–2; required for meaningful discourse, 131. *See also* Plato
Fowler, H.N., 87
Frege, Gottlob, 3
Freud, Sigmund, 106; primary and secondary process, 159–60
Frye, Northrop, 40

Gardner, Drew, 26
Gardner, W.H., 55
Garrett, John, 36
Gauss, Karl Friedrich, 15, 67, 76, 180
geodesic sphere, 63, 163
gestalt(s): aural, 157, 180; character, a gestalt, 54; comparison with Plato's forms, 75–95; conordinate, 69; different from sum of parts, 5; face(s), 11, 42, 68, 177; false, 16, 68–9, 105, 136 (see also *phi* phenomenon); family resemblance(s), 132; and gesture, 114–17; as harmonies, 159 (*see also* internal relations); and internal

relations, 63–4; metaphysical or ontological status, 9–10, 16, 50, 76, 178–84; significant and insignificant, 54; sub- and super-ordinate, 68–9, 88, 129, 171, 182; temporally extended, 180; two types, 11–14, 67, 101–2
gestalt comprehension, vii, 3–5, 16, 21, 146, 147; and absence of clutter, 60–1, 64, 66; characteristics, 17–18, 54; context-dependent, 82, 93–4, 130, 176; defined, 21; and directedness, 89–90; evolutionarily adaptive, 25, 50, 98, 184; and feeling(s) or emotion(s), 124–7, 157–8; hard to undermine, 51, 82–3, 105; and inscape or instress, 55; and internal structural relations, 69, 120, 127; and intuition, 78; and mathematical proof (*see* mathematics and proof[s]); necessary and sufficient criteria for, cannot be specified, 17–18, 32, 38, 70, 72–3, 93, 95, 176; and neuropsychology, 106, 157; not a 'chain of reasoning,' 135; not computational, 73; at odds with language-use (*see* language-use at odds with g. c. *and* 'undermined by analysis' *below*); and ontological awareness, 147, 161, 170–1; other names for, 60; practising, 53, 88; regarded as illegitimate by technocracy, 57, 71, 106, 128; and sense of certainty, 83; and sensitivity to detail, 98; synoptic, 161–74; underdeveloped, 28; undermined by analysis, 94, 128, 134, 136, 145. *See also* discernment *and* thought, resonant
'Gestalt quality' (von Ehrenfels), 4
Gestalt theory, 4–10, 16, 70, 175–7; comparison with Plato's views, 75–95 *passim*; critics of, 20, 92; 'factors' precipitating gestalts, 70, 99–100,

Index   233

105, 175–6; of learning, 69; and music, 110, 121; *Prägnanz*, 70, 176; and technocratic culture, viii. *See also* part-whole relations

gesture(s), 114–17, 121, 127, 182; and culture, 130; gestural communication, 122; and language, in Augustine, 140; meaning(s) context-dependent, 130; nonhuman, 117; not easily describable, 127

Gibson, James J., 177

Ginzburg, Carlo, 98

Goethe, Johann Wolfgang von, 19, 94, 111

Goodman, Nelson, 111

Gray, Robert, 100–1

Gretzky, Wayne, 166

Haack, Susan, 3

haecceity, 150, 158, 166; and world interdetermined, 171

Hagberg, Garry, 130–1

haiku, 63, 65–7, 68

Hanslick, Eduard, 111

Hass, Robert, 63, 65–6, 160–1, 166–7

Heaney, Seamus, 151–3

Hegel, Georg Wilhelm Friedrich, 9

Heiti, Warren: quoted, 120

Herakleitos, 47, 73, 94, 169–70

Hesiod, 61

Hirshfield, Jane, 161, 166

Homo sapiens: an ecological disaster, 71; speciation within and technocracy, 142

Hopkins, Gerard Manley, 39, 54–8, 60, 166

Howe, Marie, 96–7, 100

Hugo, Victor, 109

Huxley, Aldous, 147, 161

I Ching, 50

Idealism (philosophical doctrine), 7, 9, 76

Identi-Kit reconstructions, 177

image(s): aural, 113. *See also* logic *and* thinking

imagination, 113; tonal, 117

Imberty, Michel, 128

ineffable experience, 160. *See also* language-use at odds with gestalt comprehension *and* music

inner relations. *See* internal relations

inscape, 54–6, 60, 166–8; defined, 55

insight, 60, 72–3, 177–8; not computational, 73; spiritual (*see* spiritual insight); sudden, 85–6, 97

instress, 55, 166–7

integrity, experience of: 133–4; and meaning, 136

intelligence: interaction between gestalt intelligence and analytic or calculative intelligence, 53, 95, 134, 136, 137, 141; represented as computation by technocracy, 28; at least two kinds of, 71–2, 136, 155, 159–60, 173. *See also* analysis; gestalt comprehension; thinking; *and* thought (calculative, imagistic, resonant)

intention, authorial, 35

internal relation(s), 19–20, 63, 69, 76, 118–21; as attunement, 64, 135; human beings so related to world, 71; referred to as internal structural relations, 119, 120, 127, 133; referred to as resonant relations, 131, 159, 167; and things, 68, 141, 166–7, 168

intuition. *See* gestalt comprehension

Issa, 122

Jackendoff, Ray, 111

Jankélévitch, Vladimir, 109

Johansson, Gunnar, 115–17, 123

Jordania, Joseph, 126

joy, 58, 62, 108, 161, 173, 174

justice, 90–1; just epistemology, 144

Kahn, Charles, 170
Kant, Immanuel, 9, 94
Keats, John, 96, 107–8
Kekulé, Friedrich August, 85
Kepler, Johannes, 16, 60, 68, 69–70, 83, 85
Kivy, Peter, 111
knowledge. *See* character
Koestler, Arthur, 66–7, 76
Koffka, Kurt, 4–5, 177
Köhler, Wolfgang, 4–5, 79, 177; opposed to Idealism, 7; "What Is Thinking?" 77, 85, 90

land, relations with, 156–7, 174
landscape, 54, 117, 147; in Hopkins, 54–7
Langer, Suzanne, 109, 111, 115
language(s), 27, 139–41; enactive, 28, 43, 65, 150, 169–70; foreign to meaning, 139; Indo-European, 51; lyric, 150 (*see also* 'resonant' below); a medium of calculative thought, 141; resonant, 44, 57, 139–40. *See also* analysis
language-use at odds with gestalt comprehension, 20–1, 65, 73, 105–6, 110, 173; consequences, 49, 73; in Einstein, 18, 105–6; in Eliot, 119; in Freud, 106; in Goethe, 19; in Hopkins, 56; in Koestler, 67; in Lorenz, 19, 106; in Plato, 75, 86–8; with respect to music, 139; in Schooler, 19, 72–3, 106, 177–8; wordless thought, 149. *See also* culture *and* forms, Platonic
Lee, Dennis, 43, 167
left-hemispheric thought. *See* McGilchrist, Iain
Lerdahl, Fred, 111
"less is more," 61, 64
Levett, M.J., 87
light, 128, 153–4, 163
Lilburn, Tim, 161–2, 166

Loewi, Otto, 85
logic, 3–4, 158; deduction, 19; dream logic, 127; logic of concepts (Eliot), 42, 44; logic of images (Eliot), 42–3; syllogistic, 94. *See also* 'chain of reasoning' *and* thought, calculative
Longfellow, Henry Wadsworth, 64
Lorenz, Konrad, 19, 78, 79, 83, 106
Lund, Frederick H.: quoted, 92
lyric: art, defined, 31; artist, defined, 31; awareness displaces 'I', 163; and "less is more," 61; insight, defined, 159; language, 150; art's relationship with mathematics and science, 60; resonantly clear or coherent, 60, 120, 168; thought, characteristics, 148; thought, polyvalent, 155; thought sidelined by technocratic culture, 160

machine(s), mechanization, mechanistic epistemologies: and calculative intelligence, 136; ecologies as, 57; emancipation from, 129; ideal of, 21; meaning not mechanical in structure, 18; and philosophy, 9, 132; in poetry, 26–9; and power and control, 137; rejected by Arne Næss, 129; rejected by Plato, 78; rejected by Wertheimer, 95; and technocracy, vii–viii, 21, 141–2; world as, 50
Malpass, Roy, 177
mathematics, 15–16, 31, 63, 71, 143; and emotion, 157; Greek, 143; in Indigenous societies, 81; in Plato, 84; relationship with poetry or lyric art in general, 37, 60, 66; and visual thinking, 14, 57, 102. *See also* music; proof; Pythagorean theorem; *and* Pythagoreans
McGiffin, Emily, 103–5
McGilchrist, Iain, 155–61
meaning, 18, 49, 60, 122; abused, 57; arises from attunement of parts, 64,

131; avoidance of, 29; defined, 136; experience of (*see* meaning, experience of); and gesture, 128; neglect of, at root of planetary crisis, 49; neurophysiology of, 117; not 'personal interpretation,' 58; and tone of voice, 123, 128

meaning, experience of, 16, 20–21, 72, 135; and absence of clutter, 68–9; changes us, 53–4, 183; connection to being, 49–50; as evolutionary pleasure, 25, 29, 50, 98; gestalt phenomenon *par excellence*, vii; and gestalt shifts, 50, 111; and music, 111, 122, 127, 138, 142; in Plato, 92; in Rilke, 59–60; *vs.* sense of certainty or security, 34, 54, 95; and showing, 36, 97; and spiritual insight, 147. *See also* beauty, gestalt comprehension, *and* integrity

medical diagnosis, 35, 98

medieval thought regarding simplicity, 194

Melcher, Joseph, 177–8

melody, melodious, 4, 54–5, 110, 180

memory, mnemonic technique, 132, 177

Mesmer, Sharon, 25, 26; quoted, 58

metaphor, 20, 67, 102–5, 113; defined, 119; and internal structural relations, 120–1, 127; and myth, 127; and music, 127, 128; and Necker cube, 149, 155; and reality, 121; Roger Scruton's view of, 118–19; and truth, 119, 155

Metzger, Wolfgang, 6, 76, 176

Michaels, Claire F., 110, 143

Mies van der Rohe, Ludwig, 61, 64

mirror neurons, 117

mistake(s): concept of, 34, 39, 52–3; terror of, 34, 54, 95, 171. *See also* gestalt(s): false

Mithen, Steven, 126

modernism, high, 23

Morrow, Glenn, 87

Mozart, Wolfgang Amadeus, 60, 128

Murdoch, Jim, 22

music, 8, 47–8, 109–46 *passim*; atonal, 112, 142; and feeling(s) or emotion(s), 118–25, 134; as geometry of feeling, 114–15, 117; and gesture, 117, 121, 125, 127; ineffability of, 109, 139, 145; and mathematical proof, 127; and metaphor, 118, 121, 127–8; "the music plays you," 8, 138; musical structure of world, 50; has syntax but no lexicon, 111; tonal, 112, 142; verbal or linguistic (*see* poetry: aural dimensions of). *See also* scales *and* tone

mysticism, extrovertive, 147. *See also* spiritual insight

Næss, Arne, 63, 110, 171; sub- and superordinate gestalts, 68–9, 88, 129–30, 182

nature: natural world has meaning, 57–8. *See also* beauty; ecology; ecosystem; land; *and* landscape

Necker cube, 12–13, 17, 183; relation to metaphor, 149, 155

neuropsychological foundations of gestalt comprehension, 106, 142, 157–8. *See also* McGilchrist, Iain

Newton, Isaac, 16, 98, 194

Nézet-Séguin, Yannick, 122–3

ontology, 10; ontological awareness, 147–8, 164–74; ontological resonance, 170

optics, 9–10

Oulipo, 26

Ozawa, Seiji, 114

236   Index

Page, P.K., 31

Parmenides, 49

part-whole relations, 5–9, 131, 136, 158; analogy with symphony, 6–9; and 'inner lawfulness,' 5–6. *See also* internal relations *and* structure, resonant

patience, 53, 58, 154

perception: building block model, 11; epistemological or metaphysical status of, 9–10, 16–17, 50, 178–84; of feeling, 137; and feeling(s), 124–5, 143; and imagination, 113; modes of, 112; not distinct from thinking, 14, 83, 179–80; a form of reading, 179–83. *See also* optics

Peters, W.A.M., 55

phi phenomenon, 11, 16–17, 51, 82, 183–4

philosophy, 168, 178–9; aesthetics, 144–5; aim, 94–5; Enlightenment, 50, 95; history of, 91, 92; lyric, 168–71; North American, 73, 144–5; 'Perennial,' 147, 172; relationship to poetry, 147, 161, 168–72. *See also* epistemology

'piecewise' or piecemeal approaches, 6, 8, 51

Plato, 9, 60, 73; and character, 93; comparison of views with Gestalt theory, 75–95 *passim*; notion of *dialektikē* [dialectic], 77; dialogues as teaching aids, 94; notion of *elenkhos*, 77; notion of *epistēmē*, defined, 84; and *eros*, 88–9; Lecture on the Good, 84; method of collection and division, 77–80, 88; and taxonomy in biology, 78, 88; theory of forms, 75, 131. *See also* forms, Platonic

poetry, 19, 22–58, 148–55, 160–74; and aleatory technique, 26–7; 'anti-poetry,' 43; aural dimensions of, 42–9, 107, 150–5 (*see also*

language: resonant *and* resonance); enjambment, 47; formal verse, 40, 45, 46, 48; free prosody, 43, 45–7; free verse, 39–49 *passim*, 150; great, defined, 31, 35; L=A=N=G=U=A=G=E school of, 26; the line, concept of, 46–8; meaningful, defined, 28; meaningless poetry, causes, 29–30; as memorable speech, 36; not verse (in P.K. Page), 31; poet's task defined, 27; poetry 'buzz,' 24–5, 27, 38; relationship with mathematics, 37; relationship with philosophy, 147, 161, 168–72; rhyme, 43; rhythm, 43, 45, 47–8, 150–2; teaching, 35–6. *See also* Black Mountain poetics; cut-up technique; flarf; haiku; metaphor; Oulipo; *and* prose

Poincaré, Henri, 16, 70, 85, 157–8, 161

Pope, Alexander, 42

Pound, Ezra, 23, 30, 149, 181–2

practice, as alternative to criteria, 18, 53, 88

Pratt, Mary, 164–6

'precisation' (Arne Næss), 171

progress, 21

proof(s), 66; and internal relations, 67, 127; and lyric art, 60; π is greater than 3, 102; and poems, 36–7, 103; Pythagorean theorem, 13–14; and 'showing,' 97; and recurrent surprise, 31

prose, 41–2, 44–5, 48

prosody. *See* poetry; rhythm

Ptolemy, 67, 193

Pythagorean theorem, 13–14, 65

Pythagoreans, 143

quantum mechanics, 69, 70

quantum superposition, 50–1

Quine, Willard Van Orman, 3

Raffman, Diana, 111
rationality, 135; cult of, 141; dictatorship of, 34
reading, 28, 58, 98, 101; of gesture or tone, 137; misreading, 183; world, 179–80; written language, 180–3
reductionism, 18, 20–1, 179–84
relations, internal. *See* internal relations
relations, part-whole. *See* part-whole relations
religion, defined, 172
resonance, 19, 64, 119, 130; and being, 74, 146, 168, 170; characteristic of lyric thought, 148; and emotion, 158; and haiku, 67; and meaning, 131, 135; and metaphor, 119, 121; and right-hemispheric thought, 158; resonant language, 42–9, 57, 139; world as resonant whole, 63, 159, 162, 163. *See also* internal relations; structure; *and* thought, resonant
rhyme, 43
rhythm, 113, 123. *See also* poetry
right-hemispheric thought. *See* McGilchrist, Iain
Rilke, Rainer Maria, 59–60, 162–3, 166
Rohr, Richard, 171
Romanticism, 141, 142
Rorty, Richard, 118
Rothko, Mark, 41
Ryōkan, 168

Sartorius, Wolfgang, 15
scales, musical, 112–14
Schenker, Heinrich, 111
Schooler, Jonathan, 19, 72–3, 88, 106, 177–8
Schopenhauer, Arthur, 111
Schubert, Franz, *String Quintet in C* (D. 956), 137
science, 42, 98

Scruton, Roger, 109, 118, 121
seeing-as, 150, 167. *See also* Wittgenstein, Ludwig
seeing-into, 163, 166–7, 170
self, sense of, 159–60; ego-inhibited thought, 106–8; in Hirshfield, 161; 'me' thought, 156
Shahn, Ben, 12, 61, 64, 65
Shakespeare, William, 103
Sheldrake, Rupert, 50
"show, don't tell," 36, 65–6, 96–108 *passim*; and gesture, 125
silence, 112, 150
Simic, Charles, 155
simplicity, 59–63; as ideal, 59, 193–4
skepticism, 32–4, 166; and need for certainty, 51–4, 171, 179, 184; resisting, 40–1
sophistry, 89
space: aural, 111–14, 121; modes of, 113; tonal, 112–14
spiritual insight, 147, 171; as synoptic gestalt experience, 161–74
Stace, W.T., 147
structure, 9; effect of perceiving complex resonant structure, 53–4; in gestalt comprehension, 19, 79, 81, 120; resonant, 27–8, 45, 50, 65 (*see also* internal relations *and* resonance); resonant structure of world, 35, 50, 150; resonant thought-structure, 44, 139; tonal, 113
Sullivan, Gary, 25–6

Taoism, 60. See also *Dào Dé Jīng*
technocracy, viii, 141–2; blind to environmental crisis, 141, 173; deaf to poetry, 173; derogates visual thinking in mathematics and science, 57; dismisses Indigenous wisdom, 57; dismisses gestalt insight or gestural meaning, 57, 128, 173; and education,

238   Index

57; epistemological consequences of, 50, 134; and philosophy, 145; poetry immune to agendas of, 44; privileges calculative intelligence, 28, 71; regards art as entertainment, 57; regards spiritual insight as delusional, 173; sidelines lyric thought, 160

thing(s), 17, 68, 140, 149, 175; and internal structural relations, 119–20, 133, 141, 166–7, 168

thinking, 147; aim, 95; ego-inhibited, 107–8, 159–60; productive (in Wertheimer), 76–7, 85, 89–90; two stages in Gestalt theory and in Plato, 76–9; visual, 13–14, 57, 102; wordless, 95. *See also* intelligence; perception; *and* thought (calculative, imagistic, resonant)

Thomas Aquinas, 194

Thomas, Edward, 172–3

thought, calculative, 110, 141–5; benefits of, 95, 106–7; defined, 135; and feeling, 124; *vs.* gestalt comprehension, 136; privileged by technocracy, 71. *See also* analysis; intelligence; *and* thinking

thought, imagistic, 44, 65; in Eliot, 42–3; and verbal music, 43–6, 48; in primary process, 159. *See also* gestalt comprehension; intelligence; *and* thinking

thought, resonant, 44, 45, 139, 141. *See also* gestalt comprehension; intelligence; *and* thinking

Three Gorges Dam, 103–5

Tolstoy, Leo (*War and Peace*), 61–3, 64

tone, musical, defined, 112

Tranströmer, Tomas, 103, 137

truth: and beauty (Keats), 96, 107; as coherence, 90–1; and *eros*, 77, 89–90; etymology, 107; experience of, 97, 166; and experience of

meaning, 16; as integrity, 90–1; as justice, 90–1; and metaphor, 119, 155; necessary, experience of, 84; and philosophy, 95; and poetry, 27, 31; of prose, 45; telling the truth, 27, 37

Tycho. *See* Brahe, Tycho

Tzara, Tristan, 23

'verbal overshadowing,' 177–8. *See also* language-use at odds with gestalt comprehension

Vermeer, Jan, 148, 161

Watkins, K.W., 176

Weil, Simone, 39, 182

Wertheimer, Max, 4–21 *passim*, 95; on abstraction, 143–4; and apparent motion, 82–3; on arbitrary *vs.* necessary parts, 81–2; on directedness, 89–90; on 'factors' in gestalt comprehension, 175–7; on Indigenous mathematics, 81–2; on metaphysical status of gestalts, 6–7, 178, 184; and music, 110; and 'productive' thinking, 76–7, 85–6; trouble writing, 10, 177; on truth, 90

Wertheimer, Michael, 5, 81, 176

wholes: as individuals, 158. *See also* gestalts; part-whole relations; *and* things

Wikler Senechal, Marjorie, 66

Wilde, Oscar, 7

wisdom, 53

Wittgenstein, Ludwig, 32, 125, 141, 170; commentary on Augustine, 140; and logic of doubt, 33; and Longfellow's "The Builders," 64; on music, 109, 130, 134, 139; and Platonism, 131–3; on poetry and philosophy, 148; on seeing-as, 14, 60; *Tractatus Logico-Philosophicus*, 61, 169

Wordsworth, William, 45, 161

Index   239

world: a complex of sub- and superordinate gestalts, 68–9; as machine,
   50; embodies condition of music, 50,
   146. *See also* nature; resonance; *and*
   structure
writing, enactive. *See* language, enactive
Wulf, Friedrich, 176

Xenophon, 88–9

Yeats, W.B., 148